Praise for IT'S ALIVE

"The pace of technological change is accelerating, and the line between biology and machine is blurring. *It's Alive* clearly captures the profound impact that biologically inspired technology and technology-infused biology will have on every aspect of our economy and society." —RAY KURZWEIL, inventor and author of *The Age of Spiritual Machines*

"Holy cow! Integrating biology, management, nanotech, and evolution—if you loved James Gleick's *Chaos,* you'll love this book!" —SETH GODIN, author of *Survival Is Not Enough*

"This is the book to read for anyone concerned with business innovation at a time in which nothing seems to go right. The authors view the economy as the special kind of living organism it really is. Helped by a wide-ranging understanding of biology, they draw illuminating parallels between the systems studied by life scientists and those studied in a business school. The result is an engaging and necessary read." —ANTONIO DAMASIO, Van Allen Professor of Neurology, University of Iowa, and author of *Looking for Spinoza*

"Booms and busts do not prevent businesses and science from moving twice as fast as they did a decade ago—witness the impact of the World Wide Web. Now, the Web is marrying the biological revolution and driving change in one industry after another. Only those businesses able to adapt and evolve will be left standing. Chris Meyer and Stan Davis—two leading business minds—not only describe the coming revolution but provide a plan for prospecting in it." —JUAN ENRIQUEZ, director of the Life Sciences Project, Harvard Business School, and author of *As the Future Catches You*

"The relentless advance of technology simultaneously challenges our management models and provides powerful new tools to leverage uncertainty and accelerate innovation. Read this exciting and sweeping book to regrind your own conceptual lenses for understanding business in the twenty-first century—the age of discontinuity." —JOHN SEELY BROWN, former director of Xerox PARC

"A CEO-level guide to the forces reshaping our economy. Meyer and Davis have created an essential tool kit for future growth." —MICK YATES, former group chairman, Johnson & Johnson Asia-Pacific

ALSO BY STAN DAVIS AND CHRISTOPHER MEYER

BLUR: The Speed of Change in the Connected Economy

Future Wealth

ALSO BY STAN DAVIS

Lessons from the Future

Future Perfect

The Monster Under the Bed
(with Jim Botkin)

2020 Vision
(with Bill Davidson)

Managing Corporate Culture

Managing & Organizing Multinational Corporations

Matrix
(with Paul Lawrence)

Workers & Managers in Latin America
(with Lewis Goodman)

Comparative Management

IT'S ALIVE

The Coming Convergence of INFORMATION, BIOLOGY, AND BUSINESS

Christopher Meyer

AND

Stan Davis

CROWN
BUSINESS
NEW YORK

Published by Crown Business, New York, New York.
Member of the Crown Publishing Group, Random House, Inc.
www.randomhouse.com

CROWN BUSINESS is a trademark and the Rising Sun colophon is a registered
trademark of Random House, Inc.

Printed in the United States of America

DESIGN BY BARBARA STURMAN

Library of Congress Cataloging-in-Publication Data
Meyer, Christopher, 1948–
    It's alive: the coming convergence of information, biology, and business /
Christopher Meyer and Stan Davis.
Includes bibliographical references.
    1. Information technology—Economic aspects.   2. Life cycles (Biology).
3. Business cycles.   I. Davis, Stanley, M.   II. Title.
    HC79.I55 M49   2003
    658.4'038—dc21   2002153526

ISBN 1-4000-4641-6

10 9 8 7 6 5 4 3

First Edition

To Jennifer Cline,
for twenty years of indispensability
and fun
—CM

and

To my new grandson,
Benjamin David Davis
—SD

Contents

Introduction

This is a book about the next ten years.

Your reaction might be: "Good luck!" Both social and technological data suggest that the *rate of change itself* is doubling every ten years.[1] Recall that in 1993, President Clinton had just been elected, the CD-ROM had just been introduced, and the World Wide Web had not yet entered the general consciousness.

How can we hope to predict what will happen in the decade to come if it's going to be twice as different?

We can't, in detail, any more than when a hurricane is declared in the Gulf of Mexico we can predict precisely what's going to happen in Massachusetts a week later. But we can track the storm, and we can say in general terms where it's going, even if we can't describe the gusts and eddies that may prove horrific in Hilton Head or beneficial in Baton Rouge.

The hurricane is clear, and it's a near-perfect storm, the confluence of two major economic forces, either of which on its own would cause us to head for shore. The first is the direct outcome of the investment in networks and the advances in autonomous software of the past two decades. The connected, instantly responding world has not just accelerated—it's become more volatile. It's a cliché, though seldom honored, that change is the only constant—now change is both relentless and unpredictable. Consequently, management is shifting from a stance of predicting and controlling change to one of building an organization to sense change and to respond appropriately. We refer to this as the shift to adaptive management.

The second major economic force arises from molecular technologies, comprising biotechnology, nanotechnology, and materials science. These technologies are driving a new wave of innovation and will power an economic growth cycle comparable to the information economy. Together, these new developments will produce Joseph Schumpeter's "gales of creative destruction" and, equally, enormous opportunities for individuals, businesses, and for society as a whole.

Though we don't know just when the gales will blow, we do have ideas about how to prosper in these conditions by becoming more adaptive. At the Center for Business Innovation, we've been studying adaptive systems and evolutionary models since 1995. In *It's Alive,* we take what we've learned and put it to use to describe the "Adaptive Enterprise."

As adaptive management takes hold, and as the molecular economy matures, the two will cross-fertilize. We will take lessons about adaptation from biology and apply them to management. And we will take information tools from business and apply them to biotech (this already has a name—"bioinformatics") and to other molecular sciences. Our information systems themselves will become adaptive—otherwise, our businesses cannot be. By the end of the decade, business management, information systems, and biological concepts and technologies will converge around a common view of how change happens.

Part I of *It's Alive* describes the forces of change of the next ten years, and provides a model of how our economy evolves. We present evidence that increased connectivity and autonomy of software will lead inevitably to a permanent increase in volatility, and that molecular science will drive another wave of industrial change. We introduce *general evolution,* the idea underlying the convergence of information, biology, and business. This convergence means that adaptation can occur not only in biology but in computer code, in business, and in the economy; it means that all three operate by similar evolutionary rules.

Part II, "Code Is Code," explores the weird science going on in biotech, nanotech, and materials labs today. Then we move on to show how our computer code is beginning to behave more like a living system than an engineered one.

In Part III, "The Adaptive Enterprise," we first look at management to translate the concepts of evolution into six practical business principles for the Adaptive Enterprise. These are principles that can be implemented today. Then we test them. Since one of our principles implies harvesting diversity, we look into four very different organizations that have discovered the value of adaptive behavior. These range from Capital One Financial, one of the fastest-growing issuers of credit cards worldwide, to the United States Marine Corps, BP, and Maxygen, a young biotech firm. We sum up the lessons from these cases in "Becoming an Adaptive Enterprise," a chapter that describes ways that enterprises can become more adaptive today.

In Part IV, "Convergence," we ask: If the next ten years unfold as we envision, what will emerge next? We look for the innovation that will change people's lives the way the automobile did in the Industrial Age, or the mobile PC did in the information era. We can't hope to be right in every detail, but we can suggest how little the economy in the future will look like the one we have today.

Our preview of the decade to come is not idle stargazing. There are plenty of things we can do to take advantage of this convergence of information, biology, and business. One, of course, is to begin paying attention to biotech, nanotechnology, and materials science, as they move out of laboratories and into the commercial technologies that will change the economics of everything physical we make. If Xerox can print plastic transistors in 2006, Intel might reconsider building its next $5 billion wafer-fabrication lab. A second, wider reaching advantage is this: The tools are at hand to create organizations that adapt to change and volatility in the business environment more effectively, without the need for top-down instruction. Real-time information technology will help make this possible. The economic volatility that is already with us makes it imperative.

The specific forces we track will be challenging enough individually. Even more interesting will be a deeper shift in the way we think. As these forces combine surrounded by objects, organisms, and companies that all act alive, we will come to understand that evolution is as universal a concept as gravity. In the past decade, information technology, time, and the implementation of change have become dominant issues in business thinking and, in many respects, in society more broadly. Nonetheless, business still clings to one of the most deeply rooted assumptions in management—stability. We've been nibbling at it, prizing fast cycle time for reducing inventory, employing mass customization to lengthen the useful life of physical plants, downloading software upgrades that keep products and services fresh. But we have yet to articulate a new management system that assumes that every day will bring not stability but volatility, not predictability but continual surprise. "Return on time" has not yet replaced "return on equity" as a fundamental measure of business, though we will eventually acknowledge that time is a scarcer resource than financial capital. Designing businesses to adapt is perhaps the biggest single step toward a time-aware management framework, in which the costs of change are counted not as extraordinary charges but as a cost of doing business. Costs of "doing" will shrink, but minimizing costs of "changing" will be the next management imperative.

In 1987, in *Future Perfect*, Stan pointed out that time, space, and mass are the fundamental dimensions of the universe, and of your business, too. In the next decade, autonomous software will accelerate time, universal connectivity will banish distance, and molecular technology will miniaturize the mass of our economy. Responding to the adaptive imperative will rest not on the time, space, and mass of physics, but on the growth, recombinant creativity, and selective pressures of biology.

Where will it lead? When biology supplants physics as our dominant model of thought, when objects are smart, active, and connected, when we manage our health and agriculture at the level of atoms and molecules, what next? Complexity theorists speak of the "Adjacent Possible," the potentials that become available once the next thing has happened.

Our 1998 book *Blur* described the essence of an economy: It "uses resources to fulfill desires." *How* an economy does so changes over time. Lynn Margulis, not a management theorist but a biologist, says something very similar: "Metabolism has been a property of life since it began. The first cells metabolized: They used energy and material from outside to make, maintain, and remake themselves."[2] Sounds just like businesses. We didn't realize we were saying that the one thing that's essential is that the economy is *alive*. We say that here. We think that's the biggest blur of all, erasing the boundary between what's real and what's virtual, what's organic and what's inorganic, what's alive and what's not.

Though your company's world is highly volatile, major economic changes follow a predictable game plan. Broad economic change stems from fundamental discoveries that create new possibilities. Ten thousand years ago, agricultural knowledge transformed hunters and gatherers into village dwellers. In the last couple of decades, the science of solid-state physics gave us the cell phone, the satellite, the Web—perhaps allowing us to disperse again. Late in each cycle, new organizational approaches emerge in response to the

PART I
THE NEXT TEN YEARS

business innovations spawned by the new technologies. This time around, as the information economy matures, the world around us is becoming more connected and more autonomous, increasing volatility and accelerating change.

Just as in nature, rapid change in the environment requires rapid adaptation to ensure survival. This is the adaptive imperative. Economic change will continue to accelerate, so that only by embracing adaptive techniques will companies be able to change fast enough to survive. We call the organizational response the Adaptive Enterprise.

The best way to predict the future is to invent it.

—Alan Kay, Xerox PARC, 1971[1]

1

ECONOMIC EVOLUTION: LEARNING FROM LIFE CYCLES

I MAGINE that it's 1971 in Palo Alto, California.

You've wandered into a building at the Stanford Industrial Park, a nondescript place with cinder-block walls and rented furniture. The 3180 Porter Drive site is as plain and drab as the surface of the moon, and the guys working here seem to be living in their own private universe, speaking their own unique language. Someone's nattering on about the new "Intel 4004." Apparently, this new gadget he's talking about is called a "microprocessor." Someone else seems to think it's really great that this thing contains 2,250 transistors. They're both worked up over the fact that this "microprocessor" has an entire "CPU" on a single "chip."

As an average person living in 1971, you have no idea what they're talking about. In this ugly building on Porter Drive, also known as the Xerox Palo Alto Research Center (PARC), the computer wonks are also talking about "operating systems" and "laser printing" and "icons." Soon they will be going on about the "mouse," "point and click," and the "graphical user interface"; eventually, "bandwidth" and "network protocols."

In the early seventies, these terms were arcane jargon, but the words and the concepts they represent are as familiar to us now as "assembly line" and "mass production" were then. That's because the computer scientists at places like Xerox PARC and Bell Labs were, in fact, inventing the future—which is now our present—building the new economic engine that would overtake the industrial economy of the preceding 150 years.

3

"Computer speak" is the *lingua franca* of the world we inhabit at the beginning of the twenty-first century.

Today, in commercial laboratories with names like Maxygen, Diversa, and Nanosys, it's happening again. A new generation of scientists is inventing the next new world with its own novel nomenclature. Their terms of art, phrases such as "combinatorial chemistry," "gene shuffling," "high-throughput screening," and "MEMS" sound just as arcane to the average person now as computer terminology did in 1971.

But pay attention. In the same way that researchers at PARC and Fairchild Semiconductor and Bell Labs created technology that established a new economy based on information, scientists in labs today are inventing a future based on molecular technologies. These include not just biotechnology but nanotechnology and materials science as well. Cargill Dow Polymers is growing polymers for plastics in corn plants. PPG Industries is making nano-scale coatings that enable windows to wash themselves in the rain. Bio-Rad Laboratories is attaching naked strands of DNA to gold nanospheres and injecting them into people with a nano-BB gun.

A new "molecular economy" is on its way, while the information economy hasn't completely matured. As the information economy comes of age, a surprising thing is happening: Information systems are starting to take their cues from biological ones. Information is converging with biology, and business is following suit.

At John Deere, for example, the art of breeding—as in thoroughbreds and show dogs—has been used to evolve a schedule for a highly complex factory that makes seed planters. Using a computer, the metal-benders create a few random schedules that express the sequence of planters to be built in a digital code made of zeros and ones. That code is a set of instructions, just as DNA carries a set of instructions, its "genetic code." Deere engineers evaluate each schedule with a simulator, which is like letting the horses grow up, and then racing them—in silico. The winning sequences are then mixed, put out to stud in an approach that is essentially sex for software. Through this approach, which uses a "genetic algorithm," parts of the best schedules are recombined to create a new generation, just as horse genes are recombined, albeit through a somewhat messier process. Forty thousand new schedules run simulated races every night, and the winner is the schedule that runs tomorrow's real-life production derby on the John Deere factory floor.

Genetic algorithms are already in widespread use, improving jet-engine designs, credit-scoring forms, and stock-trading rules. The bigger story than sex for software is the abstract principle that biological behavior—in this case sex—can be written into digital code, then applied to the most intractable business problems. Stay with us, and you'll see that this translation of a biological function into a computer process is only one of many ways in which the concepts of evolution apply to business, in this case through precisely measurable operations improvements.

In 1984, a multidisciplinary group formed the Santa Fe Institute and began a research program based on a really big idea: that biology is not the only system that evolves, and that the concepts of evolution help to explain the process of change in any connected system, be it an ecology or an economy. Since then SFI has extended its work to other social systems—a business, a tribe, a crowd, a stock market, or a political party. Their work (and similar work at the University of Michigan, IBM, and many other places) has created some early tools, and a point of view that lets us see the economy as an ecology, and an organization as an organism, at the level of rigor needed to do empirical science. That's the level at which you begin to use evolutionary concepts to schedule factories.

These techniques, in time, may become as pervasive as the computerized spreadsheet is today. In fact, you can get started on your PC right now with a Microsoft Excel add-on called Evolver.

The theory of evolution through selection goes back to Charles Darwin in 1859, though the practice goes back to hunters and gatherers and their dogs. In Darwin's time, scientists recognized that biological systems evolve without any conception of the future, and yet the systems' future paths are significantly affected by their past. The new wrinkle for business today is the computing power that enables us to cast forward to test different evolutionary paths. At a startup called Icosystem, for example, former Santa Fe Institute research fellow Eric Bonabeau uses genetic algorithms to breed strategies for Internet service providers (ISP), then simulates an industry of competing strategies to observe the evolutionary adaptation of each "species" of ISP.

As these tools continue to develop, they will start to provide insight into the business problems currently reserved for senior strategists. A generation ago, the spreadsheet "deskilled" financial analysis, meaning that the most junior assistant in your company, equipped with the right software on a PC, could organize and manipulate data and enter the province of a once-highly specialized profession. In the years to come, new tools relying on the power of evolution can similarly "deskill" a wide range of activities, including strategy and planning. Today, the focus is on operations; the frontier, as at Icosystem, is strategy. Tomorrow, the boundary will move to organization, and managers will be able to test evolved organization designs and compensation systems to optimize the cultures that emerge.

Why is this worth reading about now? Well, consider what it would have meant in terms of your business, your career choices, and your investments, if you could have anticipated the impact of computers and information technology. Putting you well ahead of the curve in understanding the molecular economy is one of the ambitions of this book.

An even more urgent reason to pay attention to these converging economic life cycles is that the new technologies they are spawning hold the answer to the toughest problem business faces today: the inability of most companies to adapt to changes in the economic environment as fast as those changes occur. As we'll discuss shortly, it doesn't just *seem* that the world is changing faster and that volatility is greater than it used to be. Both are measurably and demonstrably true, and both emerge from our increasingly connected economy. Our institutions, businesses included, have been built for stability, not for change. As connectivity proceeds, business leaders face an imperative to create organizations that can adapt continually and rapidly, to keep pace with shifts in their markets, technologies, and society itself.

It is the world of biology that holds the key to meeting that adaptive imperative. Adaptation, the process by which organisms respond to volatility in their environments, has been going on for the past four billion years. As businesses today are struggling with volatility, they can look to nature's example for lessons on adaptation. And, as the Deere example makes clear, we're not talking only about language and metaphor, but about technical solutions and management approaches as well.

In this book, we'll see the lesson of PARC once again: By paying attention to what's going on in the labs of the next economy, we can find the management solutions we need to thrive in this one.

ECONOMIC LIFE CYCLES

The future is already here—it's just unevenly distributed.

—William Gibson[2]

The economy of the future derives from the science of today.

It happened this way in the information economy, and in the industrial economy before that, and it will happen again in the molecular economy. A new economic life cycle begins as science learns something new about the way the world works. Next, technology shows us how to turn new science into new productive capabilities. As a life cycle reaches maturity, every business employs the new technology to improve its performance. Ultimately, as an economy ages and the once-new technology becomes a commodity, we encode the deeper lessons from science and technology and apply them to the way work gets done and the way society is organized (see Figure 1-1).

We can use this simple four-quarter model to parse the Industrial Revolution:

Q1: Gestation. The Industrial Revolution began with scientific breakthroughs such as Maxwell's equations, which describe electricity, and

---

FIGURE 1-1   The Pattern of Economic Development

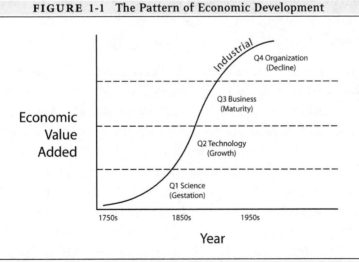

Boyle's law, which taught us about heat and pressure, the beginning of thermodynamics.

Q2: Growth. These scientific advances translated directly into the technologies that powered the industrial economy: electrical networks, steel mills, and oil companies. These technologies were the basis of enormous fortunes—the equivalent of the high-tech industry in the subsequent life cycle, the information economy.

Q3: Maturity. Entrepreneurs of the industrial economy then organized around these new capabilities, recombining them with new management concepts such as the assembly line and interchangeable parts. Expanding by way of the growth-phase industries such as railroad, petroleum, electricity, and telephone, they went on to build national, then global, firms such as General Electric, General Motors, and General Foods.

Q4: Decline. These enterprises required a new form of organization—a steel mill employed thousands, while its predecessor, a blacksmith shop, employed only a handful—and billions in capital. New ways of organizing work arose, leading to the now-familiar functional and divisional structures first observed in the railroads and at DuPont and General Motors. Even though these companies continued to thrive for a time, the period of exuberant growth ended, and industries consolidated into markets served by two or three companies, profitable not because of their growth or innovation but through their oligopoly power and their organization skills.

The pattern is straightforward: The economy transforms science into useful technology; business determines how to use the technology and then optimizes the resulting tasks organizationally. Society's trendsetters, decision-makers, and managers—sometimes unconsciously, sometimes deliberately—incorporate the concepts that bubble up and migrate out from these more fundamental, technical disciplines. Exposure to new technological capabilities alters the way we think. In the process, society, language, and politics change, too. In the industrial economy, this meant the shift of rural populations to cities, the shift of economic power to corporations, which led to the labor movement and antitrust laws, and so on. The incoming mind-set not only expands what is possible—it redefines our views of what will be possible next.

The Maturing Information Economy

In the mid-twentieth century, a new economic life cycle started. The information theory of Claude Shannon and the silicon semiconductor developed by William Shockley (both scientists from Bell Labs) gave rise to a new set of possibilities. Technology built on Shannon's and Shockley's insights enabled the manipulation of large quantities of data at high speed, building an infrastructure for providing cheap computer hardware, then software, then communications networks, and currently, an explosion of wireless devices. Today, we're in the middle of the third quarter, the Growth phase, when every kind of business incorporates the new technologies to improve their value, cost, and quality performance (e.g., through mass customization, online order confirmation, and mobile connectivity), and to launch entirely new businesses based on real-time information like Yahoo!, OnStar, and Travelocity.

The information economy is just now beginning to glimpse its organizational phase, which will come into focus much more in the decade ahead. We see it as practices like Internet-based virtual teams, telecommuting, and networked organizations start to take hold. Self-organized entities like Linux have challenged the institutional framework, but now it's consumers as well as workers who are organizing. Napster has been quashed, at least for now, by the existing power structure. But, then again, unions were at first suppressed, too. Nonetheless, Linux has been embraced. Freeware like Shockwave Player, "open source" software, and ad campaigns developed by customers are all growing. Companies have begun seeing themselves as part of economic networks rather than free-standing entities. And the World Wide Web, one of the key infrastructure technologies of this economy, isn't provided by a corporation at all.

This is the beginning of a new organizational model built around a key technology from the growth phase: networks. The resultant social changes include the blending of work and the rest of life, the growing labor force working outside of a traditional full-time employment

---

FIGURE 1-2   The Information Economy Life Cycle

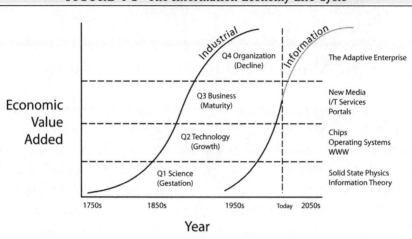

---

arrangement, the shift of economic power toward individuals, and the global economy that brings us summer vegetables year-round—and makes around-the-world terrorism possible.

Remember though, that all these aspects of today's economy were set in motion by the inventiveness of places like PARC and Bell Labs decades ago. Information technology has created cheap, intelligent, connected software agents. It has pushed miniaturization beyond the limits of ordinary comprehension. It has enabled autonomy in products and processes. It has given rise to artificial intelligence, offering a new wave of economic opportunity. And there have been other, unexpected consequences. Just as the industrial economy led to environmental degradation, the hyper-connected information economy has led to new assaults on privacy. What has been less well observed is that connectivity has created the marked increase in economic volatility that will define the key challenges of the next decade.

PERMANENT VOLATILITY

An analysis of the history of technology shows that technological change is exponential, contrary to the common sense, "intuitive linear" view. So we won't experience 100 years of progress in the twenty-first century—it will be more like 20,000 years of progress (at today's rate).

—Ray Kurzweil in "The Law of Accelerating Returns," March 7, 2001

[I]t is time to hail the new age of volatility.

—"Learning to Swing," *The Economist*, August 8, 2002

Place an order online, and your confirmation appears in your inbox before you go offline. Try to have your Walkman repaired, and you find that it's been replaced by a newer model. And the expectation of today's customers is that any feature they've seen anywhere should be available everywhere instantly. Formulate a business strategy or a new product-development cycle, and your plans are superseded by events before you can implement. The time between internal management changes and external responses is shorter and shorter. And the degree of unexpected disruption is greater.

As we said earlier, it's not just your perception—the rate of change *is* genuinely accelerating, the world is genuinely less predictable, and the swings in demand, mood, and prevailing wisdom are genuinely more volatile. And it's not just recession, the dot-com bubble, the aftershocks of 9/11, or the spate of corporate scandals. Change has become more rapid and volatility permanent. If you doubt it, consider the following indicators:

Accelerated Change

- The number of Fortune 300 CEOs with six years' tenure in that role has decreased from 57 percent in 1980 to 38 percent in 2001.[3]
- In 1991, the number of new household, health, beauty, food, and beverage products totaled 15,400. In 2001, that number had more than doubled to a record 32,025.[4]
- From 1972 to 1987, the U.S. government deleted 50 industries from its standard industrial classification. From 1987 to 1997, it deleted 500. At the same time, the government added or redefined 200 industries from 1972 to 1987, and almost 1,000 from 1987 to 1997.
- In 1978, about 10,000 firms were failing annually, and this number had been stable since 1950. By 1986, 60,000 firms were failing annually, and by 1998 that number had risen to roughly 73,000.[5]

Increased Volatility

- From 1950 to 2000, variability in S&P 500 stock prices increased more than tenfold. Through the decades of the 1950s, 1960s, and 1970s, days on which the market fluctuated by three percent or

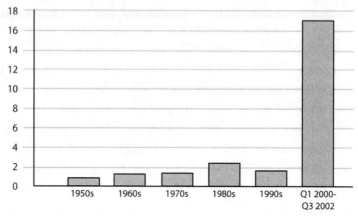

FIGURE 1-3   Stock Market Volatility on the Rise

Days Per Year that the S&P 500 Gained or Lost 3% or More (from previous close)

Source: Economagic.com time series data, CBI analysis

more were rare—it happened less than twice a year. For the past two years it happened almost twice a month (Figure 1-3).

○ The number of firms that take "special items" in their accounting has grown dramatically.[6] The number of S&P 500 firms declaring "special losses" has grown from 68 in 1982 to 233 in 2000. Special items are, by definition, an admission of being caught flat-footed by change more volatile than the normal course of the business cycle.

We need to stress that our argument here contains two distinct points. The first is that change has accelerated. That means whatever trend you look at will be proceeding more rapidly. Volatility is the degree of variability around a given trend. Our second point is that volatile events are of greater magnitude and occur more frequently. These reinforce each other, but they're not the same thing.

CONNECTIVITY AND THE CHANGE IN CHANGE

What could cause a permanent increase in volatility and the rate of change? While no single answer provides the whole explanation, one clear cause is connectivity. Without belaboring the well-known point, connectivity has transformed our world:

○ In the six years starting in 1996, the percentage of the U.S. population online grew from 14 percent to almost 52 percent.[8]

○ The maximum speed of connection in 1940 was about 1,000 bits per second; by 2000, it had reached 10 trillion bps.

○ The number of Internet hosts—important as a measure of the information a person can connect to—rose from several hundred in 1981 to about 100 million in 2001, while the cost of ISP service fell by a factor of 10 million.

○ The cost of a three-minute phone call between New York and London fell from $300 in 1930, to $60 in 1960, to about $1 today (in constant dollars).[9]

○ In 2002, the number of mobile phones worldwide reached one billion.

These leaps in the mobility of information make it possible to disseminate new ideas more quickly and cheaply than ever before. When information is codified and information technology modularized, upgrades, add-ons, plug-ins, and innovation can all happen quickly. The ease of adopting (or copying) software drives the pace of change, as does the ease of global communication, which enables rapid learning and transfer of know-how.

Every jump in connectivity—from clipper ships, to railroads, to telegraphs, to mobile phones, to BlackBerries—has shrunk the globe in space, in time, and in the effort required to support interactions among people, companies, and ideas. (Okay, maybe not the phones with cameras, but be patient.) Every jump has contributed to shrinkage in cycle time, as well as an increase in the rate at which ideas spread.

Connectivity between ideas creates the next new product, and connectivity of companies creates the next merger and change in industry structure. Connectivity between buyers, sellers, supply chains, and financial institutions shortens both the marketing cycle ("awareness, interest, purchase" is as fast as "see the ad, go to the website, research it on the Web, and order online"), and the order-to-cash cycle.

Connectivity is clearly a root cause of the acceleration of change, but in a more subtle way, connectivity must also be held accountable for increased volatility. Greater connectivity in information systems increases both the speed of communications and the permeability of boundaries that were once much more difficult to breach. This means that a signal created in any market, society, or system can propagate faster and travel farther than ever before, meaning that the climate in Brazil affects the price of coffee on the shelves more quickly and in more parts of the world. And though in a given network we can take steps to reduce the swings, we can never know when some newly made connection will create an unanticipated instability.

When networks become intensely connected, they start to become "nonlinear." Small changes can lead to disproportionately large effects. In short, they make our world more volatile. The huge power blackout that struck the northeastern United States on November 9, 1965, was caused by a single circuit breaker in Ontario, Canada, that was *functioning normally*. It did its job, which was to shut down power on a segment on the network. As expected, this caused a power surge that propagated to the parts of the system connected to it. What was not understood at the time was that the configuration of that network would amplify that surge, eventually leaving 30 million people in eight states and Canada in the dark. Today, it might be possible to simulate that network sufficiently to have found this glitch, but the principle remains: The more connected any system becomes, the harder it is to anticipate all such risks.

As more software functions autonomously, the risks escalate. Software viruses, in particular, represent the insidious side of autonomy. On November 2, 1988, at a time when the Internet was confined largely to universities and research labs, Bob Morris Jr. released into the Net a piece of code that could propagate itself from one PC to the next and reproduce with such enthusiasm that no capacity was left for the user. Six thousand computers were affected—then a large fraction of the Internet population—at a cost estimated at $10 million. Twenty-two years later, the I Love You virus cost an estimated $10 billion.

Another example of connectivity and autonomous software driving volatility comes from the financial markets. On October 19, 1987, the New York Stock Exchange lost 23 percent of its value in a single day, trading 600 million shares, nearly double the previous record volume. This cataclysm was the result not of an act of terror or even bad economic news but, rather, of the connection, in a logical sense, of a set of trading instructions that had been programmed into the accounts of institutions and individuals.

Black Monday was the wakeup call, and it led to steps by the securities exchanges to put the brakes on when such volatility starts to occur. The trend to volatility has continued, and been incorporated into investor expectations (Figure 1-4). "Mr. Market's mood swings have become more violent," *The Economist* concludes. "[I]t is not just price gyrations that have increased, but the volatility of volatility itself."[10]

THE ADAPTIVE IMPERATIVE

With autonomous software and a high degree of connectivity giving rise to big, unexpected swings and nonlinear effects, volatility will continue to surprise us, though seldom in the same way twice. While change and volatility are hard to separate when they are happening, we'll use both

FIGURE 1-4[7]   The Investor Fear Gauge

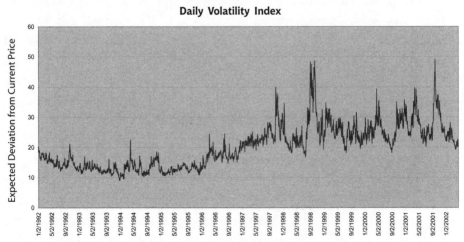

Daily Volatility Index

Source: VIX Index, Chicago Board Options Exchange

terms to refer to the core point: The increased rate of change in the economy poses the "adaptive imperative." To survive, business must learn to adapt as fast as the business environment changes. According to futurist Paul Saffo, "Business as usual has become business as unusual: unpredictable, unplannable, and above all, unmanageable . . . the stately equilibrium of Keynes has yielded with a vengeance to the unnerving creative destruction of Schumpeter."[11]

At some level, volatility has always been a part of the human condition, but our worldview and our business models belied that. We tried to forecast, always looking for the perfect plan. Then we acknowledged that there was no single best way, only probabilities and the art of decision-making under uncertainty.

Now we need to change our framework again, from one in which even these uncertain decisions are permanent, to one in which the costs and implications of continuing change are integral. This will take us from physics to biology, from engineering to evolution, from the top-down to the bottom-up, and from narrow efficiency to adaptability.

There are already examples of companies trying to act on the adaptive imperative. Businesses spent the twentieth century squeezing the fat out of industrial production, tuning processes to accomplish fixed tasks ever better, faster, and cheaper. To achieve this, however, they standardized their repertoires and put little weight on flexibility. Business became brittle. When MCI began taking customers from AT&T in droves with its "Friends and Family" marketing program, AT&T was unable to respond because its billing system wasn't built for such an offer. Worse, it wasn't built to be changed at all. Companies trying to create new strategies and capabilities are continually thwarted by the limitations of their systems. What Churchill observed about architecture is even truer of business processes: "First we shape our buildings; then they shape us."

As the costs of change become the regular costs of doing business, people's roles in organizations are shifting from doing work to managing the evolution of their companies' capacity, whether by creating new software or new relationships. There's nothing wrong in this—it means more interesting, less repetitive jobs. But it's time to acknowledge that change is not the exception, and that the costs of change are not a small part of total costs.

Quite the contrary: The costs of labor and materials that we worked so hard to minimize in the past have become much less significant, while the fixed cost of infrastructure that supports the business have become dominant. This shift has been going on for decades as we moved toward a service economy. The major cost of running the airline, the car-rental company, the franchise chain, and even the automobile company is in the management system that supports it.

Every time something changes in a business environment—a new technology, a new market expectation, or a new competitor—there's an opportunity to make a change in the business. As AT&T found out, however, if the fixed costs are supporting an equally fixed infrastructure, change doesn't happen.

Compare this with the speed of change at Amazon.com, which seems to introduce a new interface, program, or feature every week. Amazon, bred in the fast-changing environment of the Net, was built to respond rapidly to environmental volatility. AT&T, reared in an environment of regulatory oversight and forty-year depreciation schedules, was not. AT&T adapted beautifully to the environment created by the Communication Act of 1934. Every enterprise either adapts to its environment, or dies.

As the environment changes more rapidly, the costs of adapting become an ever-larger part of the total. The costs of never-ending product development as at Netscape or Microsoft, of parallel development teams as at Intel, and of "special" projects at every business are a mounting proportion of the costs of doing business.

In July 2002, for example, IBM opened a $2.5 billion chip factory in East Fishkill, New York, the company's largest capital expenditure ever.[12] This flies in the face of the current trend of relying on the assets of others. Why didn't IBM just buy chips from a fabricator in Asia? "To play to win in technology, you innovate and lead," IBM CEO Samuel J. Palmisano told the *New York Times*. "What we call the lab-to-fab time should be as close to zero as possible," according to John Kelly, senior vice president in charge of IBM's technology group. The closer the fabrication's cycle time gets to zero, the less disruptive is the market's unpredictability. This doesn't mean that volatility is made irrelevant. Quite the contrary: Market change is so relevant that it becomes the natural environment, the water to the fish. Kelly continued, "The core of our strategy is to lead in technology . . . if our strategy were anything but to be on the leading edge, we'd have put the plant in Asia."

IBM is spending extra money on the plant itself, and thus raising the unit cost of each chip it will produce, in order to have a better chance of being faster to market. Given a strategy of technological leadership, as well as the volatility of the chip business, the benefit in time of being close to the company's labs in Westchester County is worth paying for.

There's a second level to this story, and it's about flexible, adaptive manufacturing. If IBM has miscalculated the demand, it will suffer badly. High operating costs and depreciation on a huge capital investment will drag down earnings. But industry analysts say that the plant is likely to be insulated from a fall-off in one or a few segments of the semiconductor market. It is highly automated and designed to shift flexibly to produce many different kinds of chips to suit demand. "The diversity is the big difference with this plant," said Richard Doherty, director of The Envisioneering Group, a technology-assessment and research company.

IBM has devised a solution to the impossibility of forecasting demand. The new approach is to stop guessing about the future, and to build so as to adapt to it by creating a diverse set of capabilities. The intent is to deal with a volatile market, protect IBM from flux in demand, and build an adaptive factory, one that can manufacture a diverse portfolio of chips for everything from mainframes to cell phones to video game consoles. The previous generation of manufacturing stressed the "focused factory," designed to minimize unit cost by doing just one thing superbly. Presumably forever.

CEMEX, the world's third-largest cement company, faced a different adaptive imperative: intractable volatility. Fresh cement has a shelf life even shorter than that of fresh fish. Once the mixture is turning in the truck, the driver has only a couple of hours to deliver the load. Now imagine making an appointment to deliver cement to a construction site in Mexico City. The job may be behind schedule; traffic tie-ups may intervene; workers may not be available to receive the shipment.

In response to the risks of spoilage, cement makers in Mexico once charged their customers high fees to reserve a time for delivery, and even higher penalties if they were unable to take delivery as scheduled. The relationship between suppliers and customers was adversarial, costs were high, and service was poor.

CEMEX developed an adaptive solution: Treat the cement trucks like taxicabs. Station them in appropriate areas around the city, and have them respond to customers when summoned. Customers don't have to forecast, CEMEX doesn't have to commit extra resources, and the scheduling and late fees go away. CEMEX learned not to fight the volatility but, rather, to adapt to it. As a result, the company's guaranteed on-time delivery window has gone from the market-standard three hours to just twenty minutes, and it delivers loads within that window 98 percent of the time.[13]

IBM's new plant design and CEMEX's cruising cement trucks are two examples of what we call adaptive management. Information technologies (intelligent machines in IBM's case, radios in CEMEX's) support many such solutions throughout industry. Many business thinkers have noted this trend, including us in our 1998 book *Blur*. Here's the new wrinkle: As volatility and the cost of managing it become the new imperative, we need more than point solutions. We need a set of principles that support a comprehensive adaptive approach to management. We'll be developing this idea in Chapter 5, and analyzing Adaptive Enterprises in all of Part III. Yet before we're ready for that, we need to understand that the adaptive imperative is only one of two economic changes of the next ten years. Let's look at the second one.

THE NEXT ECONOMIC LIFE CYCLE

Even as the information economy matures, a new economic life cycle—the molecular economy—is reaching puberty. Watson and Crick's deciphering of the DNA molecule in 1953 marked its birth. For fifty years, the developmental curve for the molecular economy has lagged behind the curve of the information economy. At the same time, driven by the desire to scribe ever-smaller features on a silicon wafer, our power of magnification has grown from 1,000X in the 1930s—enough to see bacteria—to 300,000X in the 1980s to 100,000,000X in the 1990s—the scale of a single atom.

There are two threads here: a greater understanding of the molecules that control chemical and biological functions and the super-miniaturization of manufacturing. *They are converging to give us the ability to see, simulate, and manipulate matter at the molecular level.* The result is an enormous acceleration in biotechnology, to be followed by the development of novel materials and the takeoff of nanotechnology. Collectively, these three developments are what we call the "molecular economy."

On the day we did final proofing of the manuscript for *It's Alive*, a story appeared in the *New York Times* headlined "Scientists of Very Small Draw Disciplines Together," and began with by stating that Nanotechnology, Biotechnology, Information technology, and Cognitive science "are

FIGURE 1-5   The Next Ten Years

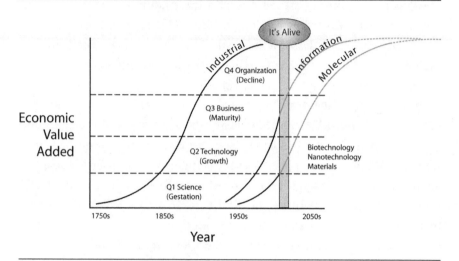

converging into a new field of science vital to the nation's security and economic clout"[14] They call it NBIC (and it's so new no one knows whether to say "NIB-bick" or "EN-bick,"). The article reported on a three-day meeting in Los Angeles that attracted participants like the National Science Foundation, Hewlett-Packard, and IBM, not to mention investors. The *Times* continued: "The organizers say the greatest opportunities lie in bridging the gaps between the rapidly growing ranks of nanoengineers and researchers in other fields . . . because all the activities of living cells are governed by nanoscale interactions of atoms and small molecules."

Call it NBIC or call it molecular science, it is the convergence at the molecular level that is new, and it's the science driving the next economic wave.

At the Xerox PARCs of today, in places like Cambridge, Massachusetts, and San Diego, California, scientists have gotten down to "the bottom" of things. Researchers now have the technological prowess to push individual atoms around, to make images of genes in action, and of individual proteins as they fold. At IBM, physicists have managed to slow down light in order to "capture" a photon. At the University of Konstanz in Germany, researchers have created an optical microscope that uses a single fluorescent molecule as its light source.

Feats of biological manipulation include genetically modified organ-

FIGURE 1-6   Four Phases of Three Economies

	INDUSTRIAL ECONOMY	INFORMATION ECONOMY	MOLECULAR ECONOMY
Q1 SCIENCE	Electrical engineering, chemistry	Solid-state physics, information theory	Biology, nanoscale science, materials science
Q2 TECHNOLOGY	Steel plants, oil, electrical equipment	Chips, operating systems, World Wide Web	Genomics, proteomics, nanotechnology, agent-based models
Q3 BUSINESS	Automobiles, consumer durables, skyscrapers	New media, information technology services, portals	**Matter compiler, personal hospital, universal mentor, experience machine, social science simulator**
Q4 ORGANIZATION	Command and control, hierarchy, "scientific management"	**The Adaptive Enterprise**	**Yet to emerge**

■ **Future developments**

isms, highly controversial creations such as corn plants endowed with pest resistance by the insertion of bacterial genes into the corn genome. Scientists, giving new meaning to the term "monkey shines," have monkeyed with the genes of a rhesus monkey to give him a gene for bioluminescence borrowed from a jellyfish.

Zeiss, an optics company headquartered in Germany, has taken the traditional electron microscope, given it a laser-powered "cut and paste" component, and turned it into, essentially, "PhotoShop" for cells. A laser can excise a piece of tissue as small as a chromosome. Then photonic pressure can catapult that chromosome directly into the cap of a microfuge tube. Future applications include transferring drugs or genetic material into cells without needles. Simply cut and paste.

This control of the very small arises in part from the desire to make even smaller electronics. IBM has developed a transistor made not of silicon but from a nanotube (a structure made of a handful of carbon atoms) that can compete at lab scale with the leading prototypes of silicon transistors. And Isaac Chuang, a professor at the MIT Media Lab's Center for Bits and Atoms, built a quantum computer that uses the spinning nuclei of atoms to represent the ones and zeros of binary code.

Despite extraordinary lab-scale developments like these, the molecular economy is today only entering its growth phase, just as the information economy was when we saw the first transistors. Initially, transistors gave us pocket radios. We had to wait until the microprocessor before the world could fundamentally change, and for the modem before the change could begin to reach its full potential.

Following the life-cycle model, today the information economy is in its third quarter, meaning that information technology has become a part of every business, and software and connectivity are becoming elements of every product. The molecular economy, as we've said, is still an awkward adolescent, just now entering its growth phase, when science moves out of the laboratory to become commercial technology. Except in a few industries like pharmaceuticals, the technology is not yet in general use.

That will come, but today, we can see the molecular economy taking off by looking at the growth of resources devoted to it.

- Biologists have replaced physicists as the leading users of super-computers, according to IBM's Life Sciences group.
- In just ten years, employment in the biotech sector has more than doubled, rising to 191,000 in 2001.[15]
- Biotechnology has attracted more investment in 2001 and 2002—two off years following the 2001 zenith—than in the entire five-year period of 1994–98, which included the previous peak in 1996.[16]
- The number of biotech patents filed each year has increased five-fold in the past ten years.[17]
- The National Nanotechnology Initiative's budget has surged nearly sixfold in the past six years, with over $700 million allocated for 2003.

During the next decade, molecular technologies will follow the same progression we've seen in the information technologies before them: They will move out from the lab and the basement, and into the fabric of enterprise itself. This will first take the form of new approaches to existing tasks, molecular tasks—a watch that reads your blood glucose level without needles, or a new class of ceramic materials that reduce the fuel consumption of jet engines. The second step is entirely new businesses such as decoding the genetic profiles of the inhabitants of Iceland, Estonia, Tasmania, and Taiwan,[18] then encoding them in a database, and then marketing the data. New capabilities for manipulating the molecules of living, evolving matter have already changed how we reproduce, how we heal, how we develop our foods and medicines and fibers.

In the third phase, molecular solutions will appear in industries outside of pharmaceuticals, agriculture, and materials. Compare the way that information content now drives value far beyond the high-tech industry. Automobiles, for example, the archetypal product of the late Industrial Age, now contain more than 100 microprocessors. The information technology sector is still a relatively small part of the economy; its share of the GDP was estimated at 8.3 percent in 2000. What proves our point is that although the information-technology industry accounts for a small portion of GDP, it accounted for almost 30 percent of overall real economic growth between 1996 and 2000 despite its rapidly declining unit costs.[19] This growth pattern will be repeated in "molectech." And in the fourth quarter of this new economy, our understanding of biology and molecular science will give shape to new and different organizational structures, more than a few decades away and still too far off to see.

Even as the pattern repeats, something unprecedented is happening. Because the molecular economy is arriving before the information economy has fully matured, the two economic waves are converging. What we learn about evolution (in this second quarter of the molecular economy) will change the way the information economy is managed in its fourth quarter. Conversely, advances in information technology, such as simulation, will accelerate our learning about evolving systems of molecules.

Anyone trying to run a business—or live a life, for that matter—over the next ten years will be dealing with two major forces: first, an environment in which change has doubled its pace and volatility has increased, creating the imperative to adapt. And second, the beginning of a new economic life cycle, in which the makeup of our GDP, which has in the past migrated from agriculture to manufactured goods, from goods to services, from goods and services to information, shifts again, this time to value created by molecular technologies.

How will management change to incorporate these developments?

In the Industrial Era, we used the technology that was creating the change to manage the change. Engineering approaches to organization used the same physics-based ideas that shaped the assembly lines to construct organizational structures and processes. Likewise, we are now using information technology—e-mail, workflow, CAD/CAM, ERP—to manage the networked organization that has emerged in the early phases of the information economy. As the industrial technologies of energy led to cities, labor unions, and suburbs; as the information technologies of networks are leading to business alliances, chat rooms, and global English; the insights of evolution will shape our society in the first half of the twenty-first century. Because the challenge is adapting to accelerated change and volatility, the concepts of evolution—tuned by nature over four billion years to cope with environmental change—are just what's needed to create the next generation of organization: the Adaptive Enterprise.

"**B**iological metaphors are used increasingly frequently to describe computing systems, and vice versa; we're finding that this connection is in fact a literal and bi-directional one all the way down to molecular scales," as Neil Gershenfeld, director of MIT's Center for Bits and Atoms, tells us.[1] We have a shorthand for this "literal connection": Whether binary or biological, code is code.[2]

Recently, computer scientists have found that they can simulate biological functions "in silico" to elucidate everything from population genetics to the functioning of heart cells. Biological systems can now be expressed in digital form, and analyzed using digital techniques. This application of information technology to biology is one of the reasons for the explosion of progress in the field.

PART II
CODE IS CODE

At the same time, computer scientists have been making the trip in the reverse direction, using the concepts of evolution in novel ways to solve real-world problems. "Genetic algorithms," for example, take the ideas of sexual recombination and selective pressure from biology, express them in simplified form in software, and apply these software tools to business problems, from factory scheduling to engine design to credit scoring. Real systems can be expressed in digital form, and manipulated using evolutionary concepts. Building on insights developed both in the world of information and the world of biology, students of "complexity theory" are finding that adaptation is a very general property of connected systems. Whether biological (Chapter 3) or binary (Chapter 4), connected systems organize themselves to evolve.

Evolution is the most profound and powerful idea to have been conceived in the last two centuries.

—Jared Diamond, author of *Guns, Germs, and Steel*[1]

2

GENERAL EVOLUTION: LEARNING FROM NATURE

NOT long ago, an artist named Eduardo Kac took a Bible verse, Genesis 1:28, and translated it into Morse code: "Let man have dominion over the fish of the sea, and over the fowl of the air, and over every living thing that moves upon the earth." He took the resulting dots and dashes and used them to create a new string of code that relied entirely on G and T and C and A, the letters used in transcribing genetic sequences. Next, he actually constructed the DNA sequence derived from this twice-coded line from Genesis, introduced it into live bacteria, cultured the bacteria in a petri dish, and put the dish in front of a video camera at a New York art gallery. That done, he projected his microbe colony onto the wall and, at the same time, broadcast it over the Web. Participants from anywhere in the world could connect to the gallery's website and zap the bacteria with ultraviolet light, which would induce mutations in the organism's genetic code, which would redirect the genetic inheritance of all the organism's subsequent generations. In the grandest, metaphorical terms, what Kac was inviting participants to do, of course, was to rewrite Genesis. To recreate Creation.

He was demonstrating the translatability of codes, through which the power of evolution can be applied to non-biological realms. We are finding that evolution is, in fact, a concept that describes many different kinds of systems and how they adapt to their environments. In this expanded view, biology is one instance of a much more general phenomenon of evolution.

Newton is said to have understood gravity from a single instance: a falling apple. This led him to a theory, not of apples but of gravity, which was useful in a broad range of situations. Up until recently, we have learned about evolution from a single instance: the biological world. Now, scientists are codifying the concepts of a more general evolution not restricted to biology, and engineers and entrepreneurs are learning to apply those concepts to virtually any system that changes in response to its environment. As you will see in Chapter 4, we already use tools that employ adaptive concepts such as breeding and selective pressure in our information systems. The next opportunity, as you will see in Part III, is to find a way to use this knowledge of adaptation in our management systems.

EVOLUTION AND ADAPTATION

In the biosphere, adaptation refers to the evolutionary process by which organisms change, both in structure and behavior, in order to succeed in the face of environmental pressures. According to Stuart Kauffman, an evolutionary biologist working at the Santa Fe Institute, generally considered the center of the world's discussion of complex adaptive systems, "whether we are talking about organisms or economies, surprisingly general laws govern adaptive processes."[2] At the SFI, researchers explore the commonalities of things you wouldn't normally think of as evolving: language, adapting to the collective minds of those who speak it through their choices of speech; a body of law, adapting to the society it governs through interpretation of the courts; or politics, in which the issues evolve along with the mood and behavior of the voters.[3] One of SFI's early books, authored by Nobel laureate Kenneth Arrow, was *The Economy as an Evolving Complex Adaptive System*.[4] The big idea is this: If you can figure out how adaptation is embedded in biological systems, and then broaden this knowledge into a theory of general evolution, you can effectively apply the theory to many complex systems—including business. Then you can begin to anticipate how your business will adapt to a changing environment and begin to influence its evolutionary path—just as Eduardo Kac lets us influence the evolution of his coded creature in its petri dish. The real value lies in directing this influence toward specific goals, less random than ultraviolet zaps (though contributors to Vault.com might say that's how management works today).

We won't dwell on general evolution per se—this is not yet another book about complexity theory. But the idea that the concepts of evolution apply to our industries, businesses, markets, and managers is fundamental to our thesis: that accelerated change creates the imperative to adapt; that adaptation is not just what biology does, it's the name of a general evolutionary process; and that if business is going to thrive in a volatile environment, it will do so by applying the lessons learned from biological evolution.

How would a business measure successful adaptation? In biology, the metric is "fitness," measured as the relative ability of an organism to breed successfully in a given environment. "Adapting" means continually improving fitness, in particular as the environment changes. In *The Beak of the Finch*, Jonathan Weiner describes finches on one of the Galapagos Islands, explaining how the birds' beaks adapted to the shapes of the flowers on which they fed, helping them to eat more, survive with greater frequency, and grow their population along with their share of the local ecology.

In business, too, growth is a reasonable measure of fitness. As the finch depends on food, business requires the ability to attract human and financial capital, customer esteem, etc. The more adaptive the individual firm, the greater its ability to improve its fitness as its market, industry, or technology changes.

The story of John Deere's planter-factory, breeding schedules moves our discussion from analogy to algorithm. The simulated throughput of each schedule is a quantitative measure of its fitness, and the later generations of schedule represent the evolution of the best schedules toward greater fitness.

John Deere's genetic algorithm leads us to another essential point. In "breeding" its production schedules, Deere has taken information about a physical process—the assembly of seed planters—and applied two evolutionary concepts—sexual recombination and selective pressure—to solve a manufacturing problem. Essential to this process are (1) the ability to represent the scheduling problem as information, coded into ones and zeros, and (2) the ability to "improve the breed" by treating this digital information the way biology treats the coded information in the sequence of Gs, Ts, As, and Cs that make up DNA, and finally (3) the ability to use the resulting information to drive the real-world process. In this way, business, information, and biology all contribute to the solution.

CODE IS CODE

As Eduardo Kac demonstrated, you can translate biology into information, and information into biology because both operate on the basis of coded instructions, and those codes are translatable. When you get down at the bottom of things, code is simply code.

So far, this ability to treat biology as information has been applied mostly to biology. Biologist Richard Dawkins comments, "Genetics today is pure information technology. This, precisely, is why an antifreeze gene can be copied from an arctic fish and pasted into a tomato."[5] Or a spider gene can be inserted into a goat to harvest spider silk from its milk, or as in another of Kac's works, a jellyfish gene can be inserted into a rabbit to make it glow in the dark.

In summer 2002, Eckard Wimmer of the State University of New York at Stonybrook demonstrated just how intertwined our information technology and the work of molecular biology have become. Wimmer created a synthetic polio virus by finding the entire gene sequence on the Net. He ordered snippets of DNA by mail, then used computer-controlled equipment to link the appropriate subsequences. "You open the Internet and lift out a sequence and go to work and make a virus without ever having seen the virus in your laboratory," said Wimmer.[6]

The interchangeability of codes has given rise to a technology marketed by a company called Cyrano Sciences, whose product, Cyranose, amounts to a kind of artificial nose. Smell, of course, is just a way for animals to crack the code of chemical structure. The brainchild of a Caltech chemist, Cyranose identifies smells by turning them into binary code that can be read by a computer. It aspires to supplant the human nose and other detection devices in sniffing out odors in the food industry, in medical diagnostics, in municipal sanitation, and in dozens of other areas in which precise identification is a must. Cyranose contains a chip embedded with thirty-two sensors. Each sensor is made of a different plastic. The entire array is covered with a conductive material such as carbon black. It turns out that each plastic has its own profile when it comes to absorbing vapor molecules. Benzene makes one type of plastic swell; water has the same effect on another. As the swelling alters the spacing between the conductive particles, each exposure creates an easily identifiable signature in the pattern of electrical resistance. The digitized molecular identification is then fed into a pattern-recognition algorithm. The chip can operate in its own handheld device, or it may become a "Cyrano Inside" component of other detection equipment. This technology will enable physicians to diagnose infections merely on the basis of a breath test, and to anticipate the onset of epileptic seizures through odor. With the ability to smell spoilage or toxicity, this kind of technology also can serve as a molecular "coal miner's canary," detecting wear and tear in machinery on the basis of smell, or detecting aircraft fluids—such as jet fuel, turbine oil, or hydraulic fluid—leaking into the cabin area.[7]

As the convergence of information and biology leads to a convergence of the information economy and the molecular economy, science and medicine lead the way.

At Emory University in Atlanta, scientists have been developing a cranial cortical implant that serves as an alternative interface between body and brain for a man named Johnny Ray. Ray suffered a stroke in his brain stem that left him with "locked-in" syndrome, meaning that his brain is intact, but he has no motor control whatsoever, not even the ability to make facial expressions.

Since 1998, however, Ray has had a new appendage very much like the plug Keanu Reeves wore in *The Matrix*. Researchers drilled a hole in his skull, just above his ear, to gain access to his motor cortex, into which they placed a narrow glass cone where electrodes terminate in an electrical contact made of gold. The cone is filled with a special tissue culture that attracts brain cells toward the contact. Over time, Ray's neurons melded with the contact.

Next, researchers asked Ray to think simple thoughts with sharp distinctions—up or down, hot or cold—so that they could record the patterns of his brain waves. By codifying these patterns, amplified and converted to USB input for a Dell Pentium box, they knew which thoughts Ray needed to think in order to move a cursor on a computer screen. By giving him feedback to reinforce these thoughts, they have taught him to spell out words, choose icons, even generate musical tones.

As John Hockenberry wondered in his *Wired* article first telling this story, where does the Dell Pentium box now end and Johnny Ray begin? His brain is now a part of a network that could extend from his motor cortex to a Web server in Australia to a lab in Tokyo and back again.

At the molecular level—where the electrons in wire trigger chemical impulses in nerves—the barriers between the born and the made are vanishing.

CONVERGENCE

Now that we are cracking the code of biology, all the power of digital technology can be used to accelerate its advance. The field of bioinformatics has been born out of this new ability to use digital code to describe molecular behavior. As Evelyn Fox Keller, who has written extensively on the relationships and differences between computer software and genetic programs, points out, "to understand the long-range impact of [recombinant DNA research] we need also to consider the effects that the introduction of powerful new computers is having on biological science."[8]

At the same time that information capabilities are affecting the way the molecular economy grows, what we learn from biology is transforming our ideas about economic growth and enterprise management itself. What we learn and codify about adaptation and evolution will, first, be modeled in digital code, so that we can simulate adaptive systems for specific purposes, as at John Deere. Next, software itself will become ever more like an ecology—books on biology-inspired software are already appearing.[9] (In Chapter 4, we will discuss both of these developments.)

When Newton worked on gravity, he developed a set of tools needed to express his theory. These became calculus, which led to the science of physics. Following the life cycle, physics was followed by the technology of mechanical and electrical engineering, industrial innovation, and the organizational approach of "scientific management." Physics, with its ideas of repeatability, predictability, and direct cause-and-effect, became a way of thinking that helped increase per-capita income for a couple of centuries.

Today, whatever their short-term doldrums, biology and information remain the economy's two growth sectors. Increasingly, both are teaching the lessons of adaptation and evolution, and as business has an ever-greater need for adaptiveness to cope with the volatility of the economic environment, business, too, will take evolution as its model. As the economic life cycle predicts, we will again have scientific management—but this time the underlying science will be "general evolution." The theories that drive biology will be adopted in the way we use information, and the way we manage our enterprises. Biology, information, and business will converge on general evolution.

CREATE, CONNECT, EVOLVE

Just as physics has core principles, so do adaptive systems. Complexity science is not sufficiently mature to have an accepted set of fundamental definitions, but we'll provide the basics here:

○ *Agents*. Atoms, software, and people can all be referred to as "agents" in a system. Agents are the decision-making units, and they have rules that determine their choices. For the atoms, the rules are the rules of chemistry. Software agents have rules that are generally clear and simple. People's rules are more complicated.

○ *Self-Organization*. An important property of agents is the ability to organize autonomously to create something more complex. Hydrogen and oxygen don't need a manager to design water for them—put them together in conducive circumstances and water simply happens. Similarly, farmers in a village sixty or six hundred years ago didn't need Wal-Mart to bring them together to form a weekly farmer's market.

○ *Recombination*. Breeding is the way biology recombines the recipes for agents. Nature recombines at random; we direct the process as, for instance, horse breeders do when hoping for faster horses. Recombination is the most efficient engine of innovation, in nature, and in human affairs. The Wright brothers created something completely new by combining the capabilities of the airfoil, the bicycle wheel, and the internal combustion engine.

○ *Selective Pressure.* "Fitness" is assessed by the environment—if your beak fits the plant, you thrive; if you're a fast horse, the breeder selects you; if your product doesn't meet the market's need, you die. Selective pressures determine which agents get the opportunity to recombine in the next generation.

○ *Adaptation.* In nature, an animal can change its behavior; over generations, a species' capabilities evolve. A business, then, can change its behavior to perform better, and an industry can evolve.

○ *Co-evolution.* "When the frog evolves a sticky tongue, flies get Teflon feet," says Stuart Kauffman. Competition, cooperation, and innovation all lead to co-evolution in business as in biology (e.g., Intel, Microsoft, and software developers all adapt continually to one another, affecting the evolution of the industry).

○ *Emergence.* The interaction of self-organization, recombination, selection, and co-evolution leads to an ecology—or an economy. The complexity of these networks is such that we are unable to predict what they will look like by examining the properties of the agents—the outcome emerges from the interactions. We don't know how a rainforest will change in one hundred years, nor the relationship between PCs and cell phones in one hundred weeks.

These concepts are helpful in pointing out similarities in the way different adaptive systems evolve. Each of them has fruitful applications in biology, in information, and in business, as we'll see in the next three chapters.

Translating back and forth among these three realms, as we will be freely doing, raises the question of how literally to interpret the parallels among these adaptive systems. In the past decade, biological metaphors have been applied to business, sometimes with care (e.g., Michael Rothschild's book *Bionomics: The Inevitability of Capitalism*), and sometimes with more flourish than rigor. Here, it is our intention to go well beyond the broadest level of metaphor to derive principles and tools that can be practically applied today.

Yet we want to be careful not to overstate the case for the parallels. For example, today we have a pretty good idea how adaptive software such as the genetic algorithm works to recombine digital information, because we made it ourselves. We are a long way from fully understanding how the DNA in a cell recombines to construct a new organism. The complexities of a single cell dwarf those of our computer systems. Our view is that although comparisons of business and biology, or economy and ecology, are often much too glib, the work of thousands of scientists has begun to codify the structural similarities of adaptive systems. The use of genetic algorithms is "metaphorical" in that the recombination of code is patterned on, rather than a model of, the way DNA recombines. It is rigorous in that it harnesses the idea of recombination to produce a measurably better result than operations research could previously achieve.

In *It's Alive*, we try to be careful to neither overstate metaphors nor soft-pedal the science that has led to useful applications. When we get to prescribing principles for business, we will necessarily be looser than we are when describing software simulations, just as the agent rules in chemistry are clearer than those for self-organizing people.

We try to use the terms defined above—agents, selective pressure, emergence—when they are precise and effective. We also use a metaphorical term for general evolution broad enough to encompass the differences among information, biology, and business: "create, connect, evolve." We use *create* as a rubric to discuss the nature of agents and their decision rules; *connect* to refer to the interactions that support both recombination and selective pressure; and *evolve* to describe the processes of both adaptation and evolution, which lead to a new set of agents, bringing us back again to *create*.

Create: Agents and Rules

The bedrock of the adaptive point of view is that the world is created from the bottom up, as agents of one kind or another organize themselves into increasingly complex and capable structures. To understand how to change the world, we need to understand the agents and the rules they live by.

A cell is a biological agent following complex chemical rules. In an electrical grid, a circuit breaker is an agent, monitoring the electrical flow by measuring physical parameters. An oxygen atom follows its rules, "deciding" whether or not to bind to a hydrogen atom. A grocer, deciding to buy more yellow peppers and fewer red ones, is an agent following rules based on business and human behavior. A financial trader or a trading program, automatically initiating a sell order, is an agent following rules in a financial market. The atom and the cell, the greengrocer and the financial trader are all agents following rules.

Biological agents self-organize according to their rules, often creating larger structures; atoms to molecules, molecules to organisms, and so on to species and ecologies. The ecology arises from the atoms, and not vice versa.

This same principle of self-organizing agents creating larger structures operates in economics as well as in biology. Semiconductors led to computers, then to modems, and then to the Internet, not vice versa. Like biology, the next economy will also derive from molecules—new molecular elements recombining from the bottom up. Our world is made up of agents, each with decision rules. Businesses are beginning to use "agent-based models"—in which each decision-maker is represented individually—in a wide range of applications. For example, to improve service at a theme park, managers can simulate foot traffic and ride capacity. Treating each customer as a separate decision-maker choosing the next activity, managers can use the model to shorten wait times, provide customers with more of what they want, and reduce staff costs. The military uses agent-based models to make choices about whether to invest in more guns or more communications equipment, how to train recruits, and when to use certain tactics, so operations can be more effective and result in fewer casualties. Policy-makers use agent-based models to assess tax policy.

We've adopted bottom-up ideas for economic management using markets—mechanisms for agent interaction—not planning, as an alternative to top-down resource allocation. The world's experience of the past fifty years has shown conclusively that distributed decision-making does a better job of satisfying demand than a centralized approach. Nonetheless, many of our businesses retain a surprisingly "Soviet" management style, using approaches developed in an assembly-line era that have more in common with a top-down mentality than with a bottom-up one.

Yet, as Adam Smith argued, distributed intelligence and action is the only way to create the capacity for adaptability. During human gestation, you can grow the 90 trillion cells that make up your body only because each cell knows what to do, according to the rules embedded in its genome. Amazon.com can give individual treatment to each customer only because software agents can follow the rules in their software to make sense of customer behavior. The U.S. Marines, as we'll see in Chapter 7, can respond to the unpredictability of battle only by teaching each marine the tactical principles he needs in order to act.

Connect: The Role of Diversity

No agent is an island. Oxygen and hydrogen atoms can't get much done on their own. But once they have the ability to connect to the ninety other elements of the periodic table, they can start forming the compounds that give us everything from bologna to benzene.

Similarly, economic progress arises from the connection of diverse elements. By the time hominids were living in caves, they had developed the essence of trade—namely, specialization and exchange. No individual made his own spears, hunted his own mammoths, or ate them by himself—groups formed to improve the odds on the hunt and make sure the carcass was consumed before it spoiled. Today, this same process continues under the name *globalization*.

RECOMBINATION

The process of "recombination," connecting ideas expressed in some form of code, is evolution's primary source of innovation. This works for technology as well as for organisms—before the airfoil connected with the bicycle and the internal combustion engine, there were no airplanes.

The enabler of recombination is connection, whether person-to-person, cell-to-cell, or atom-to-atom. To create something with more capabilities than a single agent, you have to be able to connect multiple agents. This is why the history of economic evolution is to a significant degree the history of transportation and communication, from speech, to boats, to writing, to mail, to trains, to the telegraph, to the telephone, to the airplane, to the Net. Each reduced the economic costs of recombination and therefore innovation. Each profoundly changed the scale and diversity of economic activity. And each, as we've argued above, accelerated the rate of economic change.

Evolution in biology also creates networks. One of nature's proudest innovations occurred about two billion years ago, when a virus invaded a bacterium, creating a cell with a nucleus, which is where the DNA lives. This in turn gave rise to the fundamental connection of biology beyond bacteria—sexual recombination, in which the instructions from each of two parents are combined to create the unique design for each unique child.[10] Prior to recombination, novelty arose only from random mutation. Mutation produces successful novelty only rarely, while recombination does much more frequently. So the invention of the "eukaryotic" cells—the ones with nuclei—was the establishment of a mechanism whereby nature accelerated its own evolution.

Once the cell could store the information within its boundaries, the process of sexual reproduction could begin. But why do organisms invest so much of their time and energy in some version of moonlight, roses, and rutting behavior? Given much simpler options that already existed—cloning, parthenogenesis—one might wonder why wasteful and messy sex evolved at all, much less spread throughout the biosphere. The answer is that sex, recombining genetic elements of the father and mother, is the quickest way to derive innovations that increase fitness. Sexual reproduction gives each new offspring a fresh roll of the dice in terms of inherited traits. And innovation through recombination turns out to be far more efficient than de novo invention, with far higher odds for success, and it can provide exponential breakthroughs in novelty.

Why the premium on innovation? Because the pressure to find new ways of surviving is inherent in the system. Recombination, working from existing elements, is simply the best way to get there quick.

Biologists have studied the various forms of reproduction, and the role of recombination. Ernst Mayr, one of the greatest evolutionary theorists, sums it up this way: "The ultimate explanation for the success of sexual reproduction is that it greatly increases the genetic variability of the offspring, and increased variability has multiple advantages in the struggle for survival."[11]

What happens next depends on what there is to connect to and recombine with. If all you have to start with is oxygen atoms, your outcome is limited to either ozone or the stuff we breathe. But factor in the ninety-one other elements, and you get an explosion of possibilities. The principle holds in all evolving systems: Diversity breeds diversity. One of the most powerful effects of the Net is its ability to enormously expand the diversity of backgrounds and ideas any individual can easily access.

Lou Gerstner, former CEO of IBM, began his campaign to accelerate IBM's growth by bringing the diversity of employee opinion into play, opening communicating by e-mail to every individual. And at the Center for Business Innovation, our primary approach to anticipating the future is to create as diverse as possible a network of thinkers. Recombination makes headlines when geneticists modify rice, or when AOL buys Time Warner, both cases an attempt to create new capabilities through expanded networks. Of course, some recombinations work—and some don't.

Recombinant techniques in information code have just begun to make headlines, both on the business page—John Deere's example warranted a major *Wall Street Journal* story—and the entertainment section, where reviews of Kac's work mingle with those of the movie *GATTACA*.

We have all experienced the business environment's increase in connections in the last decade, putting more diverse business capabilities in contact with one another and accelerating the rate at which they recombine. As explained in Chapter 1, that's the source of the volatility we've been speaking of. And this density of connections will only increase, as the chemical, biological, and information codes become unified. It's like bringing the gene pools of the Old World, the New World, and Australia together at a kind of universal stud farm for genetic recombination.

If our organizations don't match this external increase in connectivity and diversity, they'll fall into the trap concisely captured by Jack Welch: "When the rate of change outside exceeds the rate of change inside, the end is in sight."

SELECTIVE PRESSURE

Adam Smith's central rule is that individuals, following their own self-interest, lead to the greatest good for the greatest number in society. Charles Darwin's rule says that species adapt or die. Selective pressure is the raw truth of evolving systems. Species that are highly adaptive propagate wildly and colonize new environments with their offspring—whether animal, vegetable, or corporate. And they survive the diverse slings and arrows that a rapidly changing environment throws at them.

Markets operate the same way. If your product can't adapt to the changing environmental conditions, such as technology change or new customer preferences, it dies. Remember the Northern Spy apple, the Visi-Calc spreadsheet, and the AMC Pacer? All gone the way of the Betamax, victims of the market mechanisms that give customers the chance to create feedback, the same way that the savannah gives a lame antelope feedback. Markets are the savannah of the economy, where economic selection operates.

First agents connect to recombine and create a new idea, a new creature, or a new bit of code; then the environment applies feedback through further connection. The idea is reprinted or ignored; the creature eats or is eaten; the business process is repeated over and over until it becomes a best practice or is consigned to the dustbin of consulting reports. Successful agents become candidates for the next round of recombination. And so it goes. [12]

Evolve: How Feedback Shapes the World

Whenever molecules connect, they, and the entire system of which they are a part, engage in the continuous innovation and adaptation that collectively we call evolution. Each species faces selective pressure from the spectrum of challenges in its ecological niche—the competition for food and habitat, threats from predators, the need to adapt to changes in climate. Species may also find partners to help symbiotically exploit their niches. Each evolving part reflects and affects the evolution of the others, creating a "co-evolving" world.

In biology it's called an ecosystem; in business it's called an economy. And then there are law, government, religion, and all the other systems that put feedback into the network. Each has its own elements, connecting with others, recombining, adapting, and co-evolving.

Telecommunications services and modems, rechargeable batteries and color screens, tires and road surfaces, copyright law and communications, all co-evolve under the selective pressure. Similarly, when a new predator like the DVD separates from its CD ancestor, it affects species like the VCR and digital TV. At their most fundamental, Schumpeter's "gales of creative destruction" in market capitalism are like the continuous cycle of speciation and extinction events.

The increased connectivity of the economic world means that feedback is more immediate than ever before, and that a new, aggressive species can invade more niches more easily. (The DVD player penetrated the consumer-electronics market more quickly than any of its predecessors, for example.) Quarantines are difficult to enforce (cf. the Napster battle). Add the "code is code" connections among information, biological, and business worlds, and our economic environment changes from an isolated Iceland to an Amazon jungle, teeming with life—and teeming with volatility.

EMERGENCE

The smallest units—whether molecules, bits of software, or individuals in society—all behave according to certain rules that can be expressed in codes. Whether in information or biology, in a rainforest or an industry, agents, rules, and connections are the prerequisites for evolution. As the agents interact, the outcome emerges, not as a planned result but as the result of the evolutionary process. Some changes increase fitness; others lead to extinction.

The price of a stock, for example, is an emergent outcome of the market involving thousands of agents with their own trading rules. We are not able to look at the positions of all the traders and anticipate today's closing prices. Equally, it would be difficult to look at the periodic table of elements and predict the world's ecology—it's the emergent outcome of billions of years of elements' interactions with each other. An anthill's overall behavior emerges from the rules embedded in each ant. And we believe that profitability, rather than being an engineered feature of a business, is also an emergent outcome of the actions of the individuals within it interacting with their environment.

As we'll see more clearly in the next two chapters, not only do all connected systems evolve, but as information systems and biological systems

FIGURE 2-1　Convergence

	Biology	Information	Business
Create	• Miniaturization • Reprogramming • Self-Assembly	• Agent-Based Modeling • Object-Oriented 　Programming	• Monetize Molecules • Self-Organize
Connect	• Hybrid Devices • Combinatorial 　Chemistry • Diverse Molecular 　Libraries	• Genetic Algorithms • Evolutionary 　Programming	• Recombine • Sense & Respond
Evolve	• High-throughput 　screening as 　Selective Pressure	• Simulating Selective 　Pressure	• Learn & Adapt • Seed, Select, Amplify • Destabilize

connect to each other, radically new things will emerge. The payoff right now for the way we manage our affairs is this: As our enterprises become chiefly composed of coded messages connecting human and software agents, the concepts of evolution become more central to their behavior. Evolution will become the dominant mental model during the next ten years. Business, biology, and information will all incorporate that model, using the tools and theories of evolution. This conceptual shift is already happening. Biology is focused on evolution. Information will move to a framework of biology, as autonomous software and increased connectivity make networked systems behave as if they are alive. In business, this shift will find its expression in a different approach to management. Managers have been trained to optimize—to make the same process better—secure in the assumption that the world around them will remain stable. The emphasis will shift to designing for adaptability in a world that never stops changing. This is the adaptive management we will describe in Part III.

Biology, information, and business each express concepts of evolution uniquely. Figure 2-1 provides a framework that highlights their convergence.

In 1971, you didn't know about GUI, CPUs, or gigahertz. As today's convergence proceeds, you're going to learn terms like gene shuffling, combinatorial chemistry, and high-throughput screening, as they move into management language of the molecular economy.

In the next two chapters, we want to spend some time illustrating how create, connect, evolve is playing out in molecular science and information today. Along the way, you'll get a look at the drawing boards on which the innovations of the next decade are taking shape.

A biological system can be exceedingly small. Many of the cells are very tiny, but they are very active; they manufacture various substances; they walk around; they wiggle; and they do all kinds of marvelous things—all on a very small scale.... Consider the possibility that we too can make a thing very small which does what we want—that we can manufacture an object that maneuvers at that level!

—Richard Feynman, Nobel laureate in Physics, speaking in 1959[1]

3

BIOLOGY AND THE WORLD OF MOLECULES

ALAN Kay was originally trained as a biologist, but he combines Eduardo Kac's visual flair, intuition, and iconoclasm with a computer scientist's technical skill. As it happens, Kay was one of those guys muttering about—inventing actually—the first "graphical user interface" while at PARC in the 1970s. Now the GUI—mouse, icon, pull-down menu, "point and click"—is so intuitive that kids learn to use it before they can read.

In the past several years, Kay has nurtured another project to help us visualize and access data hidden beneath the surface. This time his medium is not pure information but the essence of all matter, viewed from the bottom up.

Working at Walt Disney Imagineering,[2] Kay developed ideas for a Disney World "ride" designed to transport visitors into the secret life of molecules. By making this experience highly visual and interactive, he wanted to help us understand the very different properties one finds at the scale of one-billionth of a meter, the "nanoscale" at which atoms move sideways faster than our nervous system can perceive motion at all.

"If an atom were scaled up to the size of a tennis ball," Kay tells us, "it would be moving at four times the speed of light."

It so happens that our conversation takes place in a taxi careening at 50 miles per hour through the streets of Rome, en route to a mutual speaking engagement at Telecom Italia.

"Bacteria spin their tails at a million RPM just to move," Kay goes on, ignoring the Space Mountain G-forces we're experiencing firsthand. "They have to, because at their scale, water has the viscosity that asphalt has at ours."

Bacteria, of course, never thought of as being particularly muscular, swim right through these molecules of double hydrogen bonded to single oxygen, the asphalt-like viscosity notwithstanding.

For all the exotic differences Kay wants to show us, his most potent observation could apply to the streams of Fiats and Vespas swirling around us as we lurch toward our destination. In the molecular world, the combination of speed, mobility, and raw numbers of units in play adds up to a rate of collision and connection that defies comprehension. The intuitions of probability that we take for granted on our individual, human scale simply don't apply at this level, nor even at the level of 100,000 people crammed into a football stadium. With so many opportunities for molecules to bash into each other and bond together, anything that can happen *will* happen, sooner than we imagine. Even such an unlikely event as the development of DNA out of the ninety-two chemical elements available when the earth first cooled down takes only a couple billion years. "The molecular world is completely outside the normal common-sense range of thinking," Kay summarizes.

It is this molecular sense that, over the next decade, will become our common understanding.

MOLECULAR TECHNOLOGIES

We know the molecular economy has begun the second phase of its life cycle because we see molecular science moving out of the laboratory and into commercial application. New technology begins the growth cycle. In 1856, Henry Bessemer patented a steelmaking process that cut the cost of rails by two-thirds, immediately spurring the growth of railroads and leading to skyscrapers, automobiles, ball bearings, and battleships. Steel was one of the high-tech growth industries of its day. Similarly, in 1959, Robert Noyce and others put two transistors on a piece of silicon, creating the first integrated circuit. As with steel and railroads, this laboratory-scale advance led to the creation of new products that radically changed the economics of production. We're living through the resulting transformation right now.

Of course, in 1856 or 1959, no one could have successfully foreseen the impact of the current technological achievements. But we can be pretty certain of the evolutionary path that leads from the lab, to processes, to products, to new businesses, to zeitgeist. Whether or not Craig Venter's work mapping the human genome is parallel to the work of Bessemer or Noyce, it shows us that the next phase has begun. Go to GeneWiz.com and you can have 700 bases of DNA sequenced for $16 and get your results back in two business days.

Here, we want to provide a tour of the enabling technologies of the molecular age, covering four technology trends that are the precursors of new economic capabilities. We don't aim to provide a complete education in contemporary science and technology, but we do hope to give you enough current "gee-whiz" examples to convince you of the importance of following these developments now.

Miniaturization

The 1966 sci-fi thriller *Fantastic Voyage* put Raquel Welch and Donald Pleasence in a submarine and used a miniaturization beam to shrink the whole affair, enabling craft and crew to cruise in the bloodstream of an injured scientist whose survival was crucial to winning the Cold War. We want to do something similar in this chapter: to shrink your perspective down to the scale needed to understand the world at the size of molecules. Our mission is to prepare you for the economic wars of the molecular economy.

At this point in the growth cycle, molecular technology advances daily. Here are items culled from just four weekly issues of a technology newsletter in late 2002:[3]

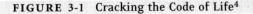

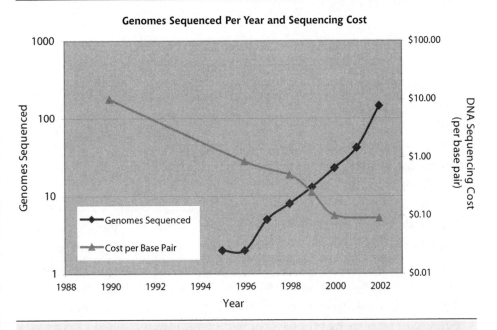

FIGURE 3-1   Cracking the Code of Life[4]

○ The unit cost of sequencing a DNA base pair has fallen from
approximately $10 in 1990 to about 10 cents today, a progression
reminiscent of Moore's Law (see Figure 3-1). Today, Celera
Genomics is able to sequence an individual's genome for $621,500;
this figure should fall to about $6,200 in ten years if this progres-
sion continues.

○ Researchers at Carnegie Mellon University have used nanotubes
to filter greenhouse gases more efficiently than today's technologies.

○ Advanced Micro Devices has fabricated circuits with transistors
inscribed at the scale of 10 nanometers.

○ Biologists and engineers recently discovered the properties that
enable the gecko's unsurpassed sticking power. This breakthrough
opens the door to synthesizing "dry adhesive microstructures that
can function underwater and even in a vacuum."[5]

○ A recent study published by IN-Stat/MDR reports that total ship-
ments of microelectromechanical systems (MEMS) for consumer

electronics will jump from 5.2 million units in 2001 to almost 190 million in 2006."[6]

How does this affect the economy today? The falling price of gene sequencing will have a significant impact on health care, and is based on molecular biology; nanotubes could affect many energy-intensive industrial processes, and is based on what we might call molecular-scale chemistry; AMD's circuits are an advance in microelectronics that enables further advance in information technology; and gecko-glue transfers knowledge from nature about how to make materials with desirable properties.

Miniaturization has been a priority, as the microelectronics industry has needed to create ever-smaller lines on semiconductor wafers to increase the power of chips. Consequently, we now have programmable devices small enough to interact with single cells. At the same time, biologists have been detailing and modeling in computers the ways cells work. The cell, biologists have observed, is already the master of nanotechnology, accomplishing its purposes through molecular machinery. When a nerve transmits an impulse, what happens can be seen as electrical or chemical. At the nanoscale, the disciplines of carbon and silicon meet and merge.

Nanotechnology is the field of research dealing with objects measured in terms of a "nano" meter—one-billionth of a meter. For reference, a red blood cell is about 10,000 nanometers (nm) in diameter. Nanotech has brought together physicists and chemists who manipulate matter at this unimaginable scale, where quantum mechanics, not classical physics, reigns, and the thermal, electrical, chemical, and structural properties create Alan Kay's non-commonsensical world. Application areas of nanotech already include pharmaceuticals and health care, materials and manufacturing, as well as electronics.

To imagine the promise of nanotech, we need only look at what nature can do with it:

Cells can do everything.... For every task that a mischievous examiner could possibly think of setting for a microscopically small something, there probably is a cell that can perform it. You want a living compass? No problem, as magneto-tactic bacteria know which way is north. A remedy against oil spills? A transport vehicle for oxygen? A molecular motor? No matter whether you want to mine for silver, dispose of organic solvents, or convert chemical energy to motion heat, or light, or vice versa, nature has a small-scale solution. Thus far, technology is unable to duplicate most of these achievements.[7]

It's not surprising that cells have the lead, given their several-billion-year head start. And until recently, working at molecular scale has been like playing poker wearing a blindfold and work gloves—it's pretty hit-and-miss trying to create winning hands with things you can't see or hold properly. This is changing rapidly.

Visualization

Louis Pasteur could never have given us pasteurized milk or safer surgery without the enabling power of the microscope to see what was going on in vitro. To scale down from the size of Pasteur's "germs"—about 2,000 nm—to that of viruses—about 50 nm—has required significant technological progress. Two cases point again to the role of information technology in driving these capabilities. X-ray crystallography—taking the molecule whose structure the scientist wants to understand, crystallizing it, shining X-rays through the crystal, and deciphering the image—has been around since Watson and Crick. But the method was straitjacketed by the sheer computation requirements of turning the X-ray image into a model of the protein. It was as if you tried to assemble the 3-D images of a CAT scan from a set of individual X-rays. By the late 1990s, the process could be achieved in a couple of days on a Silicon Graphics workstation. The result is that the resolution of X-ray crystallography has reached as low as 0.165 nm, about the size of a water molecule.[8]

The second advance is the development of the atomic force micro-scope (AFM), the "camera" that allowed IBM researchers to make an image of their company logo assembled from individual atoms. Unlike optical or electron microscopes, the AFM doesn't create an image directly. Instead, it scans a fine ceramic tip over a surface much the same way a phonograph needle scans a record. The varying attraction between the atoms on the surface to be scanned and those on the tip moves the tip, and the information about the tip's movement is translated into an image of the surface, "much like the cane of a blind person."[9] Once again, this couldn't be done at all without the information-processing capability.

AFM is no longer for publicity stunts. Veeco Instruments, a leading manufacturer of tools for operating at the nanoscale, offers four separate AFM product lines, and fifteen models. The company cites applications beyond imaging, including understanding differences in chemical forces across a surface at the molecular scale—important for setting the specs for new drugs or materials.

There are many others: The Zeiss "PhotoShop for cells" that we cited in Chapter 1 relies on something called "confocal imaging," which can see through the outer layers of the skin to give pathologists the same information they would otherwise get by looking at a biopsy under a microscope—without slicing into the patient. Unless you're going to the lab yourself, you need to know only this: The mysteries of the molecular are rapidly becoming more accessible not just to scientists in their labs but to R&D groups in any industry.

Manipulation

Once we can see molecular structures, we'd like to be able to do something with them—without damaging them. Working with researchers from the University of North Carolina, 3rd Tech has developed the NanoManipulator, which "combines the best techniques of interactive 3-D computer graphics, [virtual reality] and haptics feedback with an advanced scanning probe microscope."[10] The machine translates the force at the AFM probe tip to a push on the hand of the user—that's what "haptic" means—tactile feedback. This allows the researcher to feel the shape of a surface at atomic scale. "The NanoManipulator allows you to grab the probe in your hand and push the nanotubes around, build a structure, bend and manipulate them interactively," according to Doug Schiff, 3rd Tech's vice president of marketing.

The haptic approach is being used on a larger scale to create a simulator for medical students. At MIT, a syringe is attached to a force-feedback device attached to a mannequin, which allows students to experience the feel of inserting an epidural needle into the spinal column. At T-Medical Systems, students learn to feel the "pops" of needles and catheters piercing skin and veins. Better *in silico* than *vivo*!

A second novel manipulation capability lets the molecules do the work. It's called combinatorial chemistry, and you might think of it as molecular mass marketing. Suppose you have identified a new disease pathway, and you believe you could disrupt it if you could find a drug to bind to a particular site on a cell. In the past, pharmaceutical companies would pursue a "rational drug design" approach, isolating the binding site, perhaps using X-ray crystallography to identify its structure, and then attempting, through computer simulation, to create a new molecule that would bind to the site.

Combinatorial chemistry depends on new, automated techniques that enable researchers to arrive at a solution much more quickly and less expensively. Researchers create a population of potential solutions, a library of small molecules of enormous diversity. They can then evaluate candidate molecules in terms of their performance across a variety of factors: solubility, stability, toxicity, and so on. If you can fix the target binding site to a kind of fancy Q-Tip—in fact, to a handful of Q-Tips that are tightly packed into a tiny microchip—and swish it around in a vat containing millions of different candidate drug molecules, you have a decent chance that when you pull out your swab something has bound to it. Even better, what's attached itself has "competed" with the other molecules, which would have displaced it if they had formed stronger bonds, just the way your best potential customers respond most strongly to your advertising.

Evaluation

If we can see and touch molecules, the next step in extracting value is to assess whether manipulation—whether by man or molecule—has achieved a desired result. This requires a set of tools for "reading" molecules, especially DNA, and for sensing results.

The Human Genome Project, when it began in 1990, was compared to the Apollo program. Its objective—to sequence the human genome by 2005—was criticized on the grounds of practicality: Using the gene-sequencing technology of the time, it would have taken more than 100,000 researcher-years to complete. As the process has developed and become automated, however, the cost in time and money required to read DNA base pairs has dropped dramatically. Equipment to do this in your own lab costs about as much as an entry-level Ferrari. While we continue to learn that DNA sequences tell only a small part of the developmental story, the technology to investigate them has moved within reach of any entrepreneur with an idea.

A second foundation technology is the microarray, again a hybrid of information-technology technique and biotechnology requirement. Suppose you'd like to monitor the presence of a few thousand different compounds in a test tube, a bloodstream, or an atmosphere. Building on the combinatorial-chemistry idea, you might divide a microchip into thousands of partitions and attach a different molecule to each section, each molecule chosen because it binds to one of your targets. The chip becomes an array of microprobes. The chip can sense the change in mass caused when something binds to a section, and expresses this as a digital output. Similar technologies are in use already to assess the communication that goes on between genes within the cell. The potential for remote sensing in new ways could support control systems for industrial products that detect when impurities are present, when a bearing is wearing out, or simply when a mixture is getting out of spec.

Third, the ability to translate molecular behavior into digital code is turning simulation into an evaluation tool at the molecular scale. Many researchers are working to create simulations of human organs to allow various kinds of experiments *in silico*. One longstanding effort has been to create a simulated heart-muscle cell. Enough success has been achieved that the FDA now uses this simulation as a part of its certification process for cardiac drugs.

If Alan Kay's Wild Ride is the Life of Molecules 101, this sampling of foundation technologies is intended to be the second-level course, making the case that the next ten years will see enormous acceleration in harnessing molecules in commercial applications. In the next section, we'll look at the progress that already has been made.

APPLICATION

The technologies described above were developed to advance molecular science, but they are already in commercial use. Some of these are in the fabrication of materials, molecules, or microbes with new properties, and behaving by new rules. These are described in the section called "Create." Some are using techniques of recombination to develop even more novel solutions, or connecting molecular and information codes in new kinds of hybrids. You'll find these under "Connect." And some have accelerated and automated the forces of selection to continually improve their solutions, using synthetic evolution techniques—"Evolve."

Create

Evolution proceeds from the bottom up, but something has to be at the bottom. Here we look at the new "somethings" along with their "behavioral rules"—in the case of molecules, their properties and abilities to interact with other molecules. With the ability to visualize, manipulate, and evaluate molecules, researchers are creating new materials, some through man-made techniques, and some by reprogramming nature's existing apparatus. Molecular biology and chemistry are merging into a science of creation. In fact, in 2002, the Nobel Prize in Chemistry was awarded for work in proteomics,[11] which we would normally think of as biological.

One important breakthrough for today's entrepreneurs was the discovery in 1985 of the "buckyball," or, on formal occasions, the "buckminsterfullerene." The buckyball constitutes a third fundamental form of carbon, the other two being diamond and graphite. Named after visionary designer R. Buckminster Fuller, the buckyball is a twenty-faced structure that looks like one of Fuller's famous geodesic domes. They are hollow on the inside, and separated from the outside world by a single layer of carbon atoms linked in a way that resembles the seams on a soccer ball.

In the near future, buckyballs are projected to perform in widely varied roles. A layer of aluminum oxide turns them into superconductors at relatively warm temperatures.[12] When zapped with microwaves, buckyballs can be coaxed to form diamond crystals a few billionths of a meter in size. This smooth film is one of the world's most perfect lubricants for machines smaller than dust particles.

Cousin to the buckyball is the buckytube (also called a nanotube).

Made of carbon atoms hooked together in geodesic structures, buckytubes have the same diameter as a buckyball, which, provocatively enough given our concern with crossing codes, is the same diameter as DNA.

Combining 10^{14} of these would yield something with a diameter of one centimeter—a buckycable. Scientists predict that such a structure would be one hundred times stronger than steel, with one-sixth the weight, the electrical conductivity of copper, and the thermal conductivity of diamonds, the most efficient heat conductor known.

C Sixty, a Canadian pharmaceutical firm, has focused on buckytubes' size and structure, which allow them to sneak drugs past the human body's formidable immune system. C Sixty likens buckyballs to a molecular pincushion that can be decorated with therapeutic compounds. Since buckyballs are hollow they can carry drugs inside them, a sort of Trojan-horse approach to drug delivery. C Sixty has developed a buckyball-based AIDS treatment, currently in Stage I clinical trials. Such advances in drug delivery open up new possibilities for new medicinal agents, including proteins, which otherwise are too fragile to withstand the enzymes and pH changes found in the stomach. In more traditional industries such as transportation, consumer electronics, and textiles, the cutting edge of materials science includes these examples:

○ General Motors used nanocomposites to reinforce running boards on its 2002 midsize vans. The new nano-enhanced plastics are lighter, stronger, less brittle in cold temperatures, and recyclable. The National Science Foundation estimates that the widespread use of these nanocomposites could lead to a reduction of 400 million gallons of gasoline consumption over the life of one year's fleet of vehicles and reduce the related dioxide emissions by more than five million tons.[13]

○ Two scientists at Drexel University in Philadelphia have created a new class of ceramics that behave more like metals. They are stiff, lightweight, easily shaped or "machinable," and can support loads at upward of 1,300 degrees Celsius.[14] By contrast, our most advanced metal alloys become soft above 1,000 degrees. One application could be jet-engine turbines. Raising the operating temperature of the U.S. airlines' fleet one degree would save nearly $1 billion in fuel costs annually.

○ High-tech companies are using nanotechnology to develop next-generation computer displays and television screens. Samsung's carbon nanotube-based flat-screen television is scheduled to come on the market by late 2004. They are expected to be as inexpensive as existing cathode-ray tubes and as thin as high-priced liquid-crystal or plasma-display televisions, with significantly improved resolution.

Automobiles, aircraft, and information technology add up to a substantial proportion of the economy, and we haven't even touched on new materials used in manufacturing such as the nanocrystalline diamond-films used as lubricants. The take-home message is this: If you manufacture anything today, there are molecularly engineered materials on the drawing board that could change your game.

REPROGRAMMING

Molecular technology-enabled innovation isn't always a matter of creating entirely new compounds or materials. Other current research focuses on "reprogramming" what's already there, using genetically coded instructions to trigger a molecule or a cell to acquire new characteristics, also known as "hijacking nature's own creative machinery."[15] This sometimes involves getting cells and microorganisms to do more of what they already do, or to do it slightly differently. Quest International has created a new approach to body odor with a product that, instead of annihilating all bacteria on the skin, as most deodorants do, redirects the bacteria to change the way they digest the fats in our perspiration, which is the direct cause of the odor we find offensive. This could be an isolated application, but more likely it is an early sign of a technology revolution in the $30 billion cosmetics and body-care industries.

The most notable, and controversial, instance of reprogramming among living things is stem-cell research. Stem cells taken from embryos offer researchers a more or less "generic" state, before cells have reached the developmental stage at which they differentiate into skin cells or kidney cells, specialized to perform specific functions. Yet researchers can also redirect, or change the rules, of adult stem cells, as well as cells from other types of organisms. Under the right conditions, certain undifferentiated cells apparently can mature to match whatever a new context demands. For example, adult stem cells taken from the bone marrow of mice have been redirected to become heart muscle, kidney, and nerve cells, offering hope for those suffering from Parkinson's and Alzheimer's diseases.[16] Work directed at reprogramming bone means that knee and hip replacement, as well as periodontal surgery, could become a thing of the past. At the University of Texas, scientists already have used reengineered cells from mice to grow new teeth in the lab.

We can imagine learning enough about cellular machinery to intervene in biological systems just as effectively as we do today in mechanical systems. We're still a long way from understanding the complex workings of any single-celled organism, but when we do, the promise is even greater, especially given that cells, unlike machines, are adaptive. What if products could perform the final steps of differentiation themselves, just as stem cells do, long after they left the manufacturing facility, distribution depot, or retail shelf? What if "smart" products, sensing their surroundings, could redirect or modify their form or behavior according to the requirements of a given environment, acting on embedded rules and cues from local conditions? Scientists have created materials able to do just that. Tomorrow it will mean longer shelf life and less shelf space for a wide range of products.

- A company called Metabolix produces biodegradable plastics using "microbial factories." By modifying these microorganisms' metabolisms, researchers are growing plastics rather than manufacturing them. A similar approach creates toxin-loving organisms for environmental cleanup. These developments have significant implications for the chemical industry.
- Materials scientists at MIT and the German Wool Research Institute, citing the time and expense involved in shaping metal alloys, as well as the limited range of deformation, have developed shape-memory polymers that are much cheaper, can be programmed at the molecular level in seconds, and can withstand deformations of several hundred percent. These programmable polymers are targeted for biomedical applications, but German researcher Andreas Lendlein proposes using shape-memory polymers in auto bodies. Once you've established the "behavioral rules" at the molecular

level, should you dent your car, you simply pull out a heat gun and, essentially, "blow dry" your fender back into its original shape.

○ At the University of Illinois, researchers have created spheres 50 microns in diameter and filled them with a liquid that solidifies when it comes into contact with a catalyst. They mix these microspheres into an epoxy polymer to create a plastic. If the plastic cracks, it shatters these tiny containers, which release the liquid, which solidifies. The outcome: a self-healing plastic that is suitable for everything from durable mobile phones to spacecraft.

○ At the British company Advanced Gel Technology, scientists have combined two polymers to develop a superporous, biocompatible material called hydrogel that can either absorb or release liquids. Scientists can manipulate its molecules to make it thicker, thinner, stickier. With long, elastic molecules that trap liquids in a cage-like structure, it facilitates drug delivery through injections and medicines applied to the skin. It also helps heal burns by promoting new skin growth, and eases arthritis by slowly releasing cortisone into the joints. At the ecological level, hydrogel can be used to absorb and emulsify oil spills.

The key concept to keep in mind is "programmable." Everything has a built-in functionality dictated by some internal code. Once we crack that code, we can adjust the functionality to suit diverse purposes. Directing the function of substances by tweaking or controlling the rules of their behavior—it's all a matter of learning the natural system, modifying it, then making it a tool.

So far, the idea of programmable behavior has been applied to living systems, or information code. As we increase our understanding of the molecule, in tandem with increasingly sophisticated technology, we move closer to the goal of being able to "program" any form of matter from the bottom up.

SELF-ASSEMBLY

The next step on the path of creation at the molecular level is self-organization, which is what life does. To mass produce things at the nano scale, a top-down mind-set might envision factories—albeit incredibly clean factories—filled with batteries of computer-controlled nano-manipulators. That's not quite how nature does it. Living cells have been assembling the products and by-products of life, without external manipulation, for billions of years. It is far more likely that we'll supply the molecular economy's raw materials following nature's lead, which means from the bottom up.

In laboratories today, self-assembly is being adapted for the realms of electronic, mechanical, and chemical processes. Among other immediate applications, it offers the promise of creating fault-tolerant microprocessors without the prohibitive cost of the clean rooms used for fabrication of traditional silicon chips.

At Angstrom Medica, self-assembly is being used to meld organic and inorganic chemicals into the crystal infrastructure of human bone. Until very recently, this was a purely natural process used more often by a clam than a chemist.

Another technology can produce molecular electronic devices to supplant silicon ones, at scales so small that lithography techniques for building circuits no longer work. Organic molecules, suspended in a solution, spontaneously pack themselves together on a substrate, aligning into patterned layers a single molecule thick.

Self-assembly can also be used to create photonic crystals, thin structures that can serve as optical filters for data storage and transmission, holographic memory systems, even paints that change colors under different conditions. A team at the University of Rochester has found a way to get the crystals to stack themselves, like bricks forming their own wall.

New materials, programmed molecular factories, and self-organizing fabrication processes could change the cost and performance characteristics of everything from drugs to dragsters, paint to plastics, china to chairs. In addition, these techniques will alter production processes to require less energy, less mass in materials, and fewer waste products.

The building blocks—what we create—are changing, as they have before, with consequences for all of us. Our command of materials has progressed from stone, to iron, to bronze, to "better living through chemistry," to *in silico* chemistry, with enormous economic disruption and growth each time. We're about to take another big leap.

Connect: Recombining Codes

Genetic recombination is the single most fertile source of innovation in biology. As we saw at John Deere, the concept of recombination can be transplanted with good results. Recombination becomes even more valuable as the diversity of components increases. This is true for molecules, but, as we'll see later, the same logic applies to the diversity of ideas in a company or an industry.

In vitro entrepreneurs have already started companies to find and create diversity, and their poster child is a firm called Diversa. Founded in 1994 in San Diego as a sister company to Human Genome Sciences, Diversa has assembled a menagerie of commercially desirable products not by growing cultures in a lab or by synthesizing them from scratch but, rather, by working with genes extracted directly from the source—the natural environment.

As Diversa CEO Jay Short put it: Nature had "3.8 billion years of parallel processing across every niche of the planet. Diversa's recognized that and has developed discovery tools to tap into nature's evolution capability, and then combined that with man's *in vitro* laboratory, directed evolution . . . to come up with improved molecules."[17]

In Short's estimation, harvesting directly from nature, from what he calls "uncultured organisms," allows Diversa to accelerate the speed of discovery by a factor of 10,000, focusing not on creating the end products themselves but, rather, on the discovery of genes and gene pathways that can lead to those end products.

Diversa has collected exotic DNA from life forms inhabiting geothermal vents, from acidic soils and boiling mud pots, from alkaline springs, marine and freshwater sediments, manure piles, contaminated industrial sites, arctic tundra, dry Antarctic valleys, super-cooled sea ice, microbial mats, bacterial communities associated with insects and nematodes, and fungi and plant endophytes. Company researchers are trying to bring into their lab the full diversity of life on this planet. "We have a library of two million strains of microorganisms. For perspective, only 10,000 microbial species have been written up in the last century. There are only 100,000 species in the largest pharmaceutical collections."[18]

Connecting this vast library with the needs of drug companies and others is Diversa's goal.

Now the company that Short founded based on that idea is riding on $410 million in capitalization and has lucrative partnerships with DuPont, Novartis, and GlaxoSmithKline, as well as with other startups like Cura-Gen. Suggesting that Diversa's discoveries will come to market rapidly, Short announced that the company's goal is "to achieve double-digit royalties without having to move into clinical trials," and one "built on the novelty of our approach and our [intellectual property] position."[19]

Novel pharmaceuticals aren't Diversa's only objective. It also supplies newly evolved molecules for industrial, chemical, and agricultural applications. It's working on new plastics and on consumer products that are as "everyday" as a vastly improved high-fructose corn syrup for soft drinks. Perhaps of broadest interest right now, it's developing new ways of recycling wastes into high-value materials.

A second company that takes a more explicitly code-based approach to this whole realm of reprogramming the rules of human biology is Waltham, Massachusetts–based engeneOS, which is short for "engineered genomic operating systems." Rather than focus on a single application, the company has drilled down into what it calls "Nature's Operating System" in order to discover rules and principles that govern the modeling of proteins and engineered cells. Thus, like Diversa and its DNA collections from all over the world, engeneOS has amassed a diverse collection of biologically active components for future recombination. It's a modular strategy for recombining elements to fit diverse demands, a biological version of plug-and-play.

The operating-system part comes in when engeneOS translates the information encoded in DNA into rules for the ways molecules behave, then translates these rules and design principles into software that can model bio-molecular machines—engineered proteins, nucleic acids, cells, hybrid devices—prior to building them back in the real world of molecules. The goal is to create biosensors and drug-delivery devices by mixing and matching components from the company's proprietary library of interoperable modules. Component parts, such as molecular switches and actuators, can be used to amplify or suppress cell functions.

And, taking this idea one step deeper, biologists at Scripps Research Institute are adding an "x-nucleotide," an artificial base cooked up in the labs to expand the now-familiar DNA alphabet of A, C, G, and T,[20] the four building blocks that appear again and again in myriad combinations in the genome. It's too soon to know what properties will be created by adding this fifth letter to the genetic alphabet.

We've pointed out that in an evolving system, it's not just the agents and their rules that drive evolution—it's the way they connect. The companies above are managing the connection process. They introduce molecules that have never met before (Diversa), synthesize new ones to increase the diversity of the mix (engeneOS), or even make molecules possible that weren't in nature's repertoire before (Scripps). As we'll see in Chapter 5, the same approaches to enriching connections can work in organizational management.

JUMPING GENES

Some boundary crossings, such as in dog breeding, occur within the same domain; we might call these intra-code. Other, more exotic crossings, such as the introduction of leech neurons into a computer system we mentioned in Chapter 2, we might call inter-code. These involve recombinations across spans that would never be bridged in nature, and they are already creating commercial opportunities.

Selective breeding is as old as hybridization in agriculture. Twenty years ago, genetic engineering upped the ante by making it possible to grow therapeutic proteins in mammalian cells sustained in vats. Take the code for a desired substance—human interferon, for instance—cross the species barrier by inserting it into rapidly replicating bacteria, and you've got yourself an interferon factory. Our ability to unravel and combine DNA from disparate sources means that we can use the existing biological processes of living hosts to grow materials that we previously synthesized chemically.

○ Nexia Biotechnologies scientists upped the ante again by isolating the gene in spiders that codes for silk protein and introducing it into the mammary cells of goats. The goats produce milk that contains the spider-silk protein, the raw material for BioSteel. This "extreme performance fiber" is ultra-light, elastic, and extremely strong. A herd of Breed Early, Lactate Early goats lends new meaning to the term *mass production*. Already the U.S. Army and the Canadian Armed Forces are looking to BioSteel for soft body-armor applications.

○ In a similar development, biotechnology is shifting the locus of manufacturing not just to livestock, but from industrial "plants" to actual living plants. A collaboration between two Virginia-based startups, CropTech and ToBio, aims to use genetically altered tobacco plants to grow blood proteins, peptides, anti-cancer agents, and vaccines.[21] Obviously, this could give tobacco farmers a much-needed market alternative for their crop. Others are testing edible vaccines in potatoes, which could increase immunization rates at a fraction of the cost.

This process, called biopharming or molecular farming, lies at the boundary between medical biotechnology and chemistry, and involves modifying the "software" of a plant's genetic code by combining it with genetic code from another source.

This isn't better living through chemistry—it's better chemistry through living: essentially, outsourcing to nature. The payoff here is not only true novelty but also manufacturing processes that are cheaper, more productive, and potentially less toxic. Biopharming offers much higher output than is possible with the cultured mammalian, yeast, or bacterial cells that are widely used today. Though there are still many scientific, regulatory, and ethical hurdles to overcome, using living plants as "bioreactors" for growing protein-based drugs and reagents used in industrial enzymes could begin to address the shortage in protein production capacity. According to San Diego–based Epicyte, the annual yield of drugs from a 200-acre plot of corn (about 1.25 tons) can equal the output from a $400 million factory using mammalian cells cultured in vats.[22] At least twenty companies have entered the biopharming field and currently have drugs in clinical trials, including vaccines for hepatitis B and an antibody that would prevent tooth decay. These new molecular approaches could be a boon not only to drug development but to owners of farmland.

CROSSING CODES

MIT's Robert Langer is a pioneer in "smart" drug delivery. By crossing the boundary between information and biology, he is also crossing the boundary between life and electronics.

In the 1980s, Langer began working with special polymers that dissolve at predictable rates. In the early nineties, he made the leap to microchips. He wanted to create an implantable chip that could hold several years' worth of a medication and dispense it on an automatic schedule.

MicroCHIPS, a Cambridge startup, will soon begin testing an "intelligent drug delivery" technology developed at MIT. Its initial device is a one-centimeter square of silicon with 400 wells etched in it, each holding 150 nanoliters of medicine. A second chip controls a low-voltage electrical current that can dissolve the gold cap on each of the wells, and release the medicine held within. After implantation, blood vessels grow around the chip, facilitating the drug's reaching the bloodstream. But this is just the beginning.[23]

The ultimate delivery system would be a microchip with a biosensor that could respond to the body's needs and deliver not just a precisely timed and targeted drug but a drug in an appropriately programmed concentration. This would make the system not only smart but autonomous. Such a system would make a huge difference in the lives of diabetics, for instance, whose health depends on precisely maintained levels of glucose. Finger-prick blood testing allows you to read the levels at the moment of the test but tells you nothing about fluctuations at other times.

According to *The Economist*:

. . . the ability to release drugs within the body in precise amounts at precise intervals will eventually be combined with the ability to measure drug levels (and the body's physiological responses to them) and then to broadcast the information to data-logging equipment outside the patient. When those three functions—drug release, response, sensing and data transmission—are combined in an implantable device, physicians will, in effect, have an "intelligent agent" that can work amid the body's own tissues to do their bidding. The start, indeed, of a real-life "Fantastic Voyage."[24]

Moving even further beyond traditional boundaries, we are now more able to replicate the functions of the senses obtaining data about our world or our bodies and representing them as electronic information. Because code is code, we can use new information to add to natural structures, and we can incorporate natural structures such as neurons into newly devised information systems.

Here's an example from the $3.8 billion medical diagnostics market:[25] Burstein Technologies provides instant chemical and biological testing. Patients put biological samples into the specially designed CD-ROM disc and insert it into a CD/DVD player attached to an ordinary PC. The disk drive, acting as a centrifuge, prepares the sample; a laser reads it, translating the chemical or biological data into computer code; the software analyzes it and transmits it to a physician via the Internet. On-site biological and chemical diagnosis can happen all in one place, in a fraction of the time that a multistep process would normally require. Test sample data can include clinical diagnostics, forensic DNA testing, testing for toxicity, or even biological-warfare contamination.

Soon, the concept of cheap home sensors and remote analysis could become commonplace and move beyond health care. Mix paint to match the color of your now-faded wall? Have a (virtual) Julia Child suggest a correction to the seasoning of what's on your stove? As we develop sensors that capture what we see and taste, it all comes within the realm of possibility.

We spoke earlier of Cyranose, the artificial nose, but a similar process closer to the consumer creates "olfactory bar codes" to serve as the ultimate identifier for retail products. Supermarkets already have scanners that allow shoppers to take their own groceries through automated checkout devices. As artificial senses develop, smell, color, and shape will verify our purchases. And just like the original bar code, which went from a labor-saving device to reinventing inventory control to altering supply chains and logistics, this new technology, once introduced, will create new capabilities and ancillary products.

The penetration into mainstream culture of this code-crossing among physiology, chemistry, information, and experience doesn't stop with sight and smell. The extension of affect into electronics continues with tactile feedback. New technologies that add high touch to high tech—the "haptic" capability mentioned in connection with the AFM—includes a computer mouse that can move up and down, exerting force against the user's hand. With vibrations of up to 300 times per second, the effect can be felt as bumps and jolts or textures, such as wood or sandpaper. The feedback can be adjusted to include sensations described as crisp, metallic, spongy, and rubbery.

Not surprisingly, the world of "erotic" computing is interested in this device. For now, most applications are in the gaming world, providing the jolt of a dynamite blast or the recoil of a 50-caliber machine gun. Online chemistry students can now get the feel of folding a protein, medical students can practice inserting catheters and needles, and online shoppers can rub their fingers against a fabric.

The ability to digitize and transmit physiological dimensions opens the door to many futuristic innovations. The LifeShirt, a sleeveless garment manufactured by VivoMetrics, provides continuous feedback gathered by embedded sensors. This mobile monitoring system captures data on more than thirty physiological signs of sickness and health, and shows clinicians and doctors a "moving picture" of patients' health, rather than a snapshot.

The bodily code-crossing envisioned in the Bionic Man and Max Headroom is also becoming reality. Bionic devices that connect electronic devices to human nerves and tissues have already demonstrated great success in overcoming a range of physical impairments. Cochlear implants have been on the market for several years to address loss of hearing, artificial retinas to restore vision, and implanted electrodes attached to muscles to overcome, if only partially, paralysis; it is this approach that has restored some mobility to actor Christopher Reeve. Deep brain stimulation takes this trend to the next level of sophistication. Though still experimental, neurologists are creating direct connections to sites in the human brain to treat disorders such as Parkinson's disease and depression.

Medical researcher William Dobelle has combined these approaches in a remarkable artificial-vision system that in initial tests enabled one completely blind patient to "see" well enough to drive around a parking lot. A digital camera captures images through a specially designed pair of eyeglasses. A belt-mounted signal processor translates these images into electric signals that are transmitted up a cluster of wires and fed directly, through a penny-sized hole in the skull, to the patient's optical nerve, buried deep in the brain's visual cortex.[26] Such human-machine connections illustrate the significant, and ethically loaded, potential of converging molecular and digital technologies.

Evolve: Applying Selective Pressure to Harness Evolution

Engaging at the level of agents and rules, then connecting through recombination, are the first steps in the evolutionary process. Connection leads inevitably to innovation, but most innovations are mere curiosities, functionally no better than what we already have. Rampant innovation has no value without a means to separate the valuable from the merely novel. Evolution begins in earnest with the application of selective pressure, eliminating unpromising elements from the portfolio of possibilities.

Earlier we described Diversa's vast collection of life forms. Once that portfolio is assembled, Diversa begins directing the evolution of individual components by inducing mutations, pushing this huge variety of biological possibilities into unexplored realms.

The technology that identifies the performance—or value—is called "high throughput screening," a very efficient, automated selection process that culls from Diversa's vast array of options those life forms that seem most promising. Once the assembled biomass has been screened, Diversa cultures the selected organisms, then ranks their performance according to factors such as temperature tolerance or binding characteristics. Here we see another Darwinian horse race like the competition among evolved production schedules at John Deere. The winners in this competition get to compete again, and so on through many generations. In Chapter 10, we'll see this same "seed, select, and amplify" process applied to the financial services markets by Capital One.

The evaluation technologies such as microarrays and combinatorial chemistry, discussed earlier, are being put to use by companies like Diversa and Maxygen to create proprietary high-throughput screening techniques. Clearly, the increase of diversity enabled by connection would be overwhelming if it were not accompanied by new, sophisticated forms of selective pressure to guide the evolution of desirable molecules. Just as farmers amplified the seeds that they, not nature, had selected, in order to direct the evolution of corn or wheat, Diversa says it is "evolving the best from nature" by directing the evolution of molecules to better meet a customer's specifications.

The same process can be used in the inanimate realm as well. Instead of making organic molecules, a company called Symyx makes libraries of polymers, catalysts, and electronic materials to which it applies the same techniques of high-throughput screening. As with biosciences companies, this directed-evolution approach allows Symyx to make mistakes faster than the competition can—to "fail fast and fail cheap"—in order to find the winning solution first. Recognizing this, both ExxonMobil and Bayer have signed agreements with Symyx to leverage its directed-evolution process.

Business can practice its own version of high throughput screening, using simulations, as Deere does. As we'll see, this "fail fast and fail cheap" approach will be an important element of the Adaptive Enterprise.

CONCLUSION

The molecular world holds two different keys to the future. First, the sciences of biotechnology, nanotechnology, and molecular engineering of materials are moving out of laboratories and into commercial technologies. To repeat a crucial point from Chapter 1, whatever its investment performance at the time you read this, the biotech/nanotech sector will be the growth sector of the next decade. This growth is important not just to the pharmaceutical, chemical, and other businesses that are focused on molecules today, but to every industry, because molecular technologies will become as integral to processes and products as information technologies have in the past economic life cycle.

We will learn to monetize molecules in this next economic cycle as we have learned to monetize bits of information in the present one. As was the case with information, molecular technologies will first improve the way we do the things we already do. This means that, over time, the production economics of the things we make today will change as a result of techniques that use less energy, create less waste, and employ new materials. Next, molecular technologies will change the things we make. Products will take on characteristics impossible today, increasing their durability, strength, and customization. Some will self-assemble, or self-heal. And in the third phase, new kinds of products and businesses will arise in all economic sectors, not just the leading ones, based on new capabilities, as for example, the Web-hosting business has been created.

The second key to the future is that the molecular world is the native habitat of evolution—it's the four billion-year experiment from which we learn how adaptation works. To hammer our central theme once again, the connected economy is accelerating change, raising the bar for survival, and requiring a higher degree of adaptiveness from all of us. In particular, business needs to develop a new mental toolbox based on adaptive principles and an evolving economic and social environment. As stated recently in the journal *Science*: "Our quest to capture the system level laws governing cell biology in fact represents a search for the deeper patterns common to complex systems and networks in general."[27]

In the next chapter, we turn to what has become the most familiar of these networks: information.

HANNAH: *What I don't understand is . . . why nobody did this feedback thing before—it's not like relativity, you don't have to be Einstein.*

VALENTINE: *You couldn't see to look before. The electronic calculator was what the telescope was for Galileo.*

HANNAH: *Calculator?*

VALENTINE: *There wasn't enough time before. There weren't enough pencils!*

—Tom Stoppard, *Arcadia*[1]

4

INFORMATION AND THE WORLD OF BITS

OUR economic life-cycle chart in Chapter 1 shows us that the information economy is maturing as the molecular economy is getting under way. Not surprisingly, then, biology is being "informationalized" in the same way as every other industry. We saw a little of this in the last chapter, with artificial (digital) senses wired into natural brains. In this chapter, we're going in the opposite direction: ideas from nature converted into digital code.

We've already harped on the John Deere story to bear the standard for one big idea translated from nature: the genetic algorithm. Even though we don't yet fully know how genes work,[2] computer scientists have had no trouble taking one feature of biology—recombination—and applying it to binary code. Similarly, the idea of independent, autonomous agents has found expression in the idea of computer viruses and intelligent bots. These are as simple as the "out-of-office agent" that replies to your e-mail when you're away, or as complex as the Bosch Motronic 7.8 software that runs the engine on a new Mercedes.

With these elements in place, researchers are beginning to recombine them, creating whole ecologies *in silico*, simulated systems in which there is feedback from one agent to another. Spreadsheets were the first killer app not because the problems they solved required Einstein-like brain-power but because they amounted to an enormous increase in pencil power (which would have been a much more intuitive measure than MIPS). Spreadsheets work through equations linking one quantity to another. They fit a worldview in which relationships are known.

In biological and social systems, which are far more complex, we may know what a cell or an individual might sense and how it might respond, but we can't quantify the collective reaction of one to another, much less how the whole collection will evolve over time. With today's computing power, though, we can create models based not on linear equations but on simulating the behavior and interactions of agents.

We'll show you some of these models shortly, but first we need to clarify one fundamental point. We refer to genetic algorithms and agent-based models as evolutionary in character because they take ideas from biology—breeding and selection, for example—and express them in computer code. But these simulations, no matter how accurate or useful, are a kind of metaphor for a biological process, just as a spreadsheet is a metaphor for a business process. Many features of the reality are not captured and, often, are not even understood. Nonetheless, the ability to abstract concepts from biology to create biologically inspired models can provide a rigorous testing apparatus that can illuminate the processes of adaptive systems, including biological evolution itself. Simulation is becoming a new scientific instrument, a "macroscope" allowing us to see the structure that determines the behavior of human-scale systems the way the microscope began to reveal the cell. Rigorous experimentation can now augment intuition, conventional wisdom, and observation.

Several years ago, the Center for Business Innovation had the opportunity to test the idea of simulation as "macroscope" on behalf of Hewlett-Packard. Chuck Sieloff, a twenty-five-year HP veteran, was interested in the company's cost of knowledge. HP had a deeply ingrained belief in assessing new college graduates for loyalty, hiring people likely to remain with the company, and giving them the opportunity to learn over the course of a career. At the same time, however, the late nineties in Silicon Valley was rewarding the free agent—people taking their knowledge to the highest bidder every year or so. Sieloff wondered first whether HP's approach would be sustainable and, second, whether HP could access the knowledge it needed more cost-effectively through free agency than through its successful farm system.

This is the kind of question that leads to long conversations and occasional altercations among managers, with disagreements based on biases or value systems more than on rigorous analysis. The CBI's Kai Shih built a simulation of a labor force made up of agents, each with a given level of talent, loyalty, and capacity to learn. The model simulated the choices agents made with regard to employment during each period, and it tracked their accumulation of knowledge over time. A second component represented HP, showing the cost of employees and the knowledge available to the company from the current labor force.

Sieloff is quick to discount the model's assumptions about the productivity of knowledge, but he found that the ability to compare strategies using the model created real insights. First, it revealed that despite HP's expensive investment in individual learning, the focus on loyalty in recruiting and the subsequent low turnover led to a net lower cost of available knowledge. Second, the model was able to examine the conditions under which this would be true: For a high-tech startup with a 25 percent growth rate, free agency is essential, even though it leads to a high cost of knowledge and high turnover.

Sieloff and his colleagues were most impressed when they ran a simulation in which they changed hiring policy in midstream, shifting to free agency. After an initial increase in knowledge, there was a sharp disruption in the knowledge level, causing a rapid increase in turnover and loss of knowledgeable people. According to Sieloff, "this is not unlike Apollo Computing [which HP had bought in the 1980s] . . . it was a very disruptive process. This simulation allows us to examine what we could have done differently."[3] For example, if HP had invested in knowledge capture early in the process, the company could have limited some of its losses; it also might have seen value in a more gradual adjustment of Apollo's culture to bring it in line with HP's. "This is actually what we're trying to do with the recent acquisition of VeriFone," Sieloff added.

Spreadsheets have helped analyze the financial dynamics of acquisitions; ambitious as it seems, agent-based models are now helping to understand the behavioral aspects. The indication that this can succeed lies in the model's ability to use a few simple rules to reproduce in silicon-based individuals the high-level behavior that managers had actually observed.

Science-fiction author Arthur C. Clarke once famously observed that "any sufficiently advanced technology is indistinguishable from magic." But "magic" doesn't do you any good when you are trying to extrapolate and apply a given technology to improving your business. To do that, you need greater insight into how the results are achieved. So let's step back from this one particular business application and examine how this kind of simulation is used in a broader context.

Joshua Epstein and Robert Axtell, social scientists from the Brookings Institution, created an agent-based model called Sugarscape[4] to test a range of social and organizational policies. What would be the effect on the distribution of wealth if there were a change in the inheritance-tax law? What would be the effect on immigration of a new tariff structure? How does firm size affect the level of effort made by employees?

These are the kinds of complex questions that an agent-based model, working from the bottom up, can explore and illuminate. Just as Microsoft Excel is a tool for building simulations based on equations, Sugarscape is a tool for creating simulations based on the three elements of adaptive systems: agents, rules, and an environment that exerts selective pressure.

To explore the effects of a change in the inheritance tax, Axtell and Epstein followed the "create, connect, evolve" sequence, first creating *in silico* agents called Sugarfolk.

Represented as red dots,[5] these agents move around on a simulated landscape, a grid that looks like a primitive video game. At each point on the landscape, "sugar"—the only food—grows at a local rate, indicated by the intensity of a yellow tint. Agents try to stay alive by moving around and gathering sugar. If they run out, they die. They also die if they get too old.

Like *in vivo* humans, each of these agents has its own degree of visual acuity (how far away it can see) and its own distinctive metabolism (how fast it uses up its food). Some are speedy (able to cover a lot of ground in a single cycle of the model), and some are lethargic.

Each according to its ability, agents forage through the grid guided by three rules:

○ Look around as far as your vision permits.
○ Find the spot with the most sugar.
○ Go there and eat the sugar.

As Epstein runs his simulation through many iterations, the agents who can run to sugar fastest end up madly chasing around the high-sugar areas, while the slower agents mosey around the sugar desert. And of course, the agents with the worst eyesight combined with the highest metabolism die off the soonest. At this point, Epstein invokes the breeding technique we've already discussed in the context of John Deere. Two randomly chosen survivors connect and recombine their attributes or, as a geneticist might say, their "genomes." Over several "generations," the average rate of metabolism slows, and vision improves. The population evolves through simulated natural selection.

So far, that's all ground rules. Now for the policy analysis.

Axtell and Epstein introduce a new rule: If you die in possession of some sugar, you pass it on to your offspring. Over the next many generational cycles, they found that, compared to a world without inheritance, the population became less fit—you don't have to improve your vision or slow down your metabolism to survive if SugarDaddy left you a stash. This aligns pretty well with what folk wisdom has to say about the second generation of entrepreneurial families. Sugar, of course, is just a proxy for whatever the agents in a system find desirable. If the agents were firms, for example, the "sugar" could be employees or customers.

Axtell and Epstein use Sugarscape to investigate a range of economic behaviors that depend on individual choices and capabilities. They've analyzed income distribution, family size, and the distribution of firm sizes in the economy, always seeking to explain the economic regularities we observe (like a skewed distribution of income) and to find policies that could affect them. For example, in one experiment, sugar entrepreneurs are able to accumulate sugar. Over time, distributions of wealth appear that look remarkably like the "Pareto" patterns observed in market economies: 80 percent of the wealth ends up in the hands of an elite 20 percent. Axtell and Epstein tried many tax policies in an effort to find regimes that could redistribute income and preserve growth. They found that, even sacrificing growth, the skewed distribution of income is almost impossible to eliminate. The rich *do* get richer.

In vivid microcosm, then, Sugarscape shows how a few simple rules, a heterogeneous population, and the capacity to interact lead to the emergence of complex evolutionary social behavior.

Standard economic theory assumes that people go through life with fixed preferences, and that groups of individuals share them equally, and thus behave alike. Partly, that's because earlier models weren't precise enough to measure or account for shifts and quirks within the population. There simply weren't enough pencils. Sugarscape, however, provides a much more precise instrument for modeling what we might call adaptive learning: people's preferences, and how these evolve over time through interaction. While traditional economic models might capture the reaction of, say, the demand for mortgages to a change in interest rates, agent-based models have the potential to anticipate how the structure of the mortgage market itself might change. In other words, Sugarscape can accurately reflect how social structures and group behaviors actually emerge, which is through the interaction of individual agents.

In Sugarscape and similar approaches, the process of modeling shifts from a question of "can you explain it?" to "can you recreate it?" to "can you grow it?"—i.e., will the behavior you desire or fear emerge from a given set of characteristics?

We see this kind of *in silico* modeling as one of the "keystone" techniques of the coming molecular economy, because it helps us understand the role adaptation plays in the economy generally and in business specifically. These techniques are being used to study the diffusion of innovation, rent-control policies, the evolution of cooperation, the adoption of social norms, price volatility, civil violence, and the spread of epidemics. By creating a complex, agent-oriented microcosm rather than an aggregate or averages, they take us beyond many of the assumptions that have limited economic theory in the past, allowing us to anticipate the impact of changes in the rules used by individuals. That's the way the world really works, which is why *in silico* simulation will be one of the most useful tools of adaptive management.

CREATE: AGENTS

In computer science, a great deal of discussion surrounds the definition of "agent." What's important for our purposes is the ability to create software that acts on our behalf. A simple agent has solved the "flashing VCR" problem—it assumes we'd like our VCR to know what time it is after a power failure, and seeks the broadcast time signals in order to reset the clock. A more complex kind of agent, a "shopping bot," might take our intent to go to San Diego next week and search all available websites to find a fare that best fits our criteria. Note that both these cases take advantage of connectivity, and both displace some amount of information-oriented work.

As agents become smarter, and connectivity even more nearly universal, the next phase of automation will kick in. If agents can (1) understand our goals, (2) autonomously form or execute strategies to achieve them, (3) use networks to access information or to control some remote process, and (4) interact with other agents, many kinds of administrative and service activities that require human labor today will become far more productive. B2B marketplaces, for example, will begin to communicate with one another—when an order is received, the supplier arrangements will be taken care of in the background. If the work of coordination and administration can be turned over to agents, our economy will be transformed again, as it was when the work of manufacturing was turned over to robots.

Simple Agents

We hardly get excited when a simple software agent in our thermostat adjusts the temperature according to programmed instructions. We have become accustomed to administrative agents in workflow applications processing expense reports or benefits-change requests. And our expectations have been raised by customer-service agents, which send us automated order confirmations from Amazon.com, or call up our records for the American Airlines reservationist when we speak our AAdvantage number. Other agents filter our e-mail, alert us to stock-price changes, or keep our cars from skidding. Credit-card companies create agents to scan charges for fraud, and marketers use them to spot trends and opportunities. Agents are at the root of "collaborative filtering," the adaptive process that helps Amazon and others generate personalized recommendations based on our previous choices. An application called Do-I-Care lets a user know when to revisit a favorite website by providing an alert that there's been an interesting change to that site.[6] Soon, each package in the supply chain will be equipped with an agent designed to ensure that it takes the best route to the most valuable customer, based on local transportation and market conditions.

In other words, agents today are at the cutting edge of using software to increase productivity, particularly in services, where, historically, productivity growth has been hard to come by.

But as computing power, connectivity, and our understanding of adaptive systems all progress, entirely new classes of applications are opening up for software agents, not for automation but for providing insights into complexities through simulation. MIT's Pattie Maes developed collaborative-filtering tools to make retailers' websites more adaptive. Today, TiVo provides each subscriber viewing suggestions based on the habits of all of them, making the service more valuable to subscribers and generating marketing information for broadcasters. And BiosGroup is contributing agent-based software to help SAP's supply-chain software become adaptive.

Systems of Agents

Two hundred years ago, when Adam Smith spoke of the "invisible hand" of self-interest controlling markets, he was expressing an intuitive understanding of the force in nature that Charles Darwin would articulate a half-century later, and whose applications to human enterprise we're only now beginning to understand. It is this same force that leads to the emergence of broad phenomena, like a skewed income distribution, from individual rules in Sugarscape.

Evolutionary mechanisms in nature operate through the interactions of organisms competing for survival. Market mechanisms operate through the interaction of self-interested parties making economic decisions—like companies competing for customers or red dots foraging for sugar. All forms of evolution arise from on the interaction of independent agents following a few simple rules. This insight is difficult to exploit in nature, where the rules are not directly observable, and the interactions among agents and their environments are too numerous even to identify. But the clean, controllable environment of software presents a laboratory for investigating the relationships between rules, individual behavior, environment, and emergent outcomes. The state of the art today is in figuring out what rules can "grow" a specific behavior that fits the real world—at HP or in response to taxation.

A flock of birds is a system of agents following rules. The swooping and turning, the breaking formation to avoid objects and then regrouping, the instant changing of directions—all these complex behaviors emerge with no explicit leadership. In one of the earliest breakthroughs, in 1986, Craig Reynolds recreated the behavior of a flock of birds with an agent-based model called Boids[7] by giving each "boid" only three simple "steering behaviors":

○ Avoid crowding local flockmates.
○ Fly toward the average heading of local flockmates.
○ Move toward the average position of local flockmates.

It's hard to imagine intuitively what these rules will produce, but if you visit the website you'll see an animated flock that looks preternaturally natural. In 1992, film director Tim Burton made Boids a star, using the technique to generate swarms of bats and mobs of penguins in *Batman Returns*. "The computer-modeled 3-D penguins were cloned en masse and the set loose into the scene aimed in a certain direction. Their crowd-like jostlings as they marched down the snowy street simply emerged, out of anyone's control."[8]

Turning to larger airborne objectives, the MITRE Corp. used a similar approach to create an agent-based model of the entire airline industry and all its interactions. The goal is to provide the FAA with a better tool for conducting "what-if" policy analysis, a capability it currently doesn't have. The system is so complex that no linear analysis is useful. The Jet:Wise model incorporates factors pertaining to hub cities and markets, fleet mix, schedules, fares, response to delays, congestion, and missed connections.

In this model, airline operators use simple rules to make decisions that, over thousands of iterations, cause a rich variety of complex behaviors to emerge. The model even incorporates "personality tools" to accommodate the individual preferences of the airline personnel making the decisions. Once again, by "growing" the complexity *in silico*, Jet:Wise allows researchers to explore options and their effects.

When sophisticated graphics are added to such models, visualizations can become vivid depictions of virtual worlds. One such model was used to design the tunnels that conducted crowds from one venue to the next at the 2000 Sydney Olympics. Scottish mathematician G. Keith Still was able to show planners horrifying scenarios of trampled tourists in one design, then show pylons inserted into the path to produce an orderly flow of people. Using Legion, a program developed by Still's company Crowd Dynamics, he created a virtual-reality landscape with self-aware agents that can react to the landscape as well as to one another. "We program in simple rules and let the system replicate, evolve, and grow, " Still told *PC Magazine.* "What happens is awesome when you first see it—you get emergent behavior, something for nothing."[9]

The same tools can be used to enable businesses to map the potential consequences of their decisions into the future. Firms can also use these tools to map how a change in regulation or merger between two large rivals might affect their industry.

Complex Agents

The modeling of much more complex agents has already taken hold in the pharmaceutical industry, where a company called Physiome Sciences has used computer-based models of drugs and cells to develop a "virtual clinical trial" that can both test compounds and validate targets. With traditional, linear methods, bringing a new drug to market can take twelve years and cost $800 million. Conventional researchers can invest years of time and wads of money before discovering that they are not even in the right biochemical neighborhood for what they're trying to achieve.

Physiome's approach allows researchers to "productize" a drug early in the discovery phase. They create a simulated environment—the relevant aspects of a type of cell, a specific organ, and eventually entire systems such as the endocrine system or immune system, and the proto-drug that might affect them. This virtual "wet lab" builds a sufficiently rich multidimensional environment to allow researchers to perform simulated clinical trials from the get-go, quickly adjusting the focus to drugs with a higher probably of success. This "dry" bench experiment runs in parallel with "wet" trials. It uses *in silico* versions of the principles of general evolution (combinatorial chemistry, directed evolution) to accelerate drug discovery well beyond the *in vitro* constraints.

The most significant payoff comes from the same benefit that we saw in Sugarscape and the airline simulation: "The beauty of such models," says Physiome CEO Jeremy Levin, "is that they are nonlinear outputs, and thus they can produce results that are absolutely counterintuitive." For example, the U.S. Department of Energy asked Los Alamos National Laboratory to undertake an analysis of traffic in the city of Albuquerque. Drivers in Albuquerque were modeled as agents, choosing to travel or not at every hour of the day. The simulation was so detailed that you could zoom in on a traffic jam and learn that at the head of it was a nearsighted nonagenarian driving at 30 mph on Interstate 25, and it did an excellent job of "growing" the observed traffic pattern in Albuquerque. Because the DOE was interested in both energy consumption and air pollution, the model included the emissions performance of each automobile and the local wind patterns.

The surprise came when the Energy Department inserted a commuter rail line into the city's transportation system—and air pollution went up. After considerable skepticism and checking, the researchers concluded they had not a glitch but an insight. Commuters indeed flocked to the light-rail system, leaving their cars at home. Consequently, other family members took the opportunity to use them, in part to take care of the errands that the formerly driving commuter could no longer reach. Consequently, on average, each automobile was being driven a shorter distance, with a colder, hence more noxious, engine.

The expectation, of course, had been that the commuter-rail system would improve the energy and pollution experience. The agent-based model not only predicted a different outcome—it illuminated the string of interactions that drove the result.

Here again, we see one of the concepts of evolution emerging: It's not a predictable world of command-and-control but, rather, a world of constant surprise and volatility, created by the interactions among low-level rules, acting from the bottom up.

Entelos of Menlo Park, California, is another company using simulation for profit. It has launched PhysioLab, a disease-simulation system targeted for predictive applications in the discovery, development, and commercialization of obesity drugs, using large-scale models of human metabolism. The effects that diet, exercise, and drug therapies have on normal and obese virtual patients can be simulated. Each virtual patient represents a unique combination of genetic, physiologic, and lifestyle factors.

PhysioLab demonstrates that as molecular science and information technology continue to converge, *in silico* visualization will merge the old-fashioned file in the medical-records department with the function of the even more old-fashioned dressmaker's dummy to create a model "you." Toyota has already created THUMS, the "Total Human Model for Safety," a simulated human being. By analyzing data from 80,000 cyberparts, engineers can now zero in on skin, bones, ligaments, and tendons—something they were never able to do before. "Normally, we try to determine whether injuries will occur by combining data collected from dummies—large areas, such as the head, neck, arms, back, and legs—and from dissections of donated bodies, " said one Toyota engineer. "But we can't recreate in detail how an injury would occur; with the virtual dummy we can."[10]

In the future, the simulated "you" will be customized to your genome and medical history, and continuously updated with Web-enabled information, supplied via cardiac and other sensors, providing for telemedicine in real time. The "wet" bench and the simulation, code crossing with code, will communicate back and forth and refine each other, and the model you will continuously and autonomously update itself. Such *in silico* developments will incorporate many of the bottom-up capabilities from *in vitro* research we discussed in Chapter 3, including "smart cards" that contain an individual's entire genetic background. *In silico* simulations will revolutionize not just drug discovery but the entire practice of medicine.

We've covered agents on their own both simple and complex, and groups of agents interacting with each other at the behavioral level—that is, their behavior of one influences another's. Now we want to go a level deeper, and see what happens when agents together affect the next generation of agents.

CONNECT:
BREED EARLY AND OFTEN

Sex is one of nature's great inventions, but not for the reason you're thinking of. Forget Mickey Rourke and Kim Basinger in that alley in *9-1/2 Weeks* and think about a pair of paramecia in the puddle below them, or any other creatures that breed. A biologist will tell you, "Broadly defined, sex is simply the recombination of genes from more than one source . . . it was always crucial to the biota's 'reaction time': its ability to respond quickly to changes and emergences."[11]

In other words, the mechanism of recombining two genomes to produce a new creature is crucial to innovation. Biologists Lynn Margulis and Dorion Sagan write:

. . . natural selection by itself cannot generate any evolutionary innovation, as Charles Darwin was well aware. Natural selection, rather, relentlessly preserves the former refinements and newly generated novelty by culling those less able to live or reproduce. Biotic potential—life's tendency to reproduce as much as possible—takes care of the rest. But first, novelty must arise from somewhere. In synergy two distinct forms come together to make a surprising new third one.[12]

Random mutation is, more often than not, detrimental to the fitness of an organism, because it disturbs a solution that has worked well in the past. In sexual recombination, nature is clever enough to take chunks of code big enough to represent whole solutions, and put them together in new ways.

In the mid-1970s, the University of Michigan's John Holland learned how to teach computers the same trick, creating what we now call genetic algorithms. By experimenting with the size of the chunks and some other technical factors, he was able to evolve solutions to mathematical problems just as species evolve solutions to environmental ones.[13]

In nature, of course, each search takes a generation. *In silico*, we not only speed up the production of diversity and the effect of selection immensely—we gain the ability to direct evolution toward our specific goals.

Sex for Profit

Holland's breakthrough has allowed us to harness the power of evolution to solve problems in the real world, pointing the way to using computers to investigate evolution. As we apply genetic algorithms to practical problems, we need to recognize that none of nature's methods seeks efficiency as a goal in itself. Instead, nature's way is robust and resilient, meaning that evolved solutions can adapt to unexpected change. When the environment suddenly shifts, there's no need to go back to the beginning and redesign the whole works. Sex has produced sufficient diversity and innovation that another of the dozens or millions of other solutions within the population simply surges ahead to replace the previous best answer, and to exploit the new opportunities. Of course, efficiency is one of the characteristics that emerges: If you require a lot of food to survive, your genome will be less well represented after a famine, just as in Sugarscape. Translating sex into silicon, genetic algorithms allow us to redefine our objectives, replacing narrow individual "efficiency" with a broader concept of population "robustness"—the ability to cope with a volatile environment.

When John Deere turned to genetic algorithms, it was for a quintessentially complex problem: trying to find the optimal schedule every day for its manufacturing lines. We mentioned this example early in the book; we unpack it in detail here to illustrate the power of nature's approach to finding a good solution. Among other things, Deere makes seed planters, large machines that farmers tow behind their tractors to sow seeds, and different kinds of seed and different farming conditions demand differently configured planters. The planter's frame, for instance, can cover from four to twenty-four rows per pass. Some frames fold mechanically; others use hydraulics. They can have plastic bins attached to hold different kinds of fertilizer and insecticides, which can be either wet or dry. The options go on and on until, all told, Deere's planters can be configured 1.6 million different ways.

Into the early 1990s, Deere had people using spreadsheets—really *large* spreadsheets—to try to come up with schedules for its assembly facility. The objective was to make the best use of resources while producing the highest number of machines that could meet this incredible demand for variety. The factory's throughput was not good, affecting not only the farmers awaiting equipment but the workers and managers awaiting incentive compensation. In search of a better way, Deere turned to a company called Optimax Systems (later acquired by i2 Technologies) to "evolve" schedules by using genetic algorithms.

Optimax's system starts with the set of machines to be built and generates potential schedules. Then, an agent-based simulator evaluates each schedule, assigning it a "fitness" score based on its simulated throughput. The population is then culled based on this score—the selective pressure in this silicon environment. The best scheduling solutions within the population stay alive; the worst die off.

Next, the surviving schedules breed a new generation of schedules, and the process repeats. The breeding is done using Holland's algorithm, which is a rigorous way of taking parts of each schedule and recombining them to make a daughter schedule. Each night, this process is repeated about 40,000 times, and the fittest schedule is the one used in the factory.

This very direct transplantation of the idea of genetic recombination from living cells to silicon simulation warrants one more word on the question of metaphor. Nature has tuned sexual recombination to work as it does through billions of years of innovation and selective pressure. It has evolved to reflect the characteristics of the real-world environment, as well as the capabilities of the chemical hand as it was dealt. Holland's achievement was to see the underlying mechanism—take ideas from two reasonably successful sources, recombine them, and see if things got better or worse—and find a way to express it in software. Optimax, like many others, then figured out how to take that capability and apply it to Deere's business problem. Today, the engineering of GAs for problem solving is an active research area.

In one sense, then, "breeding" schedules is a metaphor: The *in silico* process has many dissimilarities from the natural one. In another sense, it is far more, because the transplanted idea can be applied, not just as an idea or framework, but as a rigorous operational technique. We'd call it the recombination of an idea from biology with information technology—an example of cross-breeding, if you like, or convergence, if you don't.

Regardless, it works. The results were so dramatic at Deere that there was an unexpected consequence. "Our suppliers were quite used to us being about two weeks behind schedule," said Bill Fulkerson, the engineer at Deere who championed the new system. "When we got on schedule and remained on schedule, it took them six months to learn that we wanted it there when we said we wanted it there!"[14]

"The bottom line," according to Jeff Herrmann, Optimax's CEO at the time, "is that it [the genetic algorithm] is a very effective technique for searching large, complex problem spaces because it tends to home in on the regions where it's getting good results. It's a statistical way of fanning through the search space and just shining the light where the best answers are going to be found, and thereby converging very rapidly on good results."

Farmers must wait until the next growing season to direct evolution, but users of GAs can iterate rapidly. Engineers at the University of Wisconsin's Engine Research Center, funded by Caterpillar, have used GAs to create the world's most efficient truck engine—one that pollutes less and consumes less fuel. The driving force was a genetic algorithm that rapidly sifted through billions of combinations of engine parameters and arrived at 250 combinations that were better than conventional designs but had never been used. Engineers then exercised selective pressure and focused on six specific performance measures for these finalists—fuel-injection timing, injection pressure, exhaust recirculation, and so on—into a simulator and evaluated these using a function that rated them on both emissions and fuel efficiency. Then the mating began. "We used crossover to cut the sets just like they were strands of DNA," says researcher Peter Senecal. "I actually have a screen where I can clip two six-unit strands and attach the head onto the tail of the other." (Remember "PhotoShop"? Remember "PhotoShop for Cells"? Now it's "Photoshop for DNA.") The result was an engine that reduced nitric-oxide emissions by over 30 percent, soot emissions by 50 percent, and simultaneously reduced fuel consumption by 15 percent. "It would have taken decades of conventional research to engineer the improvements that genetic algorithms discovered in just a few weeks," Senecal adds.[15]

Senecal uses the same language a molecular biologist would use to describe work in genetic engineering. Genetic algorithms can generate that same exponential level of insight, as well as novel solutions that enable evolution, for virtually any problem with many conflicting constraints. And these solutions may not be incremental adjustments: When General Electric used GAs to help design the engine for the Boeing 777, the technique changed the compressor design from seven stages to six, saving weight and increasing overall fuel efficiency.

This *in silico* is the equivalent of combinatorial chemistry *in vitro*, used to create a large library of solutions, and combined with high-throughput screening to find a winner. Both are evolving solutions, one through molecular manipulation in wet labs, the other through computer simulation. In the next chapter, you'll see the same fundamental concept applied to marketing and other social dimensions *in vivo*.

Connection and Contagion

The *in silico* work we've discussed so far applies a conceptually simple process of recombination again and again, mixing and matching different elements of many solutions in order to arrive at the best one. The more diverse the elements being recombined, the better—the Deere process starts with a generation of schedules randomized to ensure that it includes enough "ideas" to begin with. The more ideas, the greater the opportunity to interact with the environment. The greater the interaction with the environment, the more robust the solutions because they will more accurately reflect the time selective pressures. Connectivity then provides the opportunity to broadcast the answers, thus amplifying their effect.

Networks can be both the problem and the solution in directing evolution. Hyperconnectivity erases the distinction between internal and external, exposing us to "externalities," leaving us more vulnerable to selective pressures and to propagating waves of disruption. However, in the molecular economy, we should be able to use network effects to our advantage. By diffusing information faster, and sensing the environment more thoroughly, Netscape was a pioneer in this regard, distributing beta software to the public so that it would "learn" about its environment more rapidly, evolving more before it officially came to market. As software agents become more active and interconnected, this will lead, in time, to autonomous learning.

IBM and Symantec are already testing a commercial anti-virus package for computers that goes beyond the prophylactic approach of firewalls to function like a human immune system. A PC running this digital immune system connects to a central computer that analyzes code by looking at numerous factors, including system behavior, suspicious modifications to software code, or "signatures" that have been identified by studying the evolutionary lineage of known viruses. (This analysis itself could be designed using GAs.) Any program thought to be infected is copied, and the copy is sent over the network to a virus-analysis machine. The sample is then put into a "digital petri dish," software that lures viruses into infecting decoy programs, thus making the presence of the virus explicit. Decoys are then analyzed, viral signatures extracted, and prescriptions produced for verifying and removing the virus. This information is sent back to the client PC, which automatically incorporates it into a permanent database of cures for known viruses. The PC is then directed to locate and remove all instances of the virus, and like a living organism that has developed antibodies, the PC acquires immunity to that particular invader.

Once again, what we see is not metaphorical similarity but convergence. The process we just described is modeled after a living system, but it happens *in silico*. As the molecular life cycle continues to mature, the distinction between these two domains will matter less and less.

In time, rather than sending an alert signal in order to instigate remedial action, the system, like a healthy immune defense, will simply resolve any perturbations and return to normal. Computers already update software this way: Apple's Software Update feature enables Macintosh computers to complete this task autonomously. As the molecular economy advances, self-organizing, continually evolving solutions will penetrate further and further into every aspect of technology, business, and everyday life.

Let's say you're up in Vermont for some spring skiing and you stop for lunch. When you return to your BMW parked alongside the road, you find yourself stuck in icy slush. The temperature is 26 degrees, the road is sloped at a 4-degree incline, the tires are Michelin Pilots, and you're carrying a 320-pound load. Standard stuff, except that your spinning wheels are facing something that the engineers back in Munich could not anticipate: A few hours earlier, a tractor-trailer turned over, spilling its full load. This being Vermont, the load was maple syrup, which now gives the road surface and shoulder a coating more appropriate for pancakes than asphalt. Not to worry. Your BMW is already loaded with sensors that automatically upload all local characteristics to a satellite simulator. There is no one-size-fits-all answer for regaining traction, preprogrammed or dictated from headquarters. Instead, the computer runs a genetic algorithm to evolve new software to deal with the new, unanticipated problem. The computer then tests the emergent outcome in the simulator, creates the patch to the traction-control software to make the adjustment, and downloads it to your car. Off you drive, perhaps searching for a puddle of melted butter. But here a new factor enters in, which is the role of contagion. When an airline company figures out a problem with the tail assembly of a Boeing 737, it doesn't fix just the one plane that showed the defect. It upgrades the entire fleet. Since every BMW similar to yours is now connected, and the upgrade is just code, the same will happen here.

Not only will your automobile be sensing a novel set of conditions and responding accordingly—the innovation will be networked throughout the "species." An entire population of machines will learn something new about the environment and will adapt without human intervention. It's as if it were replicating mutant code derived from the Queen BMW herself.

Evolving code on board an automobile can sound slightly disturbing because we're none too sure we want some remote algorithm messing with our traction control without even telling us about it. But the concept of the product as sensor of the environment, enabling continual adaptation (read: product improvement), is already in use. When Netscape crashes, for example, it launches an application that asks the user for feedback about what was going on at the time. The information can be used to fix a bug in Netscape, or fed back to the offending website, so that it can co-evolve. This makes sense to us in the software realm; it's only when we reconceive of the BMW with its 150 microprocessors as just a bunch of software on wheels that we see the translation into the physical world.

Further along the life cycle of the molecular economy, the crossing of boundaries between information and ordinary matter will extend this capacity to sense, respond, learn, and adapt to products, processes, and people. This will only accelerate economic evolution, demanding even more urgently that our enterprises become adaptive.

EVOLVE

The utility of simple genetic algorithms is limited to problems in which the parameters can be expressed as a mathematical formula. But simple genetic algorithms still require a human programmer to establish the rules by which the algorithm recombines or mutates from the starting solution.

In 1992, however, a Stanford computer scientist named John R. Koza extended the use of genetic algorithms from specific tasks to creating entire applications. In so doing, he created a new field called genetic programming. He created a self-organizing environment in which there were rewards for programs that are somehow better, faster, or more accurate. Here the human task is limited to creating the initial conditions—a population of seed programs created by randomly combining elements from a "gene pool" of appropriate functions and program statements. After you push "enter," evolution *in silico* takes its course. Each program is run on a diet of data until it either halts or produces a result. The worst performers are culled, which is the selective pressure, the directing of evolution. The best are "bred" to produce the next generation—that is, they are broken apart and their code is mixed and matched with that of other successful programs, which can evolve into virtually any size and form.

Unlike genetic algorithms, genetic programming can generate solutions even when a problem is poorly understood. Often human programmers don't understand why a solution works, only that it does. Whether *in vitro, in silico,* or *in vivo,* what matters is what emerges, not the underlying mechanisms that got you there.

Programs evolved in this way are now used to control prosthetic limbs, to maneuver spacecraft, and to convert standard programs into parallel programs that can carry out unbelievably complex instructions simultaneously.

Employing the same biologically inspired computational techniques, Hod Lipson and Jordan Pollack of Brandeis University lifted self-assembling creatures out of the virtual world and into three dimensions. They gave a computer simulator, controlled by a neural network on a microchip, three basic parts to work with: bars for structure, synthetic muscles, and synthetic nerve cells. Starting from nothing, the simulator chooses parts at random, configures them, and puts the design through a "fitness" test measuring their mobility. The first shapes aren't good for much, but eventually they begin to move, dragging themselves along the screen like a bat unable to fly.

The shapes that work best are copied by the computer and mutated further. This process of evolution goes through hundreds of generations *in silico*. Then the designs are downloaded into a "3-D printer," a prototyping machine used in industrial design, which fabricates a model. Most prototypes contain about thirty components and are eight to twelve inches long, made of smooth, white plastic. The shapes are very different—some like an arrow, some like a crab, some like a snake.

At a certain point, researchers snap on a motor, but otherwise the process is totally hands-off. In this way, albeit a very primitive one, computer-generated self-assembly enters the physical world. With the addition of sensors, these self-assembled creatures can become far more sophisticated. For now, though, they drive home a powerful lesson about the number of different ways life could have emerged by way of agents, rules, and an environment.[16]

Computer-science pioneer Chris Langton set out to create other instances of life from which to derive a more general theory of what "Life" is and how it operates. Based not on DNA code but on the mathematical code of computer programs, his efforts gave rise to the discipline of artificial life, or "ALife."

ALife addresses the same problems explored in biology but from the opposite direction. Rather than trying to understand biological phenomena by taking apart living organisms, ALife attempts to construct, from the bottom up, coded systems that behave like organisms.

"Biology is the scientific study of life," he says, "in principle, anyway. In practice, biology is the scientific study of life on Earth based on carbon-chain chemistry. There is nothing in its charter that restricts biology to carbon-based life; it is simply the only kind of life that has been available to study."[17]

By the same token, synthetic chemistry is a well-established discipline that has contributed greatly to the theoretical understanding of the system of coded bonds within matter. It's also allowed for the fabrication of entirely new materials useful for technology and industry, such as the polymers and ceramics discussed in Chapter 3. ALife is simply "synthetic biology."

The results of the effort to generalize biology beyond the boundary of "carbon-chain chemistry" will permeate the coming molecular economy, appearing not just in computer hardware and software but in robots, medicine, nanotechnology, industrial fabrication and assembly, along with other engineering applications.

Agents, Rules, and Environment: The Artificial Stock Market

From rules found in biology to simulations *in silico*, to programming 3-D objects, we see the path to a new molecular economy taking shape. As we prepare to explore the same concepts *in vivo*, and in businesses on the hoof, we want to examine one more agent-based model, one that simulates and visualizes evolution in the financial markets, offering fresh perspective on investment strategies.

In the early 1990s, John Holland, at that time working at the Santa Fe Institute, collaborated with economist Brian Arthur and others in using an agent-based model to create a stock market *in silico*. They populated it with diverse, myopic, imperfectly rational agents, capable of making investment decisions by following investment strategies, and capable of learning from their experiences.

In the model, there are two assets: a risky stock, in finite supply, and a risk-free bond, available in infinite supply. The agents must decide how to allocate their resources. They do this by forecasting the price of the stock, and by assessing its riskiness as measured by variance in prices, as the then-widely accepted capital-asset pricing model dictated. The forecasting rules are simple "if-then" statements. If a certain market state occurs, then a certain forecast is made.

A genetic algorithm evolves the population's forecasting rules over time. The GA is invoked only when things are not going well. Whenever this happens, the GA substitutes new rules for some fraction of the least successful rules in each agent's repertoire. Thus agents learn in two ways. first, as each rule's accuracy varies from time period to time period, each agent preferentially uses the more accurate of the rules available—each agent adapts. Second, the pool of rules as a whole improves through the action of the GA—the market as a whole evolves. One of the powerful findings of this work is that, once turned on, the behavior of this artificial stock market looked very much like actual financial markets. This suggests that market behavior derives from traders interacting, adapting, and evolving their strategies, rather than from financial fundamentals.

Doyne Farmer, one of the early developers of chaos theory and famous in certain circles for having applied it to roulette in Las Vegas, recently tested this view with some rigorous observation. Studying historical stock-market data, he found patterns in price movements that would reliably persist for short periods of time—perhaps only hours. If an investor could identify the onset of these patterns, get down a bet on their persisting for a while, and cash in before the incident was over, he would win. Farmer found that, whenever such a pattern was identified, the effectiveness of the strategy of betting on it would decline over time, strongly suggesting that the market evolves in response to the introduction of a new strategy. [18]

This same kind of model has been adapted by BiosGroup, a company formed with Ernst & Young in 1996[19] to assist the National Association of Securities Dealers, parent of the Nasdaq-Amex Market Group, in evaluating possible innovations to their trading system.

The task they turned over to BiosGroup was to determine the potential effect of representing prices on the Nasdaq as decimals instead of fractions. Using decimals, they assumed, would mean a tighter spread, easing the discrepancy between bids and asking prices.

BiosGroup developed an agent-based model that allowed regulators to simulate the proposed changes, along with the responses to them made by various agents, including day traders, market makers, and institutional investors. NASD was then able to monitor the effect on overall market stability and trading volumes.

The results surprised everyone: Decimals did not improve the quality of the market as a mechanism for discovering the market-clearing price. In fact, it emerged that decimalization made parasitic trading strategies much more likely. Thus the model allowed Nasdaq to anticipate the unintended consequences of a change in policy and study the impact on the stability, nature, and volume of its business.

The message we take with us from *in silico* is this: If you can capture the "rules" of agents' behavior and translate these into code, then you can recombine the code in nearly infinite variations. If you run a simulation through large batches of scenarios, then you'll discover all kinds of dynamics that are hidden from our nearsighted human eyes. If you can identify the rules that give rise to outcomes you like, you can breed these, directing the outcome toward better performance in the real world.

CONCLUSION

Our software systems necessarily abstract from the real world. In return for the lack of verisimilitude, we receive clarity, repeatability, and a laboratory in which we can run controlled experiments.

Researchers have been running experiments to see if the ideas of biology can be illuminated by representing them in software, so that we can better understand the ways molecules, cells, and organisms work. The successes of Physiome, Entelos, and others are creating value from this convergence of information and biology at the molecular level.

At another level, the objective is not to explain biology but to apply it. Software agents, genetic algorithms, and agent-based simulations have in many instances successfully applied the core ideas from evolution—self-organization, recombination, selective pressure, and co-evolution—to practical problems in business and other fields. This work is creating new tools to deal with problems for which we had few solutions previously. Two examples are design problems with multiple conflicting constraints, ranging from diesel engines to estate taxes; and issues of behavior such as crowd control and financial-market movements. Both classes of problem are marked by nonlinear behavior (that is, a small change in the rules can lead to a big change in the outcome that emerges, the so-called "butterfly effect"), too many variables to understand how the elements will interact, and a lack of successful optimization methods. *In silico* biology is pointing the way to a new problem-solving tool kit for these and other intractable problems.

We've described these examples to show that these tools are not theoretical: The techniques apply to problems such as scheduling factories, investing in stocks, and, as we'll see in the next chapter, designing organizations and hiring policies. The translation to software of the way biology works is allowing us to use evolution to solve problems where our past methods won't do.

One intriguing application: Josh Epstein is at it again, this time using an agent-based model to try to explain the fourteenth-century disappearance of the Anasazi Indians from their best developed settlement in New Mexico. Jared Diamond assessed Epstein's effort in *Nature*, saying that his and another paper "have set new standards in archeological research by applying [an agent-based] approach to a historical problem." In summary, Diamond wrote, "Many complex systems exhibit properties that cannot be predicted by verbal reasoning, or even pure mathematics, from the behavior of their components. Human society is no exception."[20]

We think the adoption of bottom-up science will lead to a revolution to rival relativity in physics. In Tom Stoppard's *Arcadia*, the mathematician Valentine continues:

People were talking about the end of physics. Relativity and quantum looked as if they were going to clean out the whole problem between them. A theory of everything. But they only explained the very big and the very small. The universe, the elementary particles. The ordinary-sized stuff which is our lives, the things people write poetry about—clouds—daffodils—waterfalls—and what happens in a cup of coffee when the cream goes in—these things are full of mystery, as mysterious to us as the heavens were to the Greeks.[21]

Developing science to help us with the ordinary stuff of our lives is the whole point here. By learning the principles of evolution *in vitro*, and creating abstractions from them *in silico*, we have the potential to learn more about how they work in real life—*in vivo*. Read on.

A daptive management is not a new manifesto that sweeps away everything that came before but, rather, a set of ideas that extend the capabilities of the enterprise. We profile four companies that have become adaptive through very different routes, reflecting their different environments. BP is a huge global corporation in an industrial business, while Maxygen is a six-year-old biotechnology startup with 300 employees. The U.S. Marine Corps is adaptive because of the vicissitudes of war, while Capital One Financial has reinvented the credit-

PART III

THE ADAPTIVE ENTERPRISE

card business by competing on share of learning, and by learning to adapt when it learns.

Looking at what these "early adapters" have done to accelerate their own responses to change points us to measures that any company can take to make its processes, products, organization, and strategy more adaptive.

Businesses are adaptive, and economies can be analyzed as adaptive systems. Applying the concepts of evolution to economic networks and activities lets us develop management approaches for creating an enterprise designed to continually adapt. In Chapter 5, we articulate six "memes for managing" in the next ten years.

Instead of being routine and predictable, the corporate environment has grown increasingly unstable, accelerative, and revolutionary. . . . The adaptive corporation, therefore, needs a new kind of leadership. It needs "managers of adaptation" equipped with a whole set of new, nonlinear skills.

—Alvin Toffler, *The Adaptive Corporation*[1]

5.

ADAPTIVE MANAGEMENT

W E'VE just seen how "create, connect, evolve" plays out in the realm of molecules and in the realm of digital code. Now we want to turn to how the concepts of evolution play out in business. Our purpose is to build a framework for management focused not on engineering and efficiency but on evolution and adaptability. This doesn't imply that efficiency, equilibrium, and cause-and-effect are no longer important. They are underlying requirements, in the same way that natural evolution can proceed only in ways that respect the laws of chemistry and physics.

Business has always been an adaptive system. The reason that market-based economies have outperformed planned economies is that businesses sense their environments—most importantly, the market, but also regulation, technology, and social features—then move to reallocate resources to the most highly valued feasible activity. Adam Smith, at a time when large organizations were rare, viewed the individual as the economic agent. Today, economists take the corporation to be the economic decision-maker.

Inside most businesses, though, our current models of management and organization treasure stability and control, not the kind of change, diverse thinking, and experimentation that we associate with adaptiveness. There are three excellent reasons for this. First, many of the industries that built the first large organizations were harnessing energy in new ways. In these businesses, experiments were risky: A mistake could result in a chemical explosion, a spill of molten steel, two trains colliding, or a mineshaft collapse. The knowledge needed to control these risks was scarce, residing in the heads of an executive elite. No wonder engineering was esteemed so highly: Good engineering was a life-and-death issue, not a matter of an application crashing.

Second, the industrial-management priority was to reduce unit costs on the assumption of stable demand. Change requires effort from individuals and tends to divert resources from the activities for which they are rewarded. In the industrial culture, certainty is prized and change breeds uncertainty. Thus, "If it ain't broke, don't fix it" is the watchword.

Third, in the leadership style favored in the twentieth century, the individual at the top of the organization was expected to be omniscient. A CEO who couldn't predict the future of the industry, couldn't discuss every aspect of the business, or changed strategy frequently inspired suspicion, not confidence. In 1984, Alvin Toffler, author of *Future Shock*, wrote, "Managers look smart—indeed, they very often are smart—if they simply do more of the same."[2]

But, by the 1980s, this management model began to crack. Toffler, writing about his work for AT&T, noted the assumptions of the industrial corporation:

○ Most men want the same things out of life; for most of them economic success is the ultimate goal, so the way to motivate them is through economic reward.

○ The bigger a company, the better, stronger, and more profitable it will be.

○ Labor, raw materials and capital, not land, are the primary factors of production.

○ The production of standardized goods and services is more efficient than one-by-one handcraft production in which each unit of output differs from the next.

○ The most efficient organization is a bureaucracy in which each sub-organization has a permanent, clearly defined role in a hierarchy—in effect, an organizational machine for the production of standardized decisions.

○ Technological advances help standardize production and bring "progress."

○ Work, for most people, must be routine, repetitive, and standardized.[3]

Toffler went on to show that these assumptions were no longer useful. He cited information as a factor of production, and mass customization as a way to meet the differentiated needs of market segments. He also stated that "work, for most people, must be varied, non-repetitive and responsible, challenging the individual's capacity for discretion, evaluation, and judgment."[4]

Competitive Strategy by Michael Porter, published in 1980, affirmed the laws of microeconomics and competitive equilibrium, also based on assumptions from the industrial era.[5] In 1990, George Stalk and Thomas Hout of the Boston Consulting Group published *Competing Against Time*, which begins, "Time is the secret weapon of business" and concludes, "You . . . must believe that time is your number-one competitor."[6] The ideas of strategy and management have been in ferment, in other words, for the past fifteen years.

So our business culture today is schizophrenic. Executives do want their businesses to be capable of more rapid change, but they still don't want any surprises. Tom Peters has urged executives to let go, to "thrive on chaos," and Margaret Wheatley has pointed them toward quantum physics and complexity theory to provide useful insights. Managers do want to empower people to sense and respond to the market, but they still don't want to say, "I don't know." And they do acknowledge the value of diverse thinking in their organization, but they are still more comfortable with people who mirror their own thinking. These are just a few examples of the barriers to developing a management system for the Adaptive Enterprise. To be fair, these barriers aren't all internal. Consider the intense no-surprises regime imposed by financial analysts. The analysts' craving for predictability gets translated by CEOs into a culture that prizes stability.

But bowing to the external demand for stability, it turns out, doesn't pay. Take Emerson Electric, for example. Charles Knight, the company's CEO, piloted the company to twenty-seven years of consecutive earnings increases. Despite this stability, from 1991 to 2000 Emerson Electric underperformed the S&P 500 by 30 percent. In October 2000, Knight retired, and in Q2 2001 Emerson's string of consecutive quarterly earnings increases was broken. But the company was out of its rut, and since then, its stock has outpaced the S&P 500.

CEO Wendelin Wiedeking at Porsche AG has understood the potentially fatal dance with the analysts. He thinks that quarterly reporting drives short-term thinking and increases the volatility of share price. Porsche doesn't report quarterly earnings, and was kicked out of MDAX (Germany's mid-cap index) for not doing so. Nevertheless, in the first half of 2001, the company's pre-tax profits rose 40 percent, outperforming the Xetra-MDAX index by more than 200 points.[7]

In the chapters that follow, we will look closely at four organizations, each very different in size and purpose, but all working explicitly to create companies that can adapt not only more quickly but also with less top-down guidance. The U.S. Marine Corps, energy giant BP, the financial-services firm Capital One, and Maxygen, a small biotech company, despite their differences, are similar in adhering to the framework we've offered for creating the Adaptive Enterprise.

We take these examples and codify them into six simple principles to help others join these organizations on the path to the Adaptive Enterprise. We call these principles "memes for managing." *Meme* is a word coined by geneticist Richard Dawkins to convey the gene-like properties of certain ideas that reproduce, colonize niches, and adapt to the environment of a society's collective mind.[8] As the Adaptive Enterprise takes shape, we expect these ideas to recombine and evolve.

One advantage of the adaptive-enterprise approach is that it doesn't require some kind of massive, sudden change program. If leaders in an organization start embodying the memes of Adaptive Enterprise, they will spread, and over time they will change the organization's behavior.

MEMES FOR MANAGING

We'll lay out each of the six memes in a sentence, and then treat each in detail.

○ *Self-Organize*. Manage your organization from the bottom up. Influence the rules that affect individual choices rather than the overall behavior of the organization.

○ *Recombine*. Proliferating connections make recombination—of software code, product attributes, people, and markets—easier. Turn your business into an open system to capture the value and innovation of diversity.

○ *Sense and Respond*. Networks make real-time information cheap. Sensors help us filter and act on new information and even abandon forecasting altogether. Equip your business to sense changes and to respond immediately, accurately, and appropriately.

○ *Learn and Adapt*. After getting feedback on what happened when you "sensed and responded," learn from that experience and incorporate the new information into your repertoire of responses. Closing this feedback loop creates continual adaptation.

○ *Seed, Select, and Amplify*. Test many diverse options, and reinforce the winners. Experiment, don't plan.

○ *Destabilize*. The rate of environmental change demands internal instability for survival. Disrupt the static elements in your organization.

Let's drill down and explore this starter set of adaptive management principles in greater detail.

Self-Organize

A key principle of general evolution is that the bottom-up interactions of agents create adaptive systems. The agent we are most concerned about in business systems is the individual, not the molecule or line of code. This means unpacking corporate behavior into the specific rules that drive individuals' choices in order to affect the larger structures that emerge. The choices of each individual will drive the capabilities of the enterprise, and adaptation itself will be one of these capabilities: taking advantage of the creative energies, the impulses to coordinate, and the diverse ideas of people inside and outside organizational boundaries.

After a decade of focusing on process, the emphasis will shift to the individual.

Managing from the bottom up requires a shift in emphasis from controlling people's activities to influencing the choices they make, as we'll see, surprisingly, in the U.S. Marine Corps (Chapter 7). Leaders in a self-organizing company shift from managing people to managing rules.

Adam Smith in *The Wealth of Nations* argues that individual motivation will lead to the best resource allocation for the economy. This bottom-up thought was written in 1776, when other bottom-up movements were afoot, but the economic theory of the day—mercantilism—focused on the nation as the creator of wealth, not the individual. Smith was describing the macroeconomic effects of self-organization. He saw growth as the emergent outcome of the self-interest of each individual. The individual is the agent; greed provides the rules; growth is the emergent outcome.

Here's how it works in practice. Imagine a man from Mars looking down at the Manhattan streets and seeing small, yellow vehicles ingesting and disgorging people remarkably unscathed at other locations. How does the system work? A mercantilist Martian might posit some great "dispatcher in the sky" optimizing the allocation of the taxis. If he had managed a factory running a manufacturing resource planning system, he probably would. In fact, the taxi system, for the most part, operates by self-organization. Each cab is an agent, equipped with some set of rules about when to drive where; for the successful ones, the rules are adaptive, changing with the seasons and evolving over the years as neighborhoods and traffic patterns change. The emergent outcome is that everyone gets a taxi within a reasonable time.

Can factories be run this way? To a degree, they can. General Motors installed a self-organizing control system for the paint booths at its Hamtramck, Michigan, truck factory. The automated system at GM lets the paint booths themselves bid for the opportunity to work on each truck as it comes down the line. If a booth is already set up for black and a truck appears that wants to be black, it bids low; conversely, that booth would bid very high to paint a truck white, because of the cost of changeover. This auction system overcomes a management challenge—optimal sequencing of the trucks to minimize paint changeovers—and saves GM more than $1 million annually just in paint. More importantly, it improved a highly unreliable part of the production system. By letting the booths bid in the "labor" market, GM's system causes no more disruption than a few cabdrivers deciding to take a nap—the system keeps on working without stopping the line if a booth goes out of service or painting a truck the wrong color. Today, each booth could probably buy its paint on e-bay!

The U.S. Army faces a similar resource-management challenge with their fleets of unmanned intelligence gathering drones, similar to the Predators used in Afghanistan. Satellite data continually identifies new intelligence objectives, such as a newly discovered local headquarters or troop concentration. The question is how best to deploy the drones to gather the most valuable intelligence, given that new targets appear continually and that there is a significant chance of being shot down.

In classic operations research, the "traveling-salesman problem" asks how to route a salesman to all his intended calls with the least amount of travel. It is already a very challenging problem, usually solved by powerful linear-programming methods that require huge amounts of computer time. To solve this sort of problem for four drones, with uncertainty about where they will need to go next and how many will survive at a given time, is beyond any known linear methods. So the army, with the help of Bios-Group in Santa Fe, is working to develop a self-organizing solution not unlike the GM paint booths.

Each proto-Predator had a small processor capable of executing two rules, based on local information, known as "Greed" and "Repulsion." Greed motivates each drone to gather as much intelligence as it can. So each time the satellite provides new data, it may change its mind about where to go next, given time and fuel constraints. But Repulsion tells it not to get too close to any of its drone colleagues, to avoid redundant intelligence, and to reduce the risk of being felled by the same air-defense concentration.

The Greed and Repulsion idea can easily be transplanted. In fact, Adam Smith's self-interest-based economy relies on this notion of greed for profit-driving adaptive behavior; the repulsion is provided by the idea from economics that if too many people are in the same business in the same place, profits will fall. British Telecom applied this approach to managing its service fleet. Historically, phone companies have provided each service person with a schedule of work at the beginning of the day, based on the "trouble" calls received each morning. Of course, new problems arise during the day, and some jobs take more time than anticipated. Rather than having a dispatcher struggling to make real-time adjustments, BT has created a system that scores each problem for its value—a business customer with a contract guaranteeing two-hour response might score much higher than a basic residential customer with no service contract. When each technician finishes a job, he or she consults a model that evaluates the opportunity, discounted for the proximity of other service vehicles, and moves on to the next customer. A simulation tool also provides the capability to test different versions of the rules (by varying the points for service contracts, say, or by adding or subtracting trucks) to observe the effect on cost and customers' waiting times. David Lesaint, a researcher at BT Labs, notes that these tools have generated an annual savings of $170 million.[9]

In each case, a complex resource-allocation process is being handled not by centralized optimization but by the uncoordinated actions of agents following rules. No one is assigning the cars to the paint booths, the targets to the drones, the customers to the technicians, any more than the queen assigns a particular task to each ant gathering food.[10] This is what we mean by managing rules rather than people.

This management of rules becomes explicit in another simulation, created for Southwest Airlines. Southwest was dissatisfied with the performance of its cargo operations. Costs were high, and airport ramps were often piled with packages at the end of the day, entailing labor-intensive security procedures. Researchers discovered that dispatchers on the ground were treating packages as if they were passengers, putting them on the flight that would most quickly get them to their destinations, regardless of the number of times the package might have to be loaded and unloaded. Then, when freight piled up, dispatchers would load packages onto the first plane going in the right direction to reduce the backlog, often increasing even further the number of times the package would be handled.

The simulator, which treats each package as an agent, can test a vari-

FIGURE 5-1 Routing Cargo at Southwest Airlines

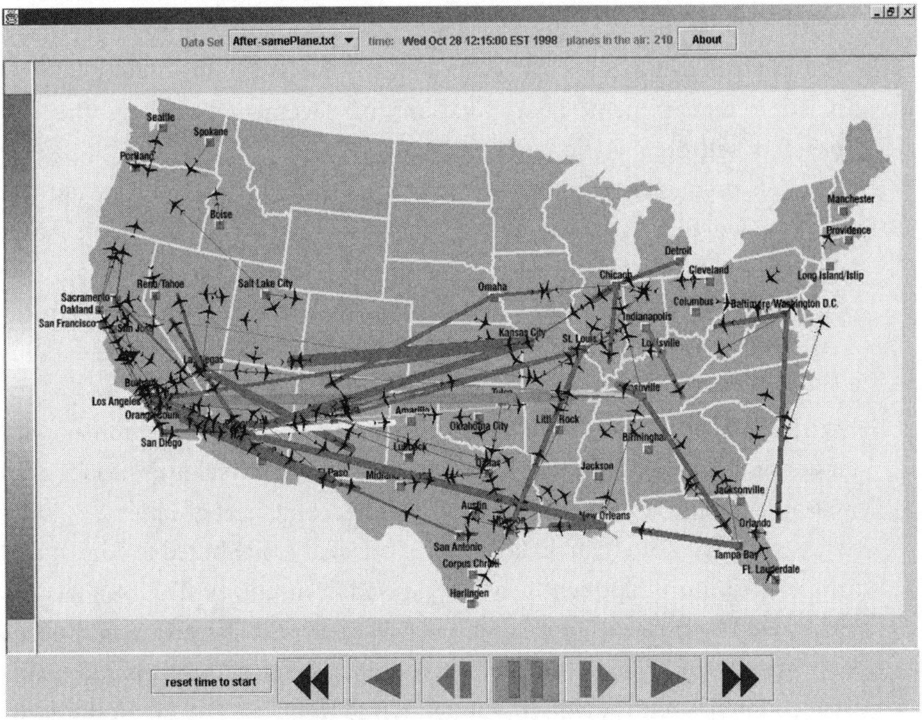

ety of different rules based on two weeks' real data. The most successful is to put each package on a plane that is going to land in the destination city, regardless of the number of stops along the way or the length of delay before getting the package airborne. Through simulation, Southwest could see that, surprisingly, this change in rules would result in almost zero degradation in service performance and a 75 percent reduction in package handling, reducing costs by 15 to 20 percent. The change requires no software or system intervention—just a change in the rules used by cargo agents.

This simulation is a precursor of the supply chain of the future. Packages will contain enough intelligence to start to behave like savvy passengers, routing themselves at every node in the transportation system to ensure they are making the best choice given a situation—stock imbalances, transportation bottlenecks—that could not have been predicted when their journey began.

Southwest Airlines and BT are narrow applications of self-organization, in that they solve quite specific problems of resource allocation. Adam Smith's vision, of course, is much broader, applying to markets as a whole, but it assumes a world of individuals, not large corporations. Organization management, not operations management, is where the real payoff of self-organization will eventually come.

Self-organizing communities, like the one formed when "free agents" flocked together to create Linux, the leader—despite Microsoft's best efforts—in providing servers to run Internet nodes, can be a boon for business. This story has been told in many places in the past five years; it's sufficient here to remind you that a Finnish programmer named Linus Torvalds took Unix, an operating system in the public domain, and began to develop it further with code contributed by any programmer who found it useful or rewarding to extend the system. Torvalds examines each submission and determines whether it will become part of Linux.

By 2001, more than 40,000 individuals had contributed to Linux, and the contributors represent a self-organized community. Their efforts are motivated by their own needs—most new code arises because a user needs it—but also by pride in their collective ability to solve problems. No financial compensation is involved, though reputations rise and fall in the community. Of course, the rule that Torvalds alone is the gatekeeper is crucial; note, though, that he is not assigning work, merely applying selective pressure to what the individuals have chosen to work on. Since 1991, when the original code was released, this self-organizing community has developed a program that accounts for over 50 percent of the Web-server market. Linux was the fastest-growing operating system in 2001, growing at 24 percent, and is projected to continue growing at a compound annual growth rate of 28 percent through 2006.[11] IBM, Sun Microsystems, and HP have all begun to support Linux, and more than one hundred companies, such as Red Hat, have arisen to participate in the industry that Torvalds and his self-organized band have created.

Given customers' preference for self-service and the ethos of the Linux community, Doug Alfred, vice president for consumer advocacy at Cisco Systems, understood as early as 1994 that the rate of Cisco's growth would require his staff of a few hundred support engineers to grow to more than 10,000. To avoid this, he established Cisco Connection Online to let customers, channel partners, and employees solve one another's problem. The result has been that thousands of technical questions are answered weekly, on a volunteer basis, and these answers are polished and added to the company's technical-knowledge base.

Great Harvest Bread Co. relies on the self-organizing behavior of its franchisees. Founded in Great Falls, Montana, in 1976, the company now has 187 locations in thirty-nine states and does $70 million in annual business. The franchise owner's manual is almost comically brief, a more extreme version of the U.S. Constitution.[12] Great Harvest's mantra is "localized innovation," and it's maximized through a few hard-and-fast rules, such as that all franchisees must share what they learn. "We're creating a community for learning," then–COO Tom McMakin told Fast Company in 1998, a "freedom based franchise" in which expansion comes from experimentation. New owners come to Montana for a week's training; then they visit two up-and-running stores. Nothing unusual so far.

Six months into the new owner's experience, he receives a check-up visit by another storeowner, paid for by the company. Great Harvest will pay half the expenses for any owner wishing to visit another's operation. "We spend most of our money on connecting owners," McMakin said, owners who create order, change rules, and direct their own evolution without rigid, centralized control or gigantic binders. Great Harvest operates an intranet used by 80 percent of their franchises for daily e-mail exchanges among the stores. As McMakin summarized, "A network of equal participants doing similar things will generate lots of new ideas."

Gifted leaders choose a few rules, make sure the memes spread, and then step back to let people do their thing as at Great Harvest. But understanding the rules gives the leader a second opportunity to alter the emergent outcome by changing the environment in which the rules operate. William Bratton, as head of the Massachusetts Transit Police in Boston and New York, and then police commissioner of New York City, understood the self-organizing nature of street crime and used this insight to reduce it, implementing the "broken windows" theory of crime control. He believed that small environmental degradations such as graffiti, noise, and abandoned lots led to an atmosphere conducive to crime (not unlike the rule-based insight at Disneyland: Tourists won't litter in a clean park, but they will in a trashy one). Bratton fixed the broken windows, erased the graffiti, and cleaned up the abandoned lots as part of a set of efforts between 1994 and 1996 that resulted in incidents of serious crime falling by 33 percent and homicide by 50 percent."[13] Essentially, he was intervening in a self-organizing behavior—groups of adolescents forming and making mischief—by understanding the agents' decision rules.

Overall, the examples cited above exploit several common benefits of self-organization, when compared with top-down direction. These include:

Flexibility—the group can quickly adapt to changes in the environment. As we get more connected, this becomes more important, as in the cases of the drones and the BT trucks.

Robustness—even when one or more individuals fail, the group can still perform its tasks. A self-organizing system functions with relatively little supervision or top-down control, and allows a community to solve problems too complex to be addressed through a system of centralized control. The GM paint booths and the New York taxis are good examples.

Innovation—the abilities of all the agents can be put to use, not just those of a centralized group. Suggestion boxes, of course, are an early example of this, but the connectivity provided in the Linux and Great Harvest examples accelerate the process enormously.

Exploration—as simulation of self-organizing processes improves, it offers the opportunity to test radically different approaches, as in the Southwest Airlines and BT examples, and discover new solutions.

The "self-organize" principle means, essentially, that leaders can alter performance by understanding the behavioral rules of individuals and intervening in either the rules themselves or the circumstances in which they are operating. We'll leave this subject with a high-stakes example: air traffic control. The Federal Aviation Agency, charged with one of the economy's most exacting functions, is now turning to a self-organizing system to free airline pilots from the narrow constraints of ground control. In the United States, routes and fares were deregulated in 1978, but airports and air traffic control were not. Now the long-established system of top-down, centralized controls is overwhelmed. In the year 2000, one-fourth of all flights were delayed, diverted, or cancelled. And passenger volume is expected to double by 2010.

"Free Flight" is the system gradually being introduced that will allow pilots at high altitudes to follow a few simple rules to determine their own course. The first step toward this self-organizing system (even when the agents at the "bottom" are 37,000 feet up) is a program already in place called the User Request Evaluation Tool. It gives controllers the computing capacity to, essentially, look twenty minutes into the future of any flight plan. When the pilot makes a request to change course, usually in response to weather, the controller punches in the data and the computer flashes either a red or green light. Until just a few years ago, such potentially life-and-death decisions were made on the basis of mental calculations and strips of paper moved around in front of the controller.

In 2004, the FAA will initiate Free Flight itself, relying on the real-time sense-and-respond capability provided by direct links between airliner navigational computers and Global Positioning System (GPS), accurate to within a few meters. European airspace is scheduled to make this same transition in 2005.

Within the rules of the system, each plane is surrounded by two concentric zones. The tighter "protection" zone must never overlap with the "protection" zone of another plane. An overlap in a wider "alert" zone immediately triggers an alarm, demanding that the pilots take action to keep their planes separated.

Planes will no longer have to adhere to zigzag routes taking them from radio beacon to radio beacon. Pilots will have greater freedom to take detours around bad weather. Voice communication between air and ground is expected to be reduced by 40 percent. As with the Army's drones, or a company's adaptive strategy, the planes will take no predetermined path, but, because the GPS information is so accurate, the vertical separation required between planes will be reduced from 2,000 to 1,000 feet. "It will be like doubling the number of lanes on the freeway," FAA spokesman William Shumann told the *San Francisco Chronicle*. Because of the far greater navigation precision, he added, "We're confident that this will be safe."[14]

Managers (and maybe passengers) often fear the loss of control that self-organization implies—they worry about potential mistakes and discount the upside. And if nothing else changed, we might agree. It is when individuals are freed to work with others and have feedback available to guide their behavior that self-organization starts to earn a return. For the Adaptive Enterprise, it becomes a prerequisite.

In a way, this gives new meaning to the term "micromanaging." Rather than seeking to control the minutiae of an organization's activities, leaders of the Adaptive Enterprise will create and manage the rules that drive operations—rules that apply to machinery, people, partners. It might be a question of tweaking the instructions for factory bidding systems, for the sales force in the field, for IT investments. Rather than creating a decision-making bottleneck or intricate chains of command—in which staff must get approval before taking an action—the adaptive leader will encourage autonomy and minimize risk by establishing the guidelines and constraints that govern independent actions. This calls for a shift in attention from function and process to creating the connected capabilities that enable autonomous action and coordination—just the approach taken by Great Harvest and, as we'll see later, all four of our case study organizations.

Recombine

As discussed in Chapter 3, nature made a breakthrough in adaptiveness by shifting from mutation to sexual recombination as its primary source of innovation. To increase its adaptiveness, business will make a similar shift.

There are both cost and benefit reasons why, historically, small changes have been favored over radical innovations. On the cost side, of course, creating both the supply and demand for a genuinely new product—the Segway, say—is tremendously expensive and uncertain; these two words are businesses' least favorite recombination. On the benefit side, once the industrial economy began to mature, competition settled down to tactical parry and thrust aimed at moving small amounts of market share. John Sculley, in his book *Odyssey*, wrote about making his name at PepsiCo by finding a new package size for Pepsi.[15]

Sculley's "odyssey" was his move from PepsiCo to become CEO of Apple, into a world where big leaps were the rule and, as he relates,

PepsiCo management skills were not all that helpful. Personal computers were in the middle of an explosion of exploration, and the market had not yet defined the success models. A company tuning its offers incrementally could not attain the rate of innovation required.

At about the same time, led by Japanese innovators, business began to increase its use of information technology to manage industrial businesses. U.S. businesses began to follow suit, leading to two of the management trends of the nineties: best practices and reengineering. Recombination ran rampant.

For example, ABB established its reputation as a superbly run and lean organization by minimizing its corporate staff; what small number of headquarters people it had spent much of their time acting as vectors of best practices from one division to another. Consultants serve a similar function within business as a whole, sanitizing information but spreading memes.

At a larger scale, companies joined industry consortia aimed at determining and sharing the most efficient way to test-market a new product, operate a production line, or manage a supplier. These small pieces of process DNA tended not to be shared across industries—a bigger combinatorial leap—until more recently.

Reengineering and best practices carried the crossbreeding of information technology and the industrial economy forward, in effect providing a "lifecycle kicker" for late twentieth-century business by increasing speed, lowering cost, and creating new value through approaches like mass customization. Recombination really got going in the late nineties, when the speed of advance in software drove companies to abandon homegrown research in favor of mating with someone who'd already done the development.

Software was evolving so rapidly that a new business strategy arose: Develop a capability on your own nickel, and sell it to a software giant, most likely Microsoft, that would rather buy than make. Among the most famous examples is Mirabilis, the company started by Israeli entrepreneur Yossi Vardi and his teenage son. Queried how his company could survive without a revenue model, Vardi replied, "Revenue is a distraction." Far from heralding a dotbust, Vardi was foretelling the acquisition of Mirabilis by AOL for $400 million in 1998. You know the Vardis' work as the instant-messaging program ICQ, which evolved into Instant Messenger.

Similarly, Pattie Maes developed collaborative-filtering technology in a company called Firefly. It duplicated the capabilities that Amazon.com had created to make recommendations to large numbers of customers based on their behavior and that of the rest of the customer group. Firefly never did business with anyone—it recombined with Microsoft in 1998 for $40 million.

Adaptive enterprises aggressively seek the ideas of others, and freely share information to ensure that others with ideas will want to come to them. Taking a practice or even a whole product from another company is a positive step, but ceding guidance of your product to the market is more extreme. Sun Microsystems took this approach to developing Java. Sun reasoned that the minds and energy of many entrepreneurial developers could do the best job of creating useful Java-based applications, ensuring the market's acceptance of Java as a standard. Consequently, in 1996 the company joined with Sun, IBM, Compaq, and others to gather $100 million to start the Java Fund. The fund was managed by the VC firm of Kleiner Perkins Caufield & Byers. Sun was creating a structure that allowed the recombination of many ideas about how to advance its cause, and outsourcing the capital budgeting decisions to the VCs.

What can you do to accelerate recombination? Following Alan Kay's molecular vision suggests two management levers. First, maximize the diversity of the ideas and capabilities that are bumping into each other. Second, increase the rate of collisions.

There is considerable organizational-development history around increasing the diversity of thought within an organization. Oticon, a Danish hearing-aid manufacturer, required each employee to take time off to study something unrelated to work, and to report back to the staff on what she had learned, to increase the pool of ideas circulating in the company. A second approach is to broaden selection criteria so that a company does not hire an endless stream of individuals just like the ones already there—AT&T managers used to refer to the "42 Long" high-potential program, referring to the jacket size of the favored (tall/athletic male) executive type. Some consulting firms have adopted a "best available athlete" hiring strategy, paying little attention to background and experience and hiring talented people with an eye to maximizing the breadth of the firm's collective mind. School admissions committees do the same thing—they speak of "filling out the class" with diverse skills, personality types, and back-grounds, seeing the entire class as a set.

Diversity also provides robustness—when the environment changes, the organization has a broad repertoire to search for a response. That's why the U.S. Department of Agriculture maintains seed banks to provide for the hundreds of "what ifs" that could undermine the few strains of currently productive food crops that dominate our agriculture. Planting all of Iowa and Illinois with a single strain of corn is highly efficient, but without the seed bank in reserve, it is not robust (i.e., it is not a strategy that could survive a sudden and dramatic change in the environment).

Regarding the rate of collisions, e-mail enables a return to the bacterial model of breeding, the exchange of idea fragments floating in an ocean of people. We can communicate more frequently, and with a larger number of people, than ever before—as we said at the outset, this is one example of how connecting accelerates innovation at the macroeconomic level, and it works for the enterprise as well.

But permeable organizational boundaries can increase both diversity and frequency of interactions simultaneously: those who joined the best-practices consortia understood this. The firewall mentality of secret competitive advantages has turned from asset to liability, as the benefits of sharing, such as faster time to market, of participating in shared conversations, have become more important than the benefits of silence—e.g., maintaining a proprietary advantage. If competition is to be about speed, permeable boundaries are essential. The U.S. economy is the most innovative in the world—and its boundaries the most permeable.

Moving to the future, molecular technologies will provide new ways to improve products and manufacturing processes, and companies that aggressively adopt them will gain the kind of advantages the Japanese enjoyed in the 1970s from information technology. This is so important that we gave it its own meme, Monetizing Molecules, which we discuss later in this chapter.

The Adaptive Enterprise focuses on recombination for three reasons: First, it is the key to rapid and original innovation; second, it increases diversity, which in turn makes the enterprise more robust, with a larger repertoire to turn to in times of rapid change; and third, it helps talented people grow faster by being exposed to and challenged by many ideas and approaches. It gives the company, and each individual in it, the best chance to create a product, practice, or strategy that's never existed.

Sense and Respond

Swimming amoeba naturally sense the direction in which the food concentration rises most rapidly, and move that way. A flower senses the sun and turns to gather the greatest amount of energy. Yet companies do not automatically sense their markets and respond to them—they have to work at it. Learning what dissatisfied someone who is no longer a customer generally requires a special effort; even if the customer makes his dissatisfaction known, the message seldom gets through. Imagine not feeling pain when a predator bit you. That definitely could be career-limiting.

Where might you be getting feedback that you currently are not?

As the information economy progresses, we are deploying tens of thousands of sensors of many types. Packages for transporting medical supplies are wired with heat-sensitive devices that warn of potential spoilage. The container trucks they're shipped in are similarly equipped, and also have embedded GPS chips so managers can identify the location of every vehicle in their fleet continuously. Cars in Singapore—and soon in half a dozen other cities—are sensed when they enter the business district, and charged accordingly. Cars equipped with navigation systems sense where they are. Faces are read and recognized by TV cameras above busy streets in England. A new regulation requires U.S. cell-phone companies to be able to identify their users' locations in case of emergency. The machine that makes disposable diapers for Kimberly-Clark takes a million readings during the birth of a single disposable diaper.[16] Red Lobster uses satellite data on the temperature of the Gulf of Mexico to predict how fast shrimp will breed, and hence what position the company should take in the futures market. What's going on?

Three developments are allowing companies to sense and respond to market shifts more quickly and accurately. First, the price of sensors is falling rapidly, allowing companies to install feedback in every product.[17] Second, the technological advance in the sensors themselves, enabling them to capture new kinds of data, more accurately, while consuming less space and energy.[18] Third, the creation of wireless networks is making the newly sensed data available anywhere in real time.

A sensor such as a thermometer has value, but a thermostat can respond by turning the furnace, oven, or air-conditioner on or off, adding a lot more. Since it's becoming inexpensive to put sensed information onto a wireless network, we can start to sense remotely and add response capabilities at the other end of the circuit. An American Airlines automaton calls to alert you of gate changes or cancellation. Home security systems are growing more rapidly as wireless, miniaturized sensors make them less disruptive. (Maybe Cyranose will become part of these systems, and its testimony about odor ID accepted in court.)

In Los Angeles, buses have been fitted with special versions of the pass that you use to go through a tollbooth. The traffic lights can sense them and have small software agents with sufficient intelligence to determine whether, by advancing or retarding their shift from red to green or vice versa, they can keep the bus from having to stop. The result has been a reduction in bus travel times of 22 to 28 percent.[19]

By continually sensing demands and reallocating inventory, new supply-chain technologies make better use of an expensive resource.

Sense-and-respond capabilities are already having a significant impact on the retail supply chain. Vendors including Alien Technology, Rafsec Oy, and Motorola are racing to create technologies for printing chips on packages to give them "RFID"—Radio Frequency Identification—capabilities so that their movement through the supply chain can be tracked. At MIT's Auto-ID program, supported by the P&Gs and Unilevers, the Wal-Marts and Costcos, and the SAPs and Intels, researchers are working out how this capability can be used to run an entire supply chain, from raw materials to your home, more effectively and inexpensively. At the store, for example, you swipe your credit card on your RFID–equipped shopping cart, put your items in, and away you go—no wait, and no markup to cover the cashier. The store knows what you took, so it can charge you, and also learn more about your preferences. And if something leaves the shelf with no corresponding signal from any cart, the surveillance cameras wake up and start recording.

The capability to sense and respond is fundamental to anything alive. The capabilities of our information technology have reached the point where we can imbue many of the objects of our everyday world with this literally vital quality. In 1999, our colleague Steve Haeckel, then director of strategic studies at IBM's Advanced Business Institute, proposed that business was too complex, and the environment too uncertain, to allow planning, and that business processes should be constructed on a sense-and-respond model; he published these ideas in a book titled *Adaptive Enterprise*.[20] In 2002, IBM launched a huge media blitz to announce its next strategy: autonomic computing, which it defines as "an approach to self-managed computing systems with a minimum of human interference."[21] But the same autonomic capabilities that will manage computing systems, once attached to sensors and networks, will be applicable everywhere. The General Electric ExtraClean dishwashers sense when the dishes are clean and adjusts the water temperature and consumption and the length of the wash cycle; Mercedes Distronic cruise control uses radar to sense the car ahead and controls the distance and closing rate.

Sense-and-respond is very powerful, as we learn from the sunflower and the amoeba. When the packages, the trucks, and the traffic lights each are part of its own sense-and-respond system, we'll start to feel that the economy has come alive. A culture of sense-and-respond can do the same for our organizations.

Learn and Adapt

Our software is becoming smart enough to go well beyond a simple response like a screaming alarm or even a delayed traffic light. Taking this capability to its logical next step, the payoff will be even greater. Now that sensors are becoming ubiquitous and connected, we have the opportunity to create software that learns from what it senses, and adapts the system to make it better.

Let's return to our thermometer (sensor) connected to our furnace (responder). Honeywell has taken the next step. When you program most thermostats for 50 degrees at night and 70 at 6 A.M. when you want to eat breakfast in comfort, they take the room to 70 and shut off. If you have a big cast-iron radiator, the temperature continues to rise to 74 or so until that radiator cools off. This is called "overshoot."

Now, Honeywell's new generation of thermostat, the CT-3600, has adaptive intelligence that analyzes heat loss daily to preserve comfort as the seasons change. The user programs the desired result (e.g., 70 degrees at 7 A.M.), and it will automatically adjust itself so your house reaches that temperature at that time. Honeywell calls this "adaptive intelligent recovery."[22]

This thermostat learns—it watches how its performance affects your home—and adapts, changing its behavior to reach a goal. Once sense-and-respond infrastructure is in place, the next development will be the creation of learn-and-adapt capabilities.

The Web has been increasing the expectations of all of us. First, we learned to expect access 24/7. Next, we were taught that order confirmation, a delay and rebooking notification, or alerts about our portfolio performance were our birthright. Soon, we will come to ask "why doesn't this product learn and adapt?" The people at Schindler, an elevator and escalator company, are among those raising our expectations. Imagine arriving at the new Cap Gemini Ernst & Young building at 5 Times Square, as usual, with your sopping umbrella in one hand and your grande latte in the other. You make your way to the "Floors 1-15" bank, where eighty-five people are waiting for the next elevator door to open; twenty-two of them will crowd in, spilling your coffee. Then the elevator will make ten stops on the way to the fifteenth floor.

What if the elevators knew where the people wanted to go before they entered the hall? As you approach the elevator bay, you stop by a kiosk and enter the floor you want, and the kiosk sends you to Elevator A, or B, or C, etc. The system batches all those who want to go to floors 12, 13, and 14 together in one elevator, the 8, 9, and 10 in another, and so on. When you get there, only the fifteen people who want to go to those floors are waiting—the rest are at their own designated elevators—and you make no more than two stops. That's sense and respond. Like the Honeywell thermostat, the control system is smart enough to watch the performance—waiting times, number of stops, etc., and continually update the algorithm that assigns the floors to the cabs—the learn-and-adapt part. As patterns change with the time of day, the seasons, the tenants of the building, etc., the system continually optimizes. Schindler claims this Miconic 10 system speeds your arrival by 30 percent. That's the payoff for tenants. For real estate owners, better performance means fewer elevators, shrinking the building core and creating more rentable area.

The "Queen BMW" described in the previous chapter illustrates the full cycle of sense and respond, learn and adapt. So does the digital immune system. One of the biggest opportunities of the third quarter of the information economy is to install learning capabilities throughout business processes. We can easily see how to do this with operations processes—inventory replenishment and supply-chain management, for example. What's harder is to integrate this feedback and learning loop into customer- and employee-related processes.

Capital One, the credit-card giant, has created a business model around learning and adapting. The company tests the market each year with 64,000 experiments, each one a precisely formulated and targeted credit-card offer. These tests are the company's sensors. The market responds, telling it whether to pursue that offer in other segments. The company learns, both from the handful of successes and the tens of thousands of failures—you've probably thrown out a thousand yourself—and updates its models of consumer segments. There is no expectation that someday its consumer models will be "right"—it recognizes that the market will change continually as interest rates, personal incomes, and other factors, shift. By taking this experimental approach, which we'll describe in more detail in Chapter 6, Capital One learns faster than the competition.

Remember the quality craze of the 1980s and its standard-bearer the Malcolm Baldrige Award? One of the key tenets, and in many ways the most powerful, was continuous improvement. Many companies instituted quality departments, which provided people to each functional group in the company to measure and advise on quality, kind of like the Communist Party advising officials in Soviet Russia. But what if you could get these groups to self-organize, to sense and respond, then learn and adapt? Each individual in the enterprise would be constantly processing information about the environment and determining whether some change would be made—and then doing something about it. This is the state of grace that startups seem to have naturally, and large businesses desperately envy.

Installing feedback loops to enable learning can happen piecemeal. The intelligence needed for learning can come from either management or effective technologies, such as neural networks. It can start in the factory, as part of a CRM system, in finance, in the benefits-administration system, or as part of a management-information system. The sensors are cheap. The integration of intelligent response and learning capabilities is challenging, but in many cases enabling technologies are available, and more are arriving daily. The *sine qua non* is the will to adapt.

Seed, Select, and Amplify

So you've just created a whole enterprise full of independent, self-organizing people. They're running around sensing the business situation and economic climate and eager to see their responses implemented. Don't we risk wasting resources at best, and chaos at worst?

Nature deals with this by rewarding effectiveness with the opportunity to breed more. This is what Darwin called "selective pressure," though biologists today would prefer to call it "nonrandom survival," emphasizing that there is no one to establish selection criteria. What works, works. Plant a lot of diverse seeds in different environments, see what thrives, and plant more of that. Or, as Capital One puts it, "seed, select, and amplify." Using this process, nature created the wolf, a superb instrument for hunting but problematic for everyday use by mankind. Humanity tinkered with wolves, through selective breeding, and produced the Norwegian elkhound, the Siberian husky, the German shepherd, the golden retriever, the Doberman pinscher, the Dandie Dinmont terrier, and the bichon frise, each carrying most of a wolf in its genes but with its unique characteristics highly adapted for different purposes. Through most of this time, the people supervising the selection process had no precise understanding of the underlying scientific mechanisms. They simply arranged for certain dogs to mate, looked at the resulting offspring to select those with promising traits, and repeated the process from within the set of offspring selected.

Mammals agonize over launching the next generation. Gestation is long, number of offspring is low, and the young remain dependent. Mollusks, on the other hand, are more nonchalant. They launch thousands of spores into the environment and trust that the selection process will sort out the fittest offspring.

Today, biotechnology companies using novel techniques can test 10,000 candidate drug molecules in a week and identify a potential winner in months, not years. As we described in Chapter 3, new recombinant technologies create huge libraries of potential solutions, which can be screened on an industrial scale. A single microarray chip can test tens of thousands of molecules all at once. A new breed of company has entered the marketplace, whose mastery of molecular processes allows them to play more like a mollusk than a mammal, to seed widely, then to select and amplify. More tests, more cheap failures, better odds for success.

The cost of testing has decreased dramatically. Almost any kind of business can use simulation to experiment with countless alternatives. The trick is to test as many "seeds" as you can afford to, in as many environments as you can find. What if you're making airplanes? You're not going to fly thousands of design variations and see which ones crash. Used to be, the best you could do was an expensive wind-tunnel test. If you're Boeing, you don't have the luxury of making twenty different kinds of airplanes, but *in silico* design and simulation now can give you the same result. You can use genetic algorithms to breed the best designs for physical objects, and use simulation to evaluate fitness. The same holds true for drugs, and, in Icosystem's case, for strategies. Seed, select, and amplify means testing for potential value across diverse economic opportunities. It means let the market select winners. Hardest of all, it means accepting a high proportion of failures. Seed, select, amplify is the adaptive principle for reproductive choice, whereas sense and respond, and learn and adapt are the adaptive principles for growing successfully after birth.

Convera, previously known as Excalibur Technologies, developed a technology for breeding computer code to read patterns in many kinds of data. The company uses "digital organisms" to detect patterns in unstructured information such as faces, fingerprints, and visual Web files. It's solution by evolution, rather than solution by design. The Convera solution is to turn loose megabytes of digital beasts, and to let them toil away, looking for patterns that help solve some portion of the overall puzzle. Those that identify patterns are allowed to survive and reproduce, passing along what they've learned to a new generation. In time, a set of capable digital organisms emerges.

Convera used this approach to create an automated system for grading lumber as it moves along through a mill at eight feet per second amid dust, vibration and poor lighting. The company used it to help United Air Lines minimize the time that its jets spend in repair facilities. Most impressive of all, Convera used it to develop software that can read handwritten Kanji, the ideographic characters used in written Japanese. The problem was to find a way to recognize 60,000 symbols, even when created by millions of different people with highly variable penmanship, types of pens, and types of surfaces. The solution had nothing to do with understanding Japanese. It involved turning loose millions of digital microbes asked to respond to "Have you seen anything like this?" Because only the successful searchers survived and passed on their knowledge, over time the expanding population of digital organisms discovered patterns that had not previously been noticed and evolved an automatic categorizing process.

The method has been particularly successful for problems beyond the computing power of the human mind, problems that consist of many variables, problems that continuously change, and problems that defy human logic. Maybe that's why they are currently focusing on knowledge management in industries ranging from media to homeland security.

The convergence of these pattern-recognition technologies—computer algorithms and microarray chips—is enabling their application to all kinds of business problems. The seed, select, and amplify principle is especially useful in the discovery process, for evolving new solutions. The sense-and-respond and learn-and-adapt principles, using connections and feedback loops, are key to evolving the solutions further and further. In the convergent world, the mammal and the mollusk are no longer either/or choices.

Above, we pointed out that nature has no predetermined, purposeful selection criteria. But enterprises do. They can choose to apply selective pressure in ways that help achieve their goals.

Branch Rickey was, according to the National Baseball Hall of Fame, "Baseball's greatest visionary executive. With the St. Louis Cardinals in the 1920s and 1930s, Rickey invented the modern farm system, promoting a new way of training and developing players [an example of seed, select, and amplify]. Later with the Brooklyn Dodgers, he pioneered the use of baseball statistics [sense and respond, and learn and adapt]. In 1945, he became the first owner to break Baseball's color line when he signed Jackie Robinson, who became the modern major leagues' first African-American player [permeable boundaries for recombination]."[23]

Already a pretty adaptive manager, Rickey had another adaptive strat-agem that the Cooperstown shrine doesn't mention: He demanded that his managers include a rookie in the starting lineup every year. He deliber-ately introduced a particular kind of selective pressure.

What does this achieve? For one thing, the team never gets old all at once, because there's a steady stream of renewal. For another, it motivates each veteran, who knows that one of the eight starters will be gone next season.

What would the right percentage be for a top management team? And what about term limits for politicians? Most organizations have poli-cies that cull the poorer-performing employees. But have you ever con-sidered retiring twelve percent of your information systems every year? What about your administrative policies? And while it's not a new idea, how many companies actually practice "firing" their least profitable customers?

Diversity and recombination create options; selective pressure evalu-ates them. Part of the job of the leader is not just to embrace a healthy turnover but to insist upon it.

Destabilize

Which of the following charts strikes you as the better-managed process?

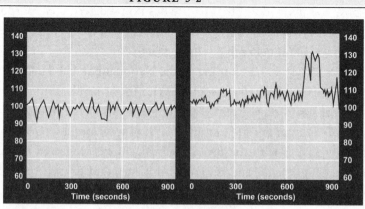

FIGURE 5-2

Most people we ask prefer the process on the left. It appears stable, under control, varying within predictable limits. The problem is that the chart on the left is the heartrate of a patient whose heart was seriously compromised and would die eight days later. The right-hand chart shows the heartbeat of a healthy person. The reason it looks irregular is that a healthy heart adapts to inputs from its environment—how much oxygen in the lungs, how much sugar in the blood—and adapts its rhythm accordingly. An overly stable heartbeat is a sure sign that the heart is unable to adapt. Stability may be comforting, but it's dangerous. How can you avoid becoming "stable" the way IBM was before its early-nineties crash?

In 1993, Lou Gerstner asked his executive team why IBM so badly missed the changes in its environment. "We saw it coming," said Senior VP Jim Cannavino. "Our strategic planners foresaw the impact of PCs, open architecture, intelligence in the network, computers on micro-processors, even the higher margins of software and declining margins in hardware." When he looked into operations rather than strategy, he found that nothing had changed in response. "The most important piece to the puzzle was a secret only insiders would know, a dose of arsenic to our diet of cyanide, and it was administered during the year-end financial reconciliation process. When we rolled up the sector submissions into the totals for the corporation, the growth of new products never quite covered the gradual erosion of margins on our mainframes. . . . But facing this possibility would have precipitated a great deal of turmoil and instability. Instead, year after year, two of our most senior executives simply went behind closed doors, quantified the gap, and raised prices to cover it."[24]

The information was in the lungs and the blood, but the heart couldn't adapt.

Complexity scientists talk about "the edge of chaos." They recognize that too much stability is deadly, but so is too little order. In the heart, the chaos is called fibrillation, the lack of an organized heartbeat. Mathematical models suggest that living as near to the edge as possible without becoming chaotic provides the greatest chance to survive a turbulent environment.

At the CBI, we did some research to see if exploring the edge of chaos was any healthier for a business than insisting on a stable heartbeat. We found some startling support for the idea that stability is analogous to designed-in aerodynamic drag. Our research showed that among the Russell 3000 companies, the companies with the most stable earnings (as defined by a common measure of volatility) achieved a ten-year compound annual growth rate of earnings of 13 percent.[25] Not bad. But consider this. The average ten-year CAGR for all the companies in the sample was 17 percent. Now here's where it gets really interesting. The 250 companies with the most unstable earnings achieved a CAGR about two and a half times better: 30 percent. Maybe stability really isn't all it's cracked up to be.

We're not suggesting that you should manage more volatility into your earnings. We are saying that you can't afford the economic drag that managing for stability induces. Sooner or later, the market analysts who prize stability because it fulfills their predictions will notice that the stable companies make less money; those who met their "no surprises" expectations will be left without the capacity to respond as quickly as those who did not.

As the life cycle of products gets even shorter, decreasing the time that firms have to reach profitability, this will become crucial. This is perhaps most visible in the high-technology arena, but it is affecting other industries as well, such as pharmaceuticals where the exclusivity of a drug has decreased from thirteen years in 1965 to as little as four months in 1999.[26] Companies that can cycle through the product-development loop faster than their competitors will be able to create an unstable market environment and exploit it to their advantage.

A faster operating loop coping with and creating instability is the essence of the strategy of the Marine Corps (Chapter 7) and a tenet of Lord John Browne's leadership at BP (Chapter 8). Branch Rickey reduced variability in the Brooklyn Dodgers by inducing instability in the organization. With the high-tech market at its all-time nadir, Dell decided to expand into three new lines of business within a matter of months. This might lower the company's earnings growth for the current year, but it sure creates selective pressure for its even more stressed competitors.

It's hard to say how much instability is the right amount for businesses, in part because we have no measures that capture the idea. We've found, in conversations with executives, that "destabilize" is the adaptive-enterprise message that they find most discomforting. Yet it should be clear by now that a more volatile external environment requires a less stable internal world. However stable we were, we should be less so now. Yet when times get hard, executives cling even more tightly to goals of unbroken earnings growth through greater control, just when they should be exploring how they will make a living in a different and more volatile world.[27]

CONVERGING ON THE ADAPTIVE ENTERPRISE

The six principles we've described above will guide managers as they take steps to make their organizations, products, processes, and strategies more adaptive. They are a response to the "connectivity, volatility, adaptation" imperative of the maturing information economy. There's an additional step on the path to the Adaptive Enterprise, less urgent for some perhaps but no less important. By anticipating the opportunities offered by newly available molecular technologies, businesses will be better prepared to employ the next wave of economic growth. During the next ten years, adaptive management will rapidly converge with the next wave of economic opportunity, now entering its growth stage. It's all about creating value at the molecular scale.

Monetize Molecules

As the molecular economy builds momentum, its technologies will radiate out from pharmaceuticals, chemicals, and agricultural companies and affect the manufacturing processes of all businesses. New molecular technologies will offer opportunities to make things "cheaper-better-greener."

American cardiologists implant about 300,000 electronic pacemakers per year, each costing the health-care system up to $40,000 (for the device, annual checkups, and battery changes).[28] A recent scientific breakthrough may change these figures dramatically, and illustrates how value in the next economy will be created by bringing molecular solutions to persistent and widespread problems, in health care, and eventually, throughout all sectors.

An adult human heart has a few thousand cells that emit electrical impulses, which prompt the surrounding muscle cells to beat in unison. When these natural pacemaker cells die or become weakened by disease, cardiologists surgically implant electronic equivalents to take over. Scientists are now testing a method of injecting a gene directly into mammalian hearts to convert muscle cells into the pacemaker cells that set the rhythm of life. The great advantage of a "biopacemaker" is that it will never need a battery change and does not require radical surgery. And a biological pacemaker adapts to the body's needs, whereas an electronic pacemaker does not.[29]

This story is an elegant example of a new technology displacing an existing product. The new materials being engineered by molecular scientists provide many others—we've already discussed spider-silk cable, and higher-temperature, ductile ceramics. Not only the products but the discovery and manufacturing processes will change, as combinatorial chemistry, directed molecular evolution, and biopharming become ever more common.

Twenty years ago, information was an almost invisible element of business. Knowledge management was an issue for corporate librarians, if anyone at all. Computers might have written payroll checks, programmable-logic controllers might have operated a machine or two, but information and the associated technology were buried deep in the organization's consciousness. So it is with molecular solutions today.

The migration of molecular solutions to other industries is a few years away, but not so far off that you shouldn't start watching now. If you run an auto-repair business, you need to know about self-healing paint and shape-memory metal alloys. If you run a car wash, coatings that shed dirt when they get rained on could put you out of business. Merely as a customer who occasionally rents a car, you might see the competitive advantage in a cheap, biologically based deodorizer. And of course, for manufacturers, composite materials, reflective compounds, new lubricants, and battery technologies have already made a difference.

When the next infrastructure matures, every company will incorporate molecular technologies into its business operations. You can already look throughout your business for opportunities to reduce costs and add more value by shrinking mass. You can seek out substitutes and opportunities to increase productivity by measuring the mass used in your business today, and getting it to decrease every year. Today's manufacturers use a lot of energy bending metal or catalyzing chemicals, and spend a lot of money dealing with by-products in an environmentally responsible way. If they could replace these processes with biopharming, such as growing plastics in corn, they would reduce their size, mass, and materials requirements. From the corn planter to the retail counter, bioplastics have a life cycle that reduces fossil-fuel consumption by up to 50 percent. In addition, the process to make bioplastics generates 15 to 60 percent less greenhouse gases than the material it replaces.[30] With such advances, the economy would become far more efficient with regard to both energy and materials—and less environmentally damaging.

Comparing the U.S. economy in 1979 and 1999, the total weight of all products contributing to the GDP has remained constant, while the value has grown by over 76 percent.[31] Put another way, a dollar's worth of stuff in 1999 weighs half of what it did in 1979 (in constant dollars). The value-to-weight ratio has nearly doubled. Per capita, you're consuming about 4,100 pounds annually—down from 5,522 twenty years earlier.[32]

A lot of that reduction is because we're paying for *information* content today, which weighs nothing, while we paid for *materials* content twenty years ago. Molecular technologies will radically shrink the mass of our economy, continuing this trend, because a BioSteel elevator cable (spider silk, remember?) will weigh less than NuCor steel cable. And it affects every kind of business because, not to be too obvious about it, everyone uses molecules, whether directly in products or indirectly in information technology, transportation, communication equipment, and energy they use.

What characteristics might your product offer that would make it more valuable? Maybe someone could design a new molecule to make it more appealing. We don't have to be new-age about this: Teflon did it for the frying pan. A coating of nano crystals could make your eyeglasses indefinitely scratchproof. What toxic chemicals does your business use or dispose of? Maybe there's a cleaner answer, or someone could breed you one. Maxygen increased the value of a certain industrial chemical from $200/kilo to $500/kilo using an enzyme the company bred rather than laboring through the ten or fifteen steps required by traditional chemistry. What's the most expensive material in your production process, and why do you use it? Maybe there is, or could be, a substitute that didn't exist last year. *Monetizing Molecules means looking at every physical transformation in your business, and searching for improvements based on emerging molecular approaches.*

Responsibility for the management of information moved from clerical staff, to a Manager of Computer Services, to a Director of Information Technology, to a VP for Information Systems, to a Chief Information Officer. Maybe in your business it would be premature to appoint a Chief Molecular Officer . . . but maybe not. The *New York Times* introduced its "Circuits" section in 1998; someday it may have "Compounds." We will reach a point at which every day, some business's economic fitness will be improved or destroyed by a molecular innovation, as clearly as when aspirin was attacked by acetaminophen, or saccharine by aspartame.

Everything reported on in Chapter 3 will accelerate the availability of custom-designed molecules to meet every business's needs for novel product characteristics, easier production processes, and lower energy and environmental costs. If you're in a health, pharmaceutical, food, agriculture, or materials business, this is already a vital part of your daily concern. If you're not, you have a chance to steal a march on those who have yet to understand the coming molecular economy.

WHY NOW?

Clockwork logic—the logic of the machines—will only build simple contraptions. Truly complex systems such as a cell, a meadow, an economy, or a brain (natural or artificial) require a rigorous nontechnological logic. . . . It is an astounding discovery that one can extract the logic of Bios out of biology and have something useful . . . it wasn't until the complexity of computers and human-made systems became as complicated as living things, that it was possible to prove this.

—Kevin Kelly, *Out of Control*[33]

We started this chapter by saying that business has always been an adaptive system. So businesspeople have been adapting all along, without the benefit of our memes for management. What has changed that demands these new solutions?

First, as described in Chapter 1, connectivity in the environment has accelerated change and increased volatility in the business environment. Business must respond with more rapid and varied adaptation, and will experience fewer periods of stability in which efficiency is the dominant source of economic health. Second, we have greater understanding of the means of adaptation than ever before, so that we can articulate these management principles more precisely, implement them more systematically, and rely less on the intuition of a few gifted leaders.

Even as they are implemented, the memes themselves will evolve. This has always been true of management, as each economic advance poses another problem. Mass production carried with it enormous productivity improvements at the cost of huge capital expenditures—"scientific management," designed to utilize this investment with maximum efficiency, was the response. When Japanese and other post-war industrial powers overtook the United States' older capabilities, the Quality movement was the focus. As information technology allowed for cross-functional coordination, reengineering became the way to get it done.

The adaptive imperative is the next business problem. But as Doyne Farmer showed, the value of knowing the pattern diminishes over time, as more investors learn it, so new patterns must be found. Similarly, while these six memes are the right ones for management today, new ones will overtake them eventually. But the next approach should be different.

Today, changing the approach of management requires a conscious effort. But if the organization can become adaptive, from then on it will create and adopt the new principles on its own, through the evolutionary processes we've described. Change will become natural—literally.

We have always recognized that rapid technological advances create an "innovation imperative." Product life cycles are getting shorter and shorter, pushing marketers to move faster and faster to stay ahead of the competition. Capital One is specifically designed for this environment. Our strategy, people, technology, operations, and culture are built to deliver on the innovation imperative.

—Richard Fairbank and Nigel Morris in Letter to Shareholders, 1998[1]

6

SEED, SELECT, AND AMPLIFY AT CAPITAL ONE

IN THE world of Capital One, ideas hatch like fruit flies, and anyone with a breakthrough has maybe six months to exploit it before the swarm of competition crowds the field and negates the advantage.

So how do you find strategic direction in such a world?

As former Capital One senior vice president George Overholser explains, "We don't write strategy—we *grow* it."

Early on, Capital One's founders, Nigel Morris and Richard Fairbank, recognized the extent to which low-cost information technology could transform the credit-card industry. They also saw the futility, in a connected economy, of continuing to use linear models from Newtonian physics and mechanics. They pursued growth relying on the very biological model of "seed, select, and amplify."

Since the company made that conceptual shift, Capital One has maintained a 45 percent compound annual growth rate, with 20 percent earnings per share and 20 percent return on equity each year.[2] With 48 million customers and a market valuation of $7.7 billion, Capital One has grown to become the sixth-largest credit-card company in the United States, in just seven years.

Capital One thinks in terms not of maximizing its share of the market but of maximizing its "share of experience." If the company can learn more about the market and its customers more quickly than its competitors, it will make more money. It knows very well that every offer, win or lose, represents an opportunity to elicit feedback from the marketplace.

At the heart of Capital One's approach to products and business concepts is the use of scientific testing on a massive scale. "We use testing to learn how to customize products and services to the individual consumer. We also use testing to build an innovation laboratory capable of creating a steady stream of new ideas to stay ahead of the competition," said Fairbank and Morris. "We have literally turned the business into a scientific laboratory. In 1998, we conducted thousands of tests of products, prices, features, packages, marketing channels, credit policies, account management, customer service, collections, and retention."[3]

This scientific approach facilitated the shift from the one-size-fits-all solution in credit lending to mass-customized offers delivered through direct marketing channels. Credit decision-making had always been done by people making informed but subjective judgments. While working at Signet Bank in the 1990s, Fairbank and Morris proposed replacing those people with computer algorithms and statistics, an approach they called "information-based strategy" (IBS). They realized that by using a "test-and-learn" approach that combined detailed information about customers and disciplined analysis, they could target market segments with great accuracy and create a product-development process that was highly flexible. When the product is essentially computer code, it's easy to change, far easier than the manufacturing specifications for an automobile or packaged good. They brought their idea to twenty-four banks; only Signet agreed to give it a try.

During the initial experiment that would test this approach, using nothing more sophisticated than a PC, Morris and Fairbank's group built the systems from scratch, pushing ahead before the competition could catch up. Risk-taking meant seizing the opportunity even when not really prepared. They launched 300 test cells with a team of 100 temps managed by a twenty-one-year-old. From these tests, they identified a breakthrough that would prove catastrophic to the industry: the balance transfer.

This was the now all-too-familiar idea of attracting new customers with the option of transferring existing debt to a Capital One credit card, only at a much lower, introductory rate. As a marketing device, "balance transfer" was, at first, a license to print money. "We took the balance-transfer product and made it the bane of the credit-card industry. Eventually we exited the product. We created it, we built it, we grew it as a monopoly for eighteen months, and we exited before everyone else did. We've re-entered it now that it's profitable again, but we didn't participate during a period of negative profitability," says Mike Rowen, Capital One's VP of e-commerce and new business development. In other words, the company has the best sense-and-respond cycle in the industry.

Rowen tells the story this way: "Our brilliant analytical guy named Matt Cooper—twenty-two years old—who ran our U.K. bank, would go to the fifty-five-year-old senior vice president of credit at Signet Bank and say, 'I need you to change credit policy: these three things, for these graphs.' And he's showing him all these analyses and the graphs—complex theory about credit policy. And the guy's reaction was 'Get out of my face, kid. You don't even know the first thing about lending. I have thirty-five years' experience, and you've got one.' "

Then the credit-card division, one of seven business units at Signet, began to contribute 85 percent of the profits. Which, nonetheless, did not earn it bouquets from corporate. As Rowen explains, "The highly analytic, scientific culture of that division became more and more at odds with the banking culture of Signet, to the point where Signet ejected the group because of all the chaos and friction it created."

Morris and Fairbank were onto something far too innovative to be woven into the traditional blue serge of an established bank. At their newly formed Capital One, they were creating in a sudden surge a totally new way to run a business, discovering the rules of the Adaptive Enterprise as they went along.

Such a business, as you might expect by now, followed the pattern of create, connect, evolve, which starts at the bottom—in this case, with the way they recruited and empowered the individual agents that are their people.

WE CAN ONLY TELL YOU
HOW TO BE

"We are a test-and-learn culture" is the refrain that loops through every aspect of Capital One, including recruiting and performance. As CEO Fairbank describes, "We have taken our entire recruiting process and used IBS in it. How you recruit people is linked back to who tested them and what tests were used. We track this information, then link it to later performance. It's exactly like soliciting a credit-card customer. You say, 'Gee, we noticed any time Sam interviews, he's got this ability to randomly predict what, later, happens.'"

"Because we're hiring thousands of people a year, we're trying to institutionalize as many things as possible, to move away from the judgmental interview process." So for efficiency and effectiveness, they company has created standardized tests—capturing both intellectual, problem-solving dimensions and behavioral ones—that correlate with future performance. Over time, Capital One has empirically linked many aspects of performance back to certain aptitudes that show up in these recruiting tests. The automated online testing of candidates has reduced the cost per hire by 45 percent and saved the company $3.7 million in the first eighteen months.

Nevertheless, senior people spend 20 to 25 percent of their time recruiting. Frank Rotman, Capital One's director of competitive lines, was initially surprised at this allocation of management resources, but he came to understand why they all take it so seriously. "Rich's attitude is, 'Would you rather spend 20 percent of your time recruiting and 2 or 3 percent of your time managing mistakes, or spend 5 percent of your time recruiting and 50 percent of your time managing mistakes?' It's really stunning how much power you can get out of hiring the right people and putting them into the right roles.

"One of the failings in corporate America is that job designs and organizational charts, by assigning a certain amount of responsibility to rigidly defined boxes, end up disempowering talented people. You end up averaging your people, which means you're not getting the output out of your high performers and you're expecting too much of your lower performers. When a responsibility gets too much, it's the box above one of those boxes. Career progression is a step function: If you do well in a given box, then they bet on whether you can fulfill the responsibility of the box one level up, which has more responsibility associated with it.

"At Capital One," Rowen continues, "we're much more organic. We find the people who are talented and structure jobs around their skills. We give people the responsibilities associated with their skill sets. We let them grow, and, as they succeed, they naturally take on more responsibility. Rather than using a career-track system, we have a tier system that goes from Tier Seven to Tier One, from entry level to most senior. I got promoted from Tier Seven directly to Tier Five. We'll do things like that at Capital One if it's the right decision. We promote people because they're already doing more than their manager assigned them, already doing a more senior job. Since they've already proven their ability, we just make it official—which is the exact opposite of the way most companies do it. We accelerate talented people very quickly, because that's where we get value. Sometimes you have to be placing bets on future value."

Capital One also makes a habit of hiring without defining a specific role in the organization. New hires spend a year participating broadly and "managing" only by influencing others across organizational lines. Much like the transmission of genetic instructions, strategy is articulated only as a process, and the functional specifics emerge within that process. "We can't tell you what to do," is the philosophy. "We can only tell you how to be."

Managers are coaches, in the vernacular of the sports team, trained to create high-performance teams by empowering them to get the job done and training them to develop the skills they need. People are given areas of responsibility and empowered to innovate, rather than being assigned rigid roles and job titles. It's all a question of imbuing the agents with a few simple rules, then letting them self-organize around ideas and resources, which then flow freely to areas of high potential.

This means crossing boundaries, changing jobs, and forming new teams to meet evolving needs. As Capital One's IT department grew, the incredibly fast pace of expansion made it more and more difficult to manage the loosely defined structure. Former CIO Jim Donehey, heading up IT at the time, needed to find simpler and simpler rules to ensure that everyone was working toward goals that were in the best interest of the entire company. He devised a game of sorts, based on four rules and a reward system of colored chips. Managers were free to dispense these chips whenever they saw someone in the IT department demonstrating one of the rules:

- ○ align with the business;
- ○ use good economic judgment;
- ○ be flexible; and
- ○ be empathetic to your colleagues.

Whether because of the Blue Chip Game or not, the four percent attrition rate in Donehey's IT department contrasted sharply with the industry norm of 20 percent.

Capital One's "on-boarding" process uses a similar approach. The idea is that if you give employees a solid foundation by teaching them a few simple rules that will guide them in their decision-making, then you will be able to assimilate them quickly into the Capital One culture, launching them with confidence into a somewhat chaotic environment, knowing that they will direct themselves toward optimal performance. Capital One calls these rules "success factors."

The success factors themselves many not sound radically different from those at many companies. What is remarkable, and what allows for a loose, self-organizing culture at Capital One, is how these success factors are instilled in the staff. Like the rules of Craig Reynolds' Boids, this is what keeps the firm flying in formation in search of new opportunities.

"Our compensation system serves to align the bottom of the organization with the overall shareholder value creation," Rowen says. "As you move up the organization, you are increasingly incented with stock options. At the very top, they work only for stock options. At my level,

TABLE 6-1 Capital One's Five Success Factors	
Builds Relationships	How you relate to and communicate with people.
Applies Integrative Thinking	How you analyze and solve problems.
Drives Toward Results	How motivated you are, how organized you are.
Leads in a Learning Environment	How you motivate and develop others.
Takes Personal Ownership	Core values such as integrity and dealing with change.

stock options are worth multiple times my cash compensation in annual wages.

"So as I look at the insights that are percolating up in my group, I look for the ones that are going to create the most shareholder value, the ones with the highest net present value. And I move resources, people, and capital to that project, to harvest that value, all the time keeping the pressure on, testing it to make sure it will deliver."

Rich Fairbank tells a story to illustrate the value of creating people rules. "Nigel and I do this annual road show, where we lay out the vision of the company and the objectives for the year. Last year, an associate in the collections department was working her way toward a big award for conducting ten perfect calls. After nine successful calls—monitored by her boss—she broke rank and risked it all, violating company policy for the sake of a customer in need. She raised the customer's credit limit to $700, a huge amount relative to the credit risk. She explained to her superiors that treating customers with compassion was not only more effective in extracting payments—it was highly effective in building trust and loyalty.

"In the end, her boss was really pleased that she had uncovered a poor policy. Rather than punishing her, he celebrated her insight and boldness, and communicated several important messages. He reconfirmed that it's okay to break the rules in the right way. And he acknowledged that, at Capital One, it's the keen, hard-working associates who are the real heroes, the ones that the company depends on."

Fairbank continues: "The key thing is they're learning. I think that in many ways failure's a better teacher than success. Our organization tries to institutionalize learning, so that we don't make the same mistakes. Failure is not great, but learning is, and allowing people to take risks. If you run a big failure, you typically don't get promoted during the next cycle, but nor do you get fired."

Mike Rowen describes how managers encourage staff to learn this way. "Because we don't have a top-down organization where it's your boss telling you what to do, it's a very odd place for new people to be interjected into. It takes them a while to get their sea legs, to orient themselves. They join what looks like just a bunch of people running around doing randomly disconnected things. Everyone has their own little mission that they're on. And so as a manager, I am more of a coach. I'm encouraging my people to just step off the cliff and jump into the organization and try to create change, try to identify value-creation opportunities."

Growing a company from 2,000 employees to 20,000 employees in seven years calls for an extraordinary commitment of resources. Dennis Liberson, executive VP of human resources, notes: "With growth like that, our organization structure was becoming a 50,000-pound amoeba. And so came the idea of disaggregation or subdividing cells. You don't have a circulatory system in an amoeba. When you get big, you can no longer develop all the peripheral relationships you need to be effective organizationally. So you have to start creating different systems and roles with specific functions."

MOLECULES IN MOTION

In an adaptive organization, rather than relying on an organization's structure to define a pattern of communication, leaders will manage their networks in a more conscious way, to make sure they have access to all parts of an organization, to all external resources.

In other words, leaders manage the connections rather than the structure. They also know how to hybridize.

At the time of the spin-off in 1994, Signet was the fiercest competitor of Capital One, bar none. It had all the same products, all of the same insights. Signet went out and hired some people from McKinsey and BCG and Bain and said, "We're going to do this all over again, but this time, we're going to do it with a little bit more sanity. We're going to let Bob in Credit make the final call on lending decisions, and we're going to let Joe in Marketing make the final call on product-launch decisions, and we're going to use this other group to come up with new ideas, which they'll pitch to Marketing and Credit." What Rich and Nigel recognized that Signet didn't was that Marketing and Credit had to become one integrated decision-making group. As a spin-off, they were renegades, and they've been renegades in the world of financial services ever since.

"Every other lending institution on earth has a marketing department and a credit department," Rowen explains. "Marketing wants more volume—for better commissions and better top-line results—and they want to loosen credit standards, they want to approve more people, in order to get that volume. The credit department wants portfolio quality, so they want to tighten credit policy—which reduces the approval rates of applicants. So these two organizations are constantly at odds."

Mike Zamsky, director of SuperPrime, points out that "the big difference between the vertical channel at Capital One and the vertical channel at most other places is that things here tend to move bottom-up rather than top-down, because ideas are generated by analysts; test results are analyzed by analysts. In many cases, managers are informed of decisions—made at the bottom of the organization, based on local information—and given veto power rather than asked to make decisions."

The horizontal process at Capital One seems to happen naturally. "Many business lines are operating independently, with people doing similar jobs in different places and they reach out to others with corresponding roles across the organization to learn and share ideas," Zamsky says.

"The cross-functional piece happens between different horizontal functions—between, for example, marketing and operations. These communications often happen on a project-by-project basis. There might be regularly scheduled sessions initiated either around functions or around projects or around tasks. People participate if they feel it adds value and might just stop showing up when they see no more value in it, the sessions just die off naturally when they're no longer necessary. It's a market phenomenon. If the meetings are valuable, people come, and if they're not, they don't. What's key is knowing who to approach to get something done, knowing which organization to get support from. This requires people to be willing to move around and to support their colleagues when needed."

These cross-functional teams keep the joint jumping, almost literally.

"People just bump into each other somewhat randomly," Mike Rowen explains, "like molecules in Brownian motion. As the organization heats up, you bump into more people. When one person bumps into another who's headed in a similar direction to pursue a similar idea, the two negotiate to determine who should continue on. You make commitments to each other and maintain contact in a customer and performer relationship." Such random encounters serve not only to eliminate redundant efforts, they enable innovation by bringing diverse elements together. Without these kinds of connections, diversity has little inherent value.

"We have this whole chaotic percolation of ideas at the bottom of the organization. The people who have their hands on what's actually happening, who are closest to the activities are empowered to say, 'Here's a better way of doing it. Let me put the case together and let me make this my mission for this month, this quarter, this year.'"

Feedback generated by thousands of such random encounters is what helps to drive innovation.

"Rarely is an innovation something that is so earth-shatteringly new that you don't even know where it came from," says Frank Rotman. "Innovation starts with a spark of an idea that's connecting disparate things together. Maybe you see a problem that consumers are having. Or you read about something in another industry, you tweak it a little and find that it solves your problem—and you have an innovation.

"That's why reading the world is so incredibly important. If innovation is a connection of disparate ideas, you need to start with a lot of ideas. And ideas could come from anywhere. I read between three and four hours a day—all sorts of stuff, not all of it business-oriented, everything from physics to modern fiction to comic books and trade journals—and this is where some of my ideas come from."

Reading is not only a resource for new ideas, a way to recombine new input with existing ideas—it's an exercise in analytical thinking, training for challenging an idea, testing a framework rhetorically, all key skills at Capital One.

Rotman continues: "You also get feedback by looking at the successes and failures of other companies, and by listening to customers on the phone. This is incredibly helpful because you're hearing about their problems, you're hearing how they react to what is actually happening. You start to think about customers as customers, not as data sitting in a computer. A customer who charged off and didn't pay us off is a real person with a real situation. And by listening to them explain their situation through their lens, hearing how they made decisions about paying their bills, maybe even by looking at the data about their transactions, we can learn. These individual data points could lead to insight. I'll sit on the phone once a month for two hours at a time; I don't get something out of it every month, but all it takes is one germ of an idea that turns into something very valuable."

Though the organizational structure allows for self-organization, it is not without discipline, not out of control. Management actively applies pressure, actively selects behaviors that are correlated to success, amplifying these through recognition and rewards, and actively reforms those that do not.

Rich Fairbank, of course, is the ultimate source of selective pressure within Capital One. He says, "We give very explicit feedback. A lot of companies give 360-degree feedback—we're just 'junkies' about it. In our performance-review system, we have cross-calibration day to prevent situations where in Richard's world everybody gets promoted really fast but, in Joe's world, they don't. We can do this because people work in all these connected networks all over the company. This is one of the ways you can kill politics in an organization. We're brutally honest, and constructively honest, and we invest huge amounts of time on cross-calibration, defining competencies required to move up to the next level, and we really preserve the sanctity of the promotion system.

"We don't just review people by their performance on the job—we also ask, 'Chris, where do you want to go in life? Do you want to write a book someday? Well, okay, to get there, you're going to need a set of competencies.' We have very high standards, and in the end, we all have a principle—that we do not let mediocrity just stay. Mediocrity's a very contagious thing. That is a key indicator of the 'prune and tune' philosophy at work. But it's done in a humane way: We actually have very 'soft landings' for the people who leave."

THE TEST-AND-LEARN WAY

So here we have young, irreverent math wizards pushing the envelope in an organic structure, with their voices as likely to be heard as anyone else's. That's because, once again, in the Capital One culture, it is the evidence, rather than place within a hierarchy, that determines the value of an idea. The "truth" emerges from the bottom up, empirically, rather than from the top down. That's the way it works in an evolving system.

At the very beginning, Capital One took its risk-assessment group, the decision-makers, and replaced them with computers. The company also filled its marketing department with a bunch of kids with 800 math SAT scores so that marketing and risk assessment were inseparable.

Then, with the profligacy of dandelions releasing spores, the company began to roll out promotional mailings, and within each mailing were dozens of tests to see where advantage might be gained. The strategy was the antithesis of "command and control." It reflected faith in the law of large numbers, and an intuitive grasp of the fundamental concepts of biology and all other complex adaptive systems: emergence, self-organization, recombination, co-evolution, and self-similarity.

In the business of revolving credit, success lies in predicting who will pay you back. The greatest success lies in finding the optimal pattern: the customer who will use your service to the maximum with the minimum risk of default. To find this ideal credit customer—the "elusive low-risk revolver"—Capital One tested the color of the envelope, the teaser interest rate, the number of months for the teaser, the annual fee, the add-ons, and the algorithms for defining credit limits. Researchers tested the "go to" rate, the hundreds of variables for selecting names, the method of delivery—whether they sent it by first-class mail or by third-class mail—and so on. In time they were doing tens of thousands of tests a year, creating a wealth of information that held a rainforest's richness of possibilities.

The response rate to each test was the "marker, " attaching to each variable much as T-cells attach to pathogens in the immune system. The mathematical wizards of Capital One began to create what they called a "fitness landscape" of offers. In effect, it's a digital replica of a natural ecosystem, a Darwinian environment in which thousands of different "species" of ideas competed with each other. As in nature, the approach was to "throw it out there and see what sticks." The best ideas would present themselves on their fitness landscape, as "local optima," at which point the task was merely to "harvest" the opportunity.

In addition, the family of models the researchers created had the same virtue as genetic diversity within a population in the wild; the variety of strategies laid out in front of them meant that Capital One was poised to adapt readily to sudden changes in its environment.

The emphasis on precise testing and measurement made the language of internal decision-making scientific rather than political. Empirical evidence, based on small tests, always carried the day.

The company took the same approach of poking, probing, and relentlessly measuring as it created other growth platforms through venture capital. Here the core vision was to attract very bright people with initial proof of concept, then plug them into the Capital One structure. The company maintained common interfaces and cross-functional capabilities that allowed work flows and value chains to talk to teach other. Thus Capital One was able to replicate success not only by sensing and responding to the marketplace, but by applying a successful concept—information-based strategy—to other value chains, all the while sticking to its core competency of risk management and financial mass marketing.

The company replicated its success with credit cards by recombining the same strategy into auto financing, a business three times the size of the credit-card industry. Capital One found another profitable way to replicate itself financing elective surgery and dental work. It didn't need to own the value chain. It was quite enough to orchestrate it.

Again, the company's strategy is the antithesis of "command and control." It focuses instead on the biological imperative "sense and respond." When a promising strategy emerges from its many tests, Capital One harvests the idea, then propagates it wildly before the mimicry of competition sets in.

Before being sent off to the lab for testing, germs of ideas are first subjected to an initial selection process; they must satisfy three value criteria: They must appeal to the consumer, they must meet Capital One's financial requirements, and they should prevent the competition from following too quickly. "If you launch a product without understanding what the value proposition is—through your lenses, through the customer's lenses, and through the competitor's lenses—it gets really difficult to get it to succeed," Rotman says. "You have to solve all of those problems at the beginning, or the chances of succeeding are diminished. So if I say it works for the consumer because it solves this problem, it works for us because of this financial outcome, and we can erect these barriers so competitors can't enter as fast, then I might have a sustainable product."

More often than not, the insights that drive the company's product innovation come from the fringe. "Last year we did 64,000 structured tests, using advanced test-theory design," says Mike Rowen. "We've developed a whole competency in test design, so that we can test very, very hostile areas of the market, where the profitability is negative. We're continually increasing the number of seeds that we plant out there for learning in the future; each one is very intelligently, thoughtfully designed to test extremes, and to test hypotheses about where value may lie, based on the last portfolio test that we just harvested and read.

"We explore the extremes, where nonlinear effects can kick in."

Sometimes, the extremes contain pleasant, nonlinear surprises. Rowen describes how Capital One discovered the teaser rate that struck an unexpected balance between margin and volume.

"All of the competition was operating at a teaser rate of around 4.9 percent, which was as low as you could go before running into negative profitability territory. We were offering different teaser rates and finding they really weren't working. Then one of our models suggested trying a 0.0 percent teaser rate. We never would have conceded to go there, but the test showed a burst of incremental responders. I think we had tested 3.0, 2.0, and 1.9 percent, but all those rates were dead. But 0.0 resonated with consumers. There was some sort of nonlinear psychological effect in consumers' minds that didn't happen at 1.9 or even 0.9—but *interest-free* resonated so strongly that we were able to penetrate a whole new section of the market and perpetuate our balance-transfer strategy for another year before exiting. Eventually, of course, our competitors came after the 0.0 rate, too."

This breakthrough led Capital One to think differently about credit policy and retention behavior. There had been a market segment of switchers that hopped from one balance-transfer offer to another—very, very unprofitable business. But this group seemed to be getting tired of doing all that hopping around, starting new account after new account, even though there was an incentive for switching each time. They were tuning out to the balance-transfer teaser. Suddenly there was a growing population who found the 9.9 percent fixed-rate product rate a fair deal.

"We took the same approach as the adjustable-rate mortgage," Rowen explains. "There's not a market today in credit cards for the fixed-rate mortgage equivalent. Someday there may be. So we continue to test it. Lending theory will tell you that you've got to be at about 10.9 percent to actually make the economics work. We could never make it work at 10.9 percent. We decided to get under the psychological umbrella of 10 percent. So we went down to 9.9 percent, and all of a sudden response and retention skyrocketed. And yet we still couldn't make a case for it. With the cost of fund and servicing and account management and all, there didn't appear to be any margin at 9.9 percent.

"When we tested it, we found a nonlinear effect that we hadn't predicted. The psychological factor was a behavioral modifier with nonlinear effects. It's the same reason why you sell something for $9.95 rather than

$10. People become a lot more loyal; they feel much better. And it's not easy to imagine things that engender loyalty in the credit-card industry."

Rowen notes that this kind of experimentation does not continue unchecked. "We have great discipline in the way we run our business, and it runs deep into the company. It's in the way we make decisions. You cannot get money to market new products and roll something out unless you have smoking-gun evidence that the economics are really as positive as they were in the test.

"And you can test like mad; you can plant as many seeds as you want when they don't put much capital at risk. Then, through experimentation with detailed measurements and discipline and logical analysis, you find profitable innovations, and you measure them actuarially and then roll them out in volume against the demographics and product sets that exist," says Rowen.

"Senior people would probably be appalled by some of the things that we test at the bottom of the organization. But some of it leads to big insights. We can harvest it. So you allow the chaos to exist. You can't move to roll-out unless you secure the funds. You can't secure funds unless you have evidence. And you also can't recruit and build the team in the internal marketplace for talent unless you demonstrate potential value. And people inside the company flock to the valuable projects."

Rowen continues; "I have an electrical-engineering background. In many ways, I think of what we do as applying the scientific method to business, with testing, experimentation, optimization. I mean, as an electrical engineer, I optimized electronic systems. Here I optimize business systems. The same disciplines: experimentation, testing, measurement. Measurement systems are important to us, and hard-core analytic optimization.

"I don't find it very much different from an engineering department, or an engineering product. Except that with financial services, the product is created in your brain, with intellectual horsepower and analytical rigor. The product is ethereal; you can just create it with electrons. You don't have to go through any physical development phase, because there are no molecules you have to assemble. So the pace of product life cycles is very fast, and you can innovate very rapidly. . . . Sixty percent of our products today didn't exist six months ago, 80 percent didn't exist a year ago, and 95 percent, two years ago."

In true evolutionary fashion, rather than taking a new technology and testing it to death before launching it, Capital One's teams build the capability and connect it to the environment, so that the environment can teach them how to deal with unpredictable problems. It's the cheapest and most effective way to learn.

When Capital One wanted to establish a process for accepting credit-card applications electronically, it was able to build on the credit policies and fraud technology it had developed for other products. Capital One was one of the first in the industry to process applications online, and it now serves more than three million customers through this Internet channel. Initially, it ran into widespread fraud, so it kept its activity volume at a low testing level, for more than two years, before scaling up. The company continued to get reads on the performance of the accounts originated to the Web, and it acted on this feedback to build better fraud defenses, learning how to detect and reject computer-submitted applications (for example, those filled out in less than a millisecond or those submitted using the same computer ID number or ISP session number).

Rather than conducting thousands of fraud-prevention tests in the lab, Capital One let the market teach it how to deal with fraud. When the company encountered new problems, it scaled back the project and returned to testing until discovering a solution. This test-and-learn cycle permeates every activity at Capital One, and underlying it is a commitment to acting on feedback, to analyzing information every way possible, and using it to make more intelligent or profitable business decisions. In doing so, it empowers the organization to grow very rapidly with very high profitability, and to outmaneuver competitors. The information flow is so close to real-time that Capital One can turn on a dime and react. In the case of fraud detection, a rapid feedback loop lets the company know within a single day that it has a problem. Without these kinds of information systems in place, it might not learn about fraud for months or, perhaps, until the quarter closes.

Mike Rowen recalls how the team would sense and respond to the signals they were getting from the marketplace, by ramping up and pulling back the launch of online processing. "We were one of the early people in our industry to take an application over the Web. We encountered massive fraud problems, so we kept our activity volume low, kept it in our testing-volume levels. We continued to get reads on the performance of the accounts originated on the Web, continued to build better fraud defenses, and kept the project in testing mode for more than two years. Then we hit the gas and cranked up the marketing.

"The fraud group kept on making advances in the technology and learning how to detect anomalies. Then we hit a hiccup. When we switched to a new-generation model that used real-time numbering, we found new fraud problems that we hadn't seen before, so I pulled back my marketing expenditures and took the group back into testing mode until we could solve it. We had a bunch of different groups working on different pieces, all using the new set of information that emerged and the new risk problems that we uncovered. Eventually we architected the entire infrastructure to operate in real time.

"The entire back end of our business is highly adaptive; we've got a whole series of account-management programs, all, again, driven by experimentation. We see certain patterns in your purchases—the types of things you buy and the cost per sale—and your behavior, and based on these, you might get interest reductions, interest increases, line extensions, line depressions. We dream up programs that might be of value to customers, and then we test them. A successful test often triggers other behaviors, and we follow these with more new offers. With 80 percent of our products new every couple of years, we're constantly abandoning things."

Once again, the evolution of success at Capital One is all about sense and respond, learn and adapt. The company even senses when and what its competition is sensing.

"It's a windows-of-opportunity game," Rowen says. "Many of our competitors just watch what we do. We have a program for catching all the mail from our competitors. Every building has a box for this. Anyone who gets any mail from another credit-card company just throws it in the box, and then teams categorize these and study our competitors' product offerings.

"They do the same to us, and they catch a lot of our testing. They can tell when we've shifted to roll-out, because all of a sudden they get a preponderance of one product from us that they've never seen before. Some of our competitors follow a strategy of watching for our roll-outs, and then following fast on our heels. First USA did that for quite a while, and it eventually blew up because they lacked one critical piece of information, something they couldn't get from our mailings: They didn't know who were we making offers to."

Rowen described how the same adaptive approach operates within the organization in the market for resources. The management hierarchy is aligned as a team across the organization to deploy people for the best, most profitable use of resources at any given time. If an opportunity for a higher order NPV shows up in another group, and they need resources, given that products in this business have a very short life cycle, it's in the manager's best interest to move her people over to that other group to harvest those opportunities as quickly as possible, to drive NPV for the organization, but also to drive her stock-option value up.

"We have a free flow of resources to where the value is," Rowen says. "I was not told to do this by my boss. I saw that the opportunity over there was better than what I could generate over here with my groups in the more experimental world. If we've been at it for six months, and I don't think it's going to happen, I'll make the decision to re-deploy my resources. I know that in time, when one of the seeds that I've planted begins to blossom and becomes one of the leading projects, I'll get a flow of resources back from other groups. This is part of the management mind-set."

In this as in everything else at Capital One, the market is the boss, and the market speaks directly. There's even a marketplace for organizational time. Anyone wishing to have a meeting with CEO Rich Fairbank, for example, must bid for a spot on his calendar. Fairbank calls it "the marketplace for time." Given the scarcity of the resource, your topic has to be more valuable than all of the others bidding for the same slot. Given that most employees have stock options, enlightened self-interest prevents turf wars. Recognizing that another colleague's issue truly is more urgent than their own, individuals routinely cede their face time for the good of all.

In this same spirit, a spirit that biologists call "reciprocal altruism" when found among genetically linked competitors, managers have been known to argue that their own operations be shut down. Moreover, at Capital One, they have sometimes been promoted for it.

Capital One's associates have permission to fail; there are no negative repercussions for trying something that doesn't pan out, as long as they behave according to the rules. Rather than penalizing people who fail, Capital One's leadership praises them for their commitment and intentions. Fairbank often asks them to explain what happened, so that others can learn. In doing so, not only does he reinforce the organization's tolerance of risk and failure—he sets expectations and helps revise best practices. Capital One separates outcome from behavior, and balances these factors when evaluating performance.

"A group had a business solution that was going to be worth over $100 million of profit to the company annually. We had supported this idea, and endorsed it about ten months ago. Well over $100 million—it was great. They came in one morning and said that recent results undermined the whole premise. They said they no longer believed in it. The guy who had originally come up with the idea got kudos, even got promoted. Today, he gave us this brilliant explanation of why a combination of flawed assumptions in a changing environment would prevent its success. He laid it out so that we could all learn, so we could all see the flaws from the original design: 'This is what we thought then, and this is what we see now.' And he never said, 'Gosh, I feel terrible we screwed up.' He wasn't hanging his head. Because that's not the way it works. In the end, they had other solutions that promised to earn us $100 million."

Fairbank's reaction was, "Thanks for not having us lose a lot more money." So a culture is created not through speeches but through interactions—particularly modeled by senior people—in which everyone learns what happens to messengers when they bring bad news.

"What we've created at Capital One is a kind of university, where people share their experiences; it's not at all unusual for people to stand up and tell everyone how they failed. We tally all the failures that we've made, and people assemble the stories. In our credit training, we teach all the really horrible mistakes that we've made."

THE PAYOFF

Don't be deceived by the extensive testing and high tolerance of failure: Capital One's operations are monitored carefully. Historically, Capital One has had the lowest losses in the industry, with a net charge-off rate lower than its competitors in four out of the last five quarters. Capital One also has the highest risk-adjusted margin. Together, these represent the biggest levers that drive a credit-card company's profitability.

Experiments are less risky when you have detailed information. Mike Rowen notes, "If you talk to people familiar with the credit-card industry, they would say, 'Capital One is a high-risk credit-card lender.' Yet the evidence shows that we're a low-risk lender."

There may be some truth in that assessment, especially when you consider that the company is using methods that are 4.8 billion years old, methods in which responsiveness to change is woven into every process. As Charles Darwin, the Peter Drucker of this type of management, once observed, "It's not the strongest of the species that survive, not the most intelligent. It's those who are most responsive to change."

No plan survives first contact with the enemy.
—Field Marshal Helmuth von Moltke (1800–91)[1]

7

BREEDING EARLY AND OFTEN AT THE U.S. MARINE CORPS

BELOW the mirrored glass building, the Pacific surf rolls and breaks against some of the most spectacular beaches in the world. But inside the Maui High Performance Computing Center, twenty or so people in Hawaiian shirts and flip-flops sit in semi-darkness, focused intently on the projected image of a computer simulation.

These are no ordinary techies ignoring the tropical paradise around them. The group includes Alfred Brandstein, former chief scientist of the U.S. Marine Corps Warfighting Laboratory; Lt. Colonel Joseph Smith, Marine Corps Combat Development Command; Major Jeremy Harker of the New Zealand Army; and Major Ash Fry of the Australian Army's Force Development Group.

The simulation that holds their attention is structurally very similar to ones used by Capital One in Falls Church. Only here, instead of breeding new credit-card offers, the computers are used to breed solutions to tactical, operational, and strategic problems in warfare.

Since the mid-nineties, the U.S. Marines have been developing a program called Project Albert (as in Einstein) that uses computer simulations to explore complex battle situations. The project is grounded in the assumption that warfare is a nonlinear process, and that everyone in the chain of command needs to be able to make on-the-spot decisions to take advantage of changing conditions as they unfold. The Marines call such improvisation-ready troops "maneuver warriors." The fact that they openly share their research with other national forces, including the Australian and New

Zealand Army Corps in Maui, speaks to the remarkably adaptive nature of the Marines, to their willingness to create organizational boundaries that are permeable, rather than impenetrable, boundaries.

Project Albert is one part of the Marines' determined effort to shape their strategy around "create, connect, evolve" fundamentals. Historically, the Corps, which was established in 1775, has been a ship-borne service skilled in amphibious landings, but its strategists spent the Cold War years internalizing the need to adapt to a geopolitical world of "permanent volatility." They refined their role and came to define themselves as "an agile force in readiness . . . prepared to respond to an infinite array of contingencies spanning the entire spectrum of conflict."[2] In other words, they are ready to deploy immediately, hold the line anywhere, and deal with unpredictable conditions as their stock in trade. This may be why the Marines, steeped in naval tradition, were the first conventional ground forces sent into landlocked Afghanistan in 2001.

The thrust of their strategy for the past forty years has been to get inside the enemy's "decision cycle," to disrupt the opponent's ability to adapt. By analyzing air combat in the Korean War, Air Force Colonel John R. Boyd envisioned the enormous advantage of destabilizing the enemy's ability to take decisive action, to complete its famous OODA loop—observe, orient, decide, act.

In Korea, the Americans had a ten-to-one kill ratio in air-to-air combat against their opponent, but not because they had superior equipment. In fact, by most measures of aircraft quality, the American F-86 was inferior to its Korean War opponent, the MiG-15. The two fighter jets differed in two critical ways—the F-86 provided greater visibility and was able to switch from one activity to another. American pilots could quickly adapt to changing circumstances and, in effect, disrupt their enemy's OODA loop. With each cycle, the destabilization mounts, the competitor falls further and further off track, and becomes less able to adapt.

To capitalize on this insight, the Marines, once known as the archetype for hierarchical organization, dispensed with conventional command-and-control long ago. Marine Corps Doctrinal Publications now define the organization's command structure as "a system that provides the means to adapt to changing conditions. We can thus look at command-and-control as a process of continuous adaptation."[3] They may not be ready to dispense with the earlier language, but their understanding of the objective has evolved.

During the nineteenth century, as the Western world embraced the industrial economy and the age of the machine, Prussian General Carl von Clausewitz derived modern military strategy from the laws of physics. During the infancy of the molecular economy, Lt. General Paul Van Riper, who recently retired after forty-one years of service in the Marines and is now a senior fellow at the Center for Naval Analyses, derived postmodern Marine Corps strategy from biology and its concepts of adaptation. "Rather than speaking in terms of operating," Van Riper says, "as in it's my job to operate this bulldozer or this plane and I'm awaiting orders on how to do that, we'd like our Marines to speak in terms of adapting to a situation as it evolves."

The quote from Helmuth von Moltke that leads off this chapter is an acknowledgment that warfare is an emergent phenomenon arising from the collective interactions among combatants. Indeed, the key problem in deploying military force today is the unpredictable co-evolution of the threat and response.

History is full of lessons about the impossibility of predicting the course of military action. Van Riper tells us, "It's an oxymoron to think of managing a battle. A battle has its own dynamics, and because it's non-linear, it's going to unfold in its own way. There's no way to predict the outcome. . . . There are those who think that microprocessors, or chips, computers at every level, are going to allow them to manage war in some businesslike way. It won't happen. The power comes from the bottom up, not from the top down. Those involved have some awareness of both what's happening around them and what's happening on a larger scale, and they will self-organize to achieve the commander's intent."

In the new Marine lexicon, the most important factors in determining outcomes are not guts and glory but the right rules of engagement. Accordingly, the organization has modified its entire high-level doctrine to allow the 174,000 Marines on active duty to adapt and thrive in a rapidly changing environment by sensing and responding, learning and adapting.

Van Riper, though recently retired, is still working to teach these ideas not just to the Marine Corps but to the entire military. As we were writing this chapter, events delivered to us a remarkable example of Van Riper putting his philosophy to work. He served as the military commander for the enemy in the Millennium Challenge 2002, the largest war game ever held, involving 13,500 people and costing $235 million. As *New York Times* columnist Nicholas Kristof put it, "The American fleet confidently steamed off to war in the Gulf recently—and promptly got creamed. . . .

"It began, key participants say, with the Americans confidently assuming that they could intercept enemy communications and predict enemy movements. But the enemy didn't cooperate. It used motorcycle couriers instead of radio and electronic messages, and sent orders as code words inserted into the muezzins' call to prayer—and this went right by the American intelligence analysts. The upshot was that the enemy 'sank' much of the American fleet as the exercise opened. Oops."

Like Capital One seeking to maximize its share of experience by launching tests in to the marketplace, the Marines rely on experimenting to learn from successes and failures. "First to fight" now means first to learn. In an evolutionary sense, then, the Marines are more like fruit flies than elephants—they go through many generations of experience in a short period of time. This allows them to rapidly evolve procedures that better conform to the threat, to the volatility of the mission, and to the unpredictable nature of combat itself.

They can, and do, establish appropriate rules for their fighting forces, rules to equip them with the decision-making power, rules that allow them to adapt to changing conditions and to self-organize when there's no one to tell them what to do. By the way, it's not clear that the entire U.S. military was as enthusiastic about experimentation as the Marine Corps. After Van Riper's enemy assault, the Pentagon, as is common in such games, re-floated its fleet and started over. "Then I asked to use chemical weapons," Van Riper recalled. "That was refused."[4]

The general complained to the *Army Times*: "Instead of a free-play, two-sided game as the joint forces commander advertised it was going to be, it simply became a scripted exercise." He protested by quitting his role as commander of enemy forces, and warning that the Pentagon might wrongly conclude that its experimental tactics were working.[5]

WHERE TACTICS MEET COMMANDER'S INTENT

"We are very good at instilling certain behaviors in our Marines," Van Riper tells us. "They understand our intent, and intent is like an algorithm in a computer or DNA in a biological system. . . . Now we must instill more tactical principles, so that instead of detailed prescriptive orders, everyone on the battlefield would inherently understand what to do. Building from the bottom up, we could have a much more powerful organization."

A Marine Corps doctrinal publication on warfighting sums up this adaptive approach: "Because we can never eliminate uncertainty, we must learn to fight effectively despite it. We can do this by developing simple, flexible plans; planning for likely contingencies; developing standard operating procedures; and fostering initiative among subordinates."

"Self-synchronization" is the term the Marines use to describe the ability of a well-informed force to self-organize complex warfare activities from the bottom up. Arthur Cebrowski, director of the Pentagon's new Office of Force Transformation and a former vice admiral in the Navy, describes it this way: "Self-synchronization . . . overcomes the loss of combat power inherent in top-down command directed synchronization . . . and converts combat from a step function to a high-speed continuum."[6] In other words, he who can best self-organize to adapt more quickly wins.

Self-synchronization pivots on the informed and coordinated decisions of forces at the bottom. It will work properly only if individual activities are aligned with the overall strategy, known in the Marines as the commander's intent. It also calls for "unity of effort" and carefully crafted rules of engagement. Sound familiar? Capital One's Jim Donehey certainly seemed to understand the value of instilling such rules. His Blue Chip Game was built on the understanding that objective and rules had to be aligned and communicated clearly.

Another Corps doctrinal publication, called *Command and Control*, dispels any confusion over the seemingly contradictory terms "bottom up" and "command and control." The Marines, now, define command as "the exercise of authority" and control as "feedback about the effects of an action taken," which doesn't sound very much like a stereotypical leather-neck barking orders. Indeed, modern commanders depend heavily on the feedback that they get from Marines in the field. Feedback allows them "to adapt to changing circumstances—to exploit fleeting opportunities, respond to developing problems, modify schemes, or redirect efforts." The result: "a mutually supporting system of give and take in which complementary commanding and controlling forces interact to ensure that the force as a whole can adapt continuously to changing requirements."[7]

FIGHTING IN A
NETWORKED WORLD

In Network-Centric Warfare, the most important asset on the battlefield is not a weapon but a sensor.[8] Sensors, connected to networks, enable greater battlefield awareness and provide continual feedback on operations.

To respond to this feedback quickly, the Marines use MAGTFs, or Marine Air Ground Task Forces, an operational structure that integrates command, air, ground, and logistics-support elements in modular fashion, on a scale ranging from a few platoons to a force of more than 100,000. The MAGTF structure allows the Marines to quickly plug together a specific set of capabilities that address any of a wide spectrum of threats. Network-Centric Warfare and a modular structure allow "decision makers and shooters to achieve shared awareness, increased speed of command, and higher tempo of operations," worthy goals for private enterprise as well.[9]

The effectiveness of the self-organizing, highly connected strategies now spreading throughout the military were amply demonstrated in Afghanistan during the winter of 2001–02. Al Qaeda's key asset of mobility and dispersion was countered by the direct connection between "spotters" and "shooters" from different U.S. military services. When an Army Special Forces soldier, for example, spotted a target, communication no longer had to traverse layers of organization to a high-level army officer before being relayed through the Air Force chain of command to the pilot circling above. Direct connection between spotter and shooter enabled an almost instantaneous, adaptive "sense and respond" cycle.

"Connection" applies not only to the Marines' networks in the field but also to an emphasis on diversity in its culture. Of all of the armed forces, the Marines are most hospitable to mavericks and new ideas. Van Riper makes a point of saying that "interesting hobbies" on a résumé carry a lot of weight with the Marines, who are a much less homogeneous bunch than one might expect. "I remember back when I was a young Marine, just enlisted, I heard this old gunnery sergeant talking about how the Marine Corps was a 'collection of characters,' a lot of unusual people pulled together only through their association with the Marine Corps. In any other context, they probably wouldn't work with each other." The Marines see this diversity as immensely valuable, not least in relation to the technology side of operations.

According to Alfred Brandstein, "We need to be multidisciplinary. Operations researchers by themselves are not creative enough. We want the social psychologists, we want the art-history majors, we want the college kid who doesn't know what he's doing, because he can be creative, or she can come up with new ideas."

The Marines have institutionalized their quest for diversity with "Time Out," a program that sends officers out to business or industry, not to be trained but to see how the private sector operates, and to bring this perspective back into the Marine Corps as a source of fresh ideas.

Van Riper notes that the Marines have also supported excursions to the New York Mercantile Exchange, because both "traders and Marines are required to make quick decisions with limited information." Observing traders at work, even Marines can learn a thing or two about making decisions and taking action under chaotic conditions.[10]

WAGING WAR IN SILICO

Meanwhile, back on Maui, the air-conditioners are having trouble keeping up with the heat generated by Project Albert's computers. "Traditionally in military operations," Brandstein says, "if you want to explore complex scenarios, you gather a group of people, you closet them in a room for eighty-seven years—this is a slight exaggeration—and they come out with a report that's a couple of years too late, and irrelevant." Project Albert is changing all of this.

Although the U.S. military has invested billions of dollars in developing traditional operations-research models, until Project Albert they have been unable to explore three fundamental phenomena of warfare: non-linearity, co-evolution, and intangible phenomena such as morale, training, and leadership. Understanding these intuitively, leaders in the Marines can now use Albert to express them *in silico*.

"I am not necessarily a proponent of complex adaptive systems approaches," says Brandstein, an unexpectedly disheveled, academic type with a doctorate in mathematics and hundreds of scientific publications to his credit. He looks somewhat like a fish out of water in the midst of clipped and shiny Marines. But appearances can be deceiving. All quirkiness fades when he discusses the huge advantages that Project Albert provides.

"These were the only techniques I knew of that could explore those issues. I wanted to have something simple, transparent, intuitive, and adaptable to what the decision-maker wants."

Whereas war games consume an enormous amount of time and resources and allow for the exploration of only a narrow set of outcomes, Project Albert captures, in simulation, the unpredictable outcomes that emerge from the interactions of combatants. Agent-based models can be run millions of times to test a vast landscape of possibilities, and they can reveal counterintuitive phenomena that could never have been discovered on a real-world battlefield until it was too late. They allow commanders to model self-organizing forces and how they interact, and to study the impact of intangible factors such as courage and fear that are themselves inherently unpredictable.

The human dimension is now recognized as the most important factor in warfare, and Albert has simulation models for exploring all-too-human intangibles such as determination and trust. *Marine Corps Doctrinal Publication 1, Warfighting* is very explicit: "Because war is a clash between opposing human wills. . . . [I]t is the human dimension which infuses war with its intangible moral factors. . . . No degree of technological development or scientific calculation will diminish the human dimension in war. Any doctrine which attempts to reduce warfare to ratios of forces, weapons, and equipment neglects the impact of the human will on the conduct of war and is therefore inherently flawed."[11]

Project Albert presents users with multiple parameters that represent two aspects of the Marines. First, its capabilities; how far and straight a

Marine can shoot, how far can his walkie-talkie communicate, how fast can he move, and so on. Second, Brandstein models aspects of his troop-agent's personality: Would he rather kill an enemy, save a comrade, defend his base, attack the hill? By varying these parameters and running countless simulations, the Marines learn where to spend money improving experiments—sensing versus responding, for example—and what mix of real-life combatants to select, and how to train them. The model runs through thousands of combinations, and the results shed light on complex trade-offs that would stymie even the sharpest analytical mind. In a war-fighting world that is constantly evolving, it makes no sense to try to affect outcomes directly.

One unique feature of Project Albert is its ability to delve into regions of a model that are of specific interest, regions of nonlinearity that cannot be grasped intuitively. Such Data Farming, invented by Gary Horne, director of Project Albert at the Marine Corps Warfighting Lab, works by conducting millions of runs and then "harvesting" the data.[12] Akin to but very different from data mining, this approach represents a decisive shift away from exploiting existing data in known scenarios, and toward exploring unknown data and scenarios. The military applies the same approach to determining when troops should engage the enemy directly and when they should maneuver, or which weapons to use in which situations. They even use the model to make procurement decisions and to determine appropriate force mix ratios.

Project Albert allow users to easily manipulate how data are displayed, to produce truer representations and access to the data behind them. For decision-makers, this feature is crucial. Visualization tools provide a transparent, versatile interface between intuition and raw computing power. In Project Albert, this means that the Marines and their ANZAC friends are looking at screens with hundreds of red and blue dots representing Marines moving around the display in a way that experienced commanders can relate to viscerally and immediately.

Modeling is not the only way the military is following the create, connect, evolve pathway. From networked swarms of Marines on the ground to technology that groups clusters of satellites according to the flocking behavior of birds, the Marine Corps is using the power of self-organization and the study of natural systems to cope with the next generation of military threats.

Battleswarm is one result, a new approach that lays out a framework to enable a "seemingly amorphous but deliberately structured force" to remain dispersed so as to avoid engagement, self-organize quickly to critical mass in order to strike the enemy, and then disperse again.[13] This strategy is very similar to the way that opportunistic bacteria behave. In isolation, small groups of bacteria mounting an attack would be easily squashed by the host's immune system. So, bacteria stay under the radar and use a chemical-signaling capability called quorum sensing to determine when they have reached critical mass. Only when they have reached a certain density will they gang up on their host and begin to produce their toxins.

The Armed Forces are investing heavily in breakthrough molecular technologies, "monetizing molecules" in the form of space-age materials, artificial muscles, and miniscule sensors.

One of the more intriguing examples is the Smart Dust project sponsored by the Defense Advanced Research Projects Agency. Researchers are working to create a network of thousands of distributed sensors, each measuring only a few millimeters yet containing its own power supply and communications hardware. Eventually, they hope to build a floating, electronic dust cloud that would gather and transmit all kinds of data. If a single sensor malfunctions, or goes down, the network itself would not be compromised.

Meanwhile, MIT researchers working with the military are busily creating the uniform of the future at the $50 million facility called the Institute for Soldier Nanotechnologies. Combining the smarts of several local partners in private industry, they are developing super-light battle suits using many of the technologies that we discussed in In Vitro, such as shape-memory, photo-sensitive and other dynamic materials, and biosensors, to enhance the twenty-first-century soldier's strength and protection, battlefield awareness, and camouflage. They're even working on automated medical treatments, molecular chain mail, and instant body shields. If all goes well, researchers at the Institute will create battle gear that will reduce the load on each Army soldier from about eighty pounds to forty-five.[14]

The Payoff

The Marines deeply believe that by working on the rules and capabilities of their agents, the connections among them, and the diversity of their ideas, and observing selective pressure and co-evolution *in silico* a superior fighting force will emerge. But "destabilize" is still the most important meme in the military business. The Marines aim to have the fastest OODA loop in the world. Smart Dust will improve the "observe" step, the results of Data Farming will translate into a greater capability to "orient," and self-synchronized, networked troops will "decide."

Collectively, this puts volatility on the side of the Marines. Even if you can't predict what will happen next, if you can adapt faster than the other guy, you'll probably win. You can create the volatility yourself, exploiting destabilized situations, which is just what the Marines know how to do. For us in the private sector, operating in an economic world of permanent volatility, the ability to exploit instability represents a similar competitive advantage.

All we can do is watch carefully, to keep an open mind ... and be ready to move. Giving up the illusion that you can predict the future is a very liberating moment. All you can do is give your-self the capacity to respond.... The creation of that capacity is the purpose of strategy.

—Lord John Browne of Madingley[1]

8

CREATING THE CAPACITY TO RESPOND AT BP

ALMOST nothing could be farther from the Maui High Performance Computing Center, either literally or figuratively, than the precisely clipped gardens of London's Finsbury Circus. Ascending the worn marble treads of Brittanic House, world headquarters of BP, formerly British Petroleum, a visitor there might be hard-pressed to find anything suggesting a common bond with the U.S. Marine Corps. Yet Lord John Browne, director and CEO of the venerable energy giant, is fighting the same war as General Van Riper: developing the organizational capacity to respond to volatility better than his competitors. The objective is to make volatility BP's friend, not its enemy.

The oil industry is famous for glacial change and hundred-year scenarios. Most oil companies' strategies (and lobbying efforts) have emphasized global stability. The sheer size of the global corporations in the business of extracting, refining, and marketing fossil fuels creates colossal inertia. BP, with revenues second only to ExxonMobil, in the industry, had sales of $174 billion and $103.5 billion in assets in 2001, and the company had 110,000 employees; for ExxonMobil, these figures were $188 billion, $143 billion, and 98,000, respectively. We don't expect a corporation of

162

such mature proportions to be acting like a frisky teenager, but BP has by many measures (reserves, production, market capitalization) tripled its size in the past four years. Acquisitions of Amoco, Arco, Burmah Castrol, and others have exponentially increased the complexity of managing BP's operations, which comprise ninety-eight business units in one hundred countries. After this growth spurt, you might expect the company to be focusing on a return to stability.

But Browne thinks that way madness lies. During his seven years as CEO, he has worked to give BP the "capacity to respond" to a volatile world. To do this, like the Marines, he's trying to create the shortest OODA loop in the industry, then create instability that BP can handle but the others can't.

Browne was the first to go on the offensive, to get aggressive about being green, not because BP had to at the time, but because he believes it can beat its competitors by adapting faster. For example, a few years ago the state of California was set to impose new standards for sulfur emissions from diesel fuel. BP urged the state to issue *more* stringent regulations. Why? BP had already developed a low-sulfur diesel product that no competitor could match. By planning for change, the company had put itself in a position to profit from it while others were still resisting.

Browne acknowledges that "the industry will be dominated by oil and gas for the next thirty to fifty years," but he chooses to focus not on the stability but on the *in*stability. "Decisions change. Attitudes change. While the regulations may say one thing, it doesn't say how long it takes to apply them. Politics move, and oil and gas are at the heart of politics. You only have to look at what's going on right now. Today, everyone says, well, it's all very unusual. I say, actually, it's just the same again in a different place. Whether it's Alaska, Alabama, Azerbaijan, Abu-Dhabi, Aberdeen, Angola—to name just the A's—everything moves."[2]

Five years ago, you might have thought his emphasis on volatility premature; by now you may find it prescient.

Consistent with the strategy of embracing volatility, BP has not been afraid to take steps that have made the oil patch a less stable place. Browne has also deviated from conventional practice by banning his company from making political contributions in the United States and so-called "facilitation payments" in developing countries. He also declared BP's support for both sustainable development and ethical conduct. In 2000, BP changed its logo to a representation of the sun, changed its name from British Petroleum to BP, and rolled out "Beyond Petroleum" as a strap line for its values. Although all the oil majors are working on solar energy, BP's efforts are notable—solar output at BP grew 35 percent in 2001, and the company produces about 20 percent of the world's new solar-energy capacity.[3]

The industry analysts did not take kindly to the "Beyond Petroleum" message, suggesting tartly that BP stick to its knitting and improve its return on equity, which at 13.1 percent has trailed industry leader ExxonMobil's 17.5 percent during Browne's tenure.[4] BP turned down the volume on its ad campaign in response, but the strategic intent remains intact.

And whatever the analysts' reactions, BP has done handsomely by its shareholders. Though BP and ExxonMobil frequently exchange the lead in the stock-price sweepstakes, from the time Browne took office in 1995 through August 2002, BP's stock price appreciated 141 percent, compared with 127 percent at ExxonMobil and 95 percent for the S&P 500. Similarly, pre-tax earnings have grown 217 percent to ExxonMobil's 135 percent. This rate of growth has been achieved through acquisitions in both companies' cases—BP acquiring Amoco and Arco, and Exxon acquiring Mobil—but BP has grown from 53 percent of Exxon's size in 1995 to 93 percent today. Clearly, Browne is paying attention to today's results as well as tomorrow's possibilities. It's the combination that *Business Week* recognized when the magazine voted him one of the Top 25 Managers of the Year in 2002.[5]

Like the CEOs of both Capital One and Maxygen, Browne was trained as a scientist, receiving an undergraduate degree in physics from the University of Cambridge, then earning an MBA at Stanford. Lately, he's expressed deep interest in complexity theory, so it's not so surprising that he has taken to heart the lessons of evolution. What *is* surprising is the unique blend of rigor and management intuition with which he is applying the lessons to BP. Despite his willingness to experiment, he's not about to abandon standard measures. "We believe in the power of rational analysis. So everything has to start there, and only when that is completed do we depart into judgment. If you don't go through that step, you will unleash huge forces very quickly that will go in the wrong direction."

BP's steady performance underscores our argument that, while accepting the unpredictability of nonlinear processes, adaptive management is far from a mystical exercise. Techniques such as data-farming and simulation employ evolution in addition to efficiency, augmenting intuition while amplifying rational analysis. By adding adaptation to business, BP is adding biology to physics, evolution to efficiency, and extending the analysis that informs judgment.

Why is Browne willing to make the stretch? Because, like the U.S. Marines, he has come to recognize the same irreversible shift that marks our connected, twenty-first-century world. "As we've grown in scope and scale and become more global, I think we've begun to realize that instability is the norm, not the exception—and that we have to adapt to that reality without sacrificing performance."

Senior managers at BP are keenly aware that in operating measures, the company is not the industry leader. While they focus intently on these performance measures, they also believe that issues like declining reserves, rising environmental and social concerns, and alternative-fuel developments are not subjects to be treated at the margins while doing business as usual. Instead, they see these as sources of instability that demand adaptability—and will reward it in the long run. Based on the appreciation of BP's shares, the markets support this view: BP is ranked third in the industry for volume, but second in market capitalization.

BP's corporate website clearly positions this element of corporate strategy. If you search for information about the organization, you quickly come to a description of the emergent properties of the enterprise:

One enduring characteristic of the oil industry has been change. As a company with a long history in oil and natural gas, petrochemicals and more recently in renewable and alternative energy technologies, BP has learned to be responsive to change and indeed to be at the forefront of the change process. Today's organization described here is well suited to a modern, global, learning corporation. It enables us to remain responsive and flexible, to spread success across the company and to ensure our core values and objectives are embedded everywhere within the organization.[6]

In contrast, ExxonMobil stresses a more traditional set of criteria for success:

Our success is built on a number of factors. Chief among them is the quality, dedication and professionalism of our employees. Their work is based on a number of long-held ExxonMobil strategies—maintaining investment discipline and lead-ing-edge operating efficiency over the business cycle. By continuing to focus on capital productivity, we have achieved better shareholder returns than the market. We have known for many years that a cornerstone of success is flawless opera-tions—which include strict financial controls, reliable operations, and sound safety and environmental performance.[7]

BP management has no doubt whatsoever that success depends on excellence in doing the operational work of running the business. Every senior leader we have spoken with stresses that plans, measures, and com-mitments are paramount in BP's management culture. They simultane-ously state that survival depends on the work of changing the business, and that this can be accomplished only through creating a company in which adaptation is an essential part of management. The "Beyond Petro-leum" positioning is, among other things, a message to BP staff that excel-lent management of the status quo is not the whole job. To repeat the thought that signals a step forward in strategic leadership, "the creation of the capacity to respond is the purpose of strategy."

THE ATOMIC STRUCTURE
OF A GIANT

Most CEOs of corporations the size of BP think of structure in terms of organization charts—group vice presidents, geographic leaders, func-tional lines—and all the matrix messiness they engender. John Browne, perhaps drawing on his physics background, has a different frame of refer-ence. "We decided to invent an atomic structure of the company, or the business unit. . . . We did a lot of experimentation, which is what BP does on an organizational basis, back in the late eighties, early nineties. How could we get people to work in smaller units—which allows us, on the one hand, to have atomic structures, on the other hand, to bring through the benefits of being in one organization?"

The "atomic structure" approach places the business unit in the role of agent, and the rules for their behavior are determined in significant part by the goal-negotiation process. Yet BP pays equal attention to the individ-ual as agent.

Bob Dudley, former executive assistant to Browne, now group vice president of gas and power and renewables, describes the benefits of BP's atomic structure: "You have these many different pieces of the organization; as the industry changes, as your portfolio changes, you can just pull things out and stick them in. It's a model that's very adaptable to change."

In 1999, BP was looking for ways to drive synergies after its merger with Amoco. "When it comes time to rationalize the portfolio, you can rationalize a piece of it, simply and easily. You can move people around; sometimes the people go with the asset. Or you can acquire, as with Arco, some new oil fields, and quickly create a new business unit that then becomes one of a collection of business units and put a BP person at the head of it and, as second-in-command, someone from the heritage company to get a rapid mix of experience. So if you're going into a new region, you can create another one of these modules.

"The North Sea, for example, had nine separate business units. Amoco ran it as one," Dudley continues. "But BP took very big oil fields and put in each one a business-unit leader who's got a management team around him to manage that asset. There were nine of those in Aberdeen, and they have very clear objectives. They also had federal behavior responsibilities to share [knowledge] across."

Dudley sees the power of the atomic approach as stemming from the behavior of individuals. "When you carve up the organization, you create mini-CEOs of businesses that are small enough to drive performance down to somebody who is really accountable."

Browne agrees. "People have to have accountability" to harness the "passion, drive, or aspiration" that mark human motivation.[8] He adds, "Organizations are human. They're societies; they're social. What's really important is to continuously create a great state of mind for everybody. We call it a great place to work."

Browne has an unusual ability to think simultaneously at the levels of the corporation, the business unit, and the individual. "We set up thematic behaviors: It's all right not to know the answer to a question. It's absolutely wrong not to ask for help." He reinforces this kind of message by sending senior managers to seminars at JMW, an executive-development organization that "works with organizations worldwide to accomplish things that have never been done before." Of course, many leaders frustrated by the conservatism of their executives have tried such approaches. Like Jim

Donehey of Capital One, Browne uses the power of his position to determine what BP stands for and, thus, what each of BP's employees should strive to embody, and then gives them the room to act.

The company has established four BP values: green, innovative, progressive, performance. "It is the state of mind that, on the one hand, the company is progressive, it thinks about the future—we made it one of our brand values. It's a very complex word, 'progressive.' It's not about status. It's not about conservatism. It's not about today. It's about *progress*. Creating a great state of mind, while thinking about not just today but about progress for tomorrow, enriching yourself in many dimensions, the company, too, and being proud of all that, is the way to motivate."

If ideas often come from the top, their implementation can emerge only from the cumulative actions of those at the bottom. In 1998, Browne pledged to reduce greenhouse-gas emissions to 10 percent below the company's 1990 standards by 2010; by 2002, it had already fulfilled that pledge. "That achievement is the product not of a single magic bullet but of hundreds of different initiatives, carried through by tens of thousands of people across BP over the past five years," said Browne when he announced the company's progress at Stanford University Graduate School of Business in March 2002.[9]

BP invests heavily to inculcate the four BP values and its thematic behavior. In the summer of 2001, we found many executives in the process of packing their bags, preparing to relocate to exotic parts of the globe— Luanda, Louisiana, or Ljubljana—and that's just the L's. After half a dozen interviews, we were still in the dark about the purpose of what appeared to us a major reorganization. It was not until we spoke to Browne himself that we understood that the intent was not about the organization structure but, rather, about training the executive team.

What was happening was in fact a part of the successful growth-by-acquisition strategy discussed earlier. "When we did this series of acquisitions and mergers," Browne told us, "I felt very concerned that the top leadership should become one culture. So we moved everyone back to London, and they got to know each other. They understood, at a very high level, how the company worked. When we were satisfied that this had been achieved, we then went back and said, 'You've really now got to go back to where the action actually is, most importantly, where the people are—

where our customers are, where our governments are—so that the work can be done with much more insight into the texture of what is going on.' "

None of the management actions described here is itself unique. Taken together, they show a leader "managing rules, not people" at the level of the business unit and the individual. By articulating the behaviors that will be successful (e.g., "ask for help") and the achievements that will be rewarded (green, innovative, progressive, performance—the "sugar" in BP-scape), he is working to create individuals who will organize themselves to achieve the company's objectives, as in the greenhouse-gas reduction. By training executives to "lift outdated limitations," he is trying to remove impediments to individuals doing all they can to succeed; by creating BP's atomic structure, he is harnessing their ambition to do so.

CONNECTING PEOPLE, CONNECTING MARKETS

One might look at bringing the BP, Arco, Amoco, Castrol, and other senior managers together in Finsbury Circus as a kind of breeding, recombining the behavioral norms of these previously distinct cultures in countless collisions at the corporate center. (As we've pointed out, nature does not direct evolution. BP's leadership, on the other hand, has been open to both positive recombinations and using selective pressure to encourage desirable behavior.) Globally, BP is extremely conscious of the network of connections within the company. Where at most big companies managers acknowledge the importance of an informal network that supplements the hierarchy, among the BP managers we spoke to, networks *were* the management structure. "Horizontal communication is the best way to get learning and understanding. There are a lot of people who are, roughly, doing the same thing—the richness of what they're doing is huge. Peers don't just provide information—they actually provide argumentation. Everything is tested again and again." Browne strongly believes in this kind of selective pressure provided by peers, which is why it is unsurprising that BP has three distinctive team-structured interventions that help organize horizontal communication.

The first, HIVE (for Highly Interactive Virtual Environment), is named in part for the idea of "hive mind." Just as in Jim Donehey's language—"you can't teach an anthill to fetch," but the colony nonetheless efficiently feeds itself—a hive of bees or other social insects can solve a problem no individual can manage. At BP, you might find a hive of geologists, seismographers, construction leaders, drilling-technology experts, and a dozen other specialists standing around in a darkened room the size of a school gym, wearing 3-D glasses and looking at an enormous curved screen. They'd be seeing—actually, more like "wandering around in"—a three-dimensional simulation of an oil deposit somewhere, constructed on the basis of seismic data. Or they might be figuring out the best process for dismantling an oil platform in the Gulf of Mexico. The point is to improve the quality of decision-making when many kinds of expertise are needed, according to Browne. "HIVEs give us something we've never had before—the ability to give all the people involved in a project a common mental picture of the structure on which they are working. A rapid and common understanding of something they will never actually see."[10]

That common mental picture doesn't come cheap—a HIVE in Houston cost BP $1 million to build—but the payoff is huge. According to some estimates, using a HIVE can save a drilling project as much as $45 million.[11] HIVEs save time as well, Browne says. "As a result of the technology, we are able to reach decisions in a matter of days rather than weeks or months."[12]

The two other team interventions, DELTA and ALERT, support BP's emphasis on performance measurement and management, the close cousins of selective pressure in nature. An internal group developed these tools to facilitate bottom-up decision-making and to encourage teams to monitor their own performance autonomously.

DELTA (Dialogue Enabled Learning & Team Alignment) supports project teams by enabling them to assess their own readiness and (mis)alignment by calibrating against the experience of other teams. The Web-based system solicits input from individual members of a project team by asking a series of questions (see Figure 8-1) and has already been applied in more than one hundred investment projects.

The team's responses illuminate readiness and alignment relative to best-in-class projects. Based on this feedback, a project team can change its priorities, assess its weaknesses, re-balance its makeup, and learn from its mistakes or flawed assumptions. From the team's point of view, DELTA

FIGURE 8-1   Sample Questions from DELTA

(Detail of Team Integration Enquiry Theme)

Business Strategy and Objectives

How well understood are the project's business objectives?

Project Execution Plan

What is the status of the project execution plan?

Change Control Process

What is your process for managing change?

Team Integration

How integrated is the project team?

Where We Are		Best in Class
❏	*I believe the level of team integration for the project is poor.*	❏
✖	*I believe the level of project integration is mixed. Communication between various project disciplines is ad-hoc. Team members' roles and responsibilities are underdefined.*	❏
❏	*I believe the level of project integration is adequate but there is room for improvement. The project is addressing communication issues across the project. Team members' roles and responsibilities have been communicated across the project.*	❏
❏	*Project integration is good. There is regular communication and consultations on interface issues, roles and responsibilities, and understanding of project goals, objectives and boundaries.*	✖
❏	*The project works very well in an open, honest, supporting and challenging relationship. The project is fully aligned on project objectives and there is ownership of project goals, objectives and boundaries.*	❏

Holistic Uncertainty Assessment

How does the project manage outstanding key project opportunities and downside risks and continue to assess and quantify new issues?

Capturing Lessons Learned from Project

How well does the project identify, capture and communicate lessons learned?

Startup/Operations Plans

What is the status of startup/operations planning?

---

guides them in what to sense and how to respond. At the company level, DELTA learns from each team that uses it and can adapt its feedback accordingly.

One of the intriguing things about DELTA and ALERT is that they support formal horizontal communication, rather than upward vertical communication. David Schofield, productivity interventions team leader, who was instrumental in sponsoring these self-organization tools, explains, "One of the rules of the game for anyone using DELTA and ALERT is that the information they contain belongs to the team. These tools are intended to help the team direct itself. Clearly, upward communication is important; however, decisions about how best to communicate the key issues within the team, horizontally across the company and upward, remain under the control of the team itself. There is no automatic upward transparency of this information whatsoever. Most people who have been involved in both risk and team quality assessment know—but rarely admit—that if you make such information vertically transparent, it's axiomatic that you'll get gaming. When the detailed data is not transparent to senior levels in the organization, team members can be much more realistic about capabilities and the range of outcomes. If your team learns that there's great uncertainty about a particular regulatory or technical issue, you'll want the space to get together with the experts to understand and manage that risk in a calm and professional manner. You'll want to focus on solving the problem rather than fending off eagle-eyed staff from headquarters."

ALERT (Asset & Opportunity Leverage through Early Risk mitigation in Teams) is a workshop-based tool for assessing risk by identifying both downside risks to be managed and upside opportunity to be captured. The intervention tool has already been applied to more than $25 billion of potential investment projects and is designed to help the organization adapt and thrive in the face of uncertainty.

ALERT is a tool for applying structured and selective pressure, applied in the form of cross-functional peer challenge. The payoff? It enables making early value-based trade-offs, it supports the creation of risk management plans throughout the life of a project, and ultimately, it enables using a "portfolio" rather than "parochial" project perspective.

Schofield notes, "With the right cross-functional team, ALERT is a tool which can provide you an unbiased portfolio perspective on what you're doing. So if, for example, you've identified specific country risk issues, ALERT provides a simple, common language for creating action plans, and for sharing the challenges with other teams and specialists across the group. ALERT also helps to build up risk correlations so that with the right leadership, the project team is equipped to treat the fifth or sixth project in China, for example, differently from the first entry into a new country."

Browne is comfortable with this lack of top-to-bottom transparency, and has moved toward horizontal communication at the business-unit level as well. "The big thing was, how do we actually get [the business units] to work together? So we said that the best way for people to test what they were doing was to have peers review what they were doing. So we invented peer groups. Heads of business units came together and reviewed each other; we had networks for learning. Very powerful for learning and understanding."

Bob Dudley describes how the peer-group structure connects similar kinds of assets. "An example might be figuring out how to improve the cost of North Sea helicopter operations. To do this efficiently, you get people from the Gulf of Mexico and South China Sea together because they all run helicopters, and suddenly, wow, there's a way to do this. Maybe it's a common helicopter contract with the same company, maybe it's scheduling software, but suddenly pretty quickly, information flies across. And I think the key is using these peer groups and common assets. Because in the oil company we have everything—from the beginning of upstream to the end of downstream and in everything in between."

The kind of investment in horizontal communication implied by mechanisms such as HIVE, DELTA, and ALERT are necessary enablers if self-organization is going to have a chance of overcoming the top-down tendencies in any big organization. However, this is not the only kind of connectivity that helps to overcome bureaucratic tendencies. BP has made another crucial connection, this time to break the chain, not of vertical communication but of vertical integration, and replace it with direct connections to the global market.

Oil companies think in terms of "upstream," which locates oil and raises it out of the ground (in BP, the Exploration and Production business stream) and "downstream," which markets it through gas stations—55 percent of a barrel of oil goes into gasoline—and other channels (BP's Refining and Marketing business stream). Since none of the oil companies is exactly in balance between upstream output and downstream needs, the companies sell excess production or buy products they can't source internally, or even swap production to reduce the need to ship product around the globe.

For most of the majors, the end-to-end throughput is primary, and the trading market is secondary. At BP, the trading market is the only market. All upstream production is sold to the internal traders, who then view downstream BP business units as just another customer in the global market. Likewise, downstream units source products from the world market, using the BP traders as their access point. The advantage of this is that it ensures that the business units, which in a more normal structure would be trading with one another, hear the voice of the market instantly. This means they are not making choices based on old data or internal relationships. In most companies, integrated value chains lead to endless bickering and occasional open warfare about transfer prices, and consequent misallocation of resources. In BP, the resources go to the highest bidder, inside or out. Like the military, which is working to make the relationship of the "spotter" and "shooter" independent of its command structure, BP is deliberately separating organizational functions to accelerate response time by exposing them to the outside signal of the market. Creating a trading mechanism between the upstream and downstream businesses effectively connects each spotter of oil to all the shooters in the global market, and each BP shooter not just to BP spotters but to everyone else who discovers oil and gas.

There's a simple logic behind this move: By dealing with the world market through the internal trading operation, each business unit can act on data from the world market, and the market is the world's biggest sensor.

Simon Orebi Gann, a particle physicist turned CIO, directs the IT side of BP's trading operation. He is as quick as the market he presides over, or the hand-built Morgan Plus 8 sports car he races on weekends. "The commodity market cannot *work* unless the participants know about the product," he notes. "If we don't know it's coming out of the ground, we can't sell it. So our trading group serves to stitch together information flows about our own business. Do you know that's one of the hardest things to do in the world? We're an unusual business; most value chains don't have a transparent price point in the middle. Oil prices have a highly transparent middle. So selling to an open market, which may include your own people in the downstream, is actually a more efficient process.

"Because it serves as a knowledge interface between the different pieces of the business, a market makes a more efficient transfer mechanism between big units in the company. The market often gives information about ourselves before we know it any other way. Trading could become the glue for holding the next generation of the BP organization together, because it represents a natural interface. It may become a knowledge hub, because it's a natural point at which information collects and from which information can be sourced." The trading operation enhances BP's ability to sense market conditions broadly and respond quickly.

The market is the best sensor for supply and demand, but BP uses sense, respond, learn, and adapt techniques in more physical fashions as well. We've made the point that molecular engineering and ubiquitous connectivity make it practical and economical to create new sense-and-respond capabilities in every business. BP is aggressively taking advantage of this potential. BP has developed a fiber-optic distributed temperature sensor system that gives accurate temperature readings for every meter along production tubing that runs from the surface down to the oil reserve and back up again. The data that the sensors generate help engineers monitor the inflows of oil, gas, and water and measure the reservoir's production (real-time as opposed to last time checked, and digital rather than paper-based). Field engineers also use near-infrared sensors to identify the precise blend of crude oils flowing through the pipelines. In time, sensors may even provide real-time seismic data.

At BP's Grangemouth refinery in Scotland, the company now uses a combination of sensors and visualization software to monitor wear and tear on pipelines. BP's sensor network can withstand temperatures up to 350 degrees Celsius, and it is so sensitive that it can detect metal loss measuring mere thousandths of a millimeter. The newly developed sensor technology is now being deployed at a number of other sites across the world.[13]

Whether connecting people, business units, or players in a market, BP seems to appreciate that sensing and sharing information drives adaptation. The company depends on connection for learning and communication. It structures business units and, ultimately, the entire organization around the experience of learning that occurs at the individual level. Group VP Ralph Alexander sums up the company's philosophy: "Data transparency in this world actually generates adaptation. Without transparency you cannot be adaptive, quick, and responsive, nor can you act with the confidence to be creative."

THE EVOLVING ENERGY COMPANY

In our "memes for managing" list, applying selective pressure (or "Seed, Select, and Amplify") and destabilizing the situation are the two management ideas for accelerating evolution. BP, more than any company of its scale that we know of, makes active use of both.

In the four years ending in 2002, BP merged with Amoco and made two major acquisitions—Arco in 1999 and Burmah Castrol in 2000—increasing BP's total staff by approximately 12 percent. At the same time, BP divests itself of 3 to 5 percent of its asset base every year. How does the company achieve any sort of constancy of purpose with all this churn going on? You might expect an emphasis on top-down control, but BP's philosophy is the reverse. John Browne emphasizes the feedback loops that guide the behavior of BP's managers: "Much of what is happening at a business-unit level need not be touched so long as it's within certain levels. But there are some things which, if they begin to trend out, are indicators of something happening—bad or good—and we are trying harder and harder to identify the few things that actually make a difference, without taking away the wherewithal of the business unit leader to do trade-offs and manage. And that's very important, because the more you look at the wrong things, the worse the leadership becomes. Because you take away those things the organization can self-correct. We don't want to teach it to self-correct in the wrong way." In other words, if leaders can stop asking questions about things that don't really govern success, managers can stop wasting their efforts on unproductive issues. How long have you been waiting for your CEO to say that?

"I argue that the Federal Reserve understands how to manage the economy without actually having a balance sheet for every component of the economy," Browne continues. "They do it with a variety of indicators, statistically, and that's basically what we're doing. And the impact has been clear, if you look at the way we handle the monthly operating review. We're using a much finer set of data to send better signals to the organization. . . . It's improving the resolution of our sensing system and the relevance of it. So less is more."

In a volatile environment, of course, there will never be a perfect feedback system. New information, filters, and sources will become useful as the external world changes. BP understands that the feedback loops that guide business decisions must themselves not only sense and respond but also learn and adapt. With strategic management, as with operations, it's not enough to be excellent at *doing*. BP wants to be excellent at *changing*, too.

As noted earlier, one of the most unusual things about BP is that, in an industry that prizes stability, it is an agent of instability. In fashion, companies are rewarded for this behavior, but in capital-intensive industries, stability is insurance against obsolescence of expensive investments. In an industry that has been widely criticized for its negative impact on the environment, BP re-branded itself as environmentally friendly and backed up this assertion with definitive steps—publicly acknowledging the risk of global warming and voluntarily setting measurable targets to reduce BP's greenhouse-gas emissions. Again, BP took advantage of instability in its sector and leaped ahead of competitors.

The Beyond Petroleum publicity campaign positioned BP as an innovator, looking beyond traditional sources of hydrocarbon energy. To some, this implied abandoning hydrocarbons—an unsettling thought for most in the business. To others, notably environmentalists, it implied accountability to do just that. Browne notes wryly that BP inevitably stirred up conflict by launching itself down this path. And the payoffs have been surprising. Not only has the company differentiated itself, it has reduced waste and cut costs in its own operations. According to a report from the Worldwatch Institute, a BP chemicals plant in Korea cut costs by $4.5 million and CO_2 emissions by 49,000 tons.[14]

Since taking these steps, Browne notes, "there's been a sea change in attitude" among BP's competitors. Once BP had demonstrated that it could achieve such an ambitious goal, without any net economic loss, its partners were prepared to follow suit. Many had no choice since, as Browne has pointed out, "When we're in partnerships [with other companies], we insist that our environmental standards are adhered to."[15] Though accused of "leaving the church" when he first publicly acknowledged the risks of global warming, Browne has been able to set his own benchmark with an aggressive plan for emissions reduction, nearly twice the reductions called for in the Kyoto Protocol. Meanwhile, ExxonMobil chairman Lee Raymond was telling shareholders, "We see the Kyoto Protocol as unworkable, unfair, ineffective and potentially damaging to other vital economic and national interests. The debate over Kyoto has distracted policymakers for too long. I am encouraged to see more constructive discussions focusing on more realistic approaches."[16]

Browne, elsewhere,[17] has stated that this is "an issue which is about leadership as well as science. . . . We're not just an outcome of somebody else's decisions. We have a way of making these decisions ourselves."

In breaking with the industry, BP embraces "destabilization" in order to live closer to the "edge of chaos." This means being agile enough to change as the environment does, but not so fluid as to lose its defining structure. And Browne balances destabilization with coherence. What Van Riper calls intent, Browne calls the plot. "One of the big things in any organization, I believe, especially in an open organization like ours, is that people can lose the plot very easily. The noise of the day lets people lose the plot. One of the roles, for example, of the group vice presidents is to keep setting the context, so that people don't lose the plot. This allows, therefore, the focus to occur and the noise to be reduced. There's always noise, there's always random noise in an organization. The key is how do you reduce it, not eliminate it. Eliminating it is very bad."

The role of senior management is to apply selective pressure by reaffirming the direction, not to choose the actions that business units will take. The diversity of ideas and perceptions that gives BP the capacity to find new responses is in the noise. Eliminate the noise, and you get too much stability. Eliminate the feedback, and you get randomness. Balance the two, and you get effective directed evolution.

THE PAYOFF

One of the most profound current hypotheses in evolution is that too much stability is dangerous—better to be just stable enough, at the edge of chaos, than to be unable to move. Browne's bold experiment, overall, is to push BP closer to that edge, distancing the company from its industry sisters. Even more challenging is BP's attempt to become more adaptable in the long run with no sacrifice in current financial performance.

The adaptive BP should reap two streams of benefits. First, as the industry inevitably changes in an increasingly volatile world, the costs of change—extraordinary items, restructuring charges, disposition of business units at distressed prices, inability to attract first-rate talent—should be lower for BP than for its less adaptable competitors. Second, because of its greater agility, BP should be the leader in seizing the opportunities presented by change. The "capacity to respond" has both upside—faster growth—and downside—lower cost to change—benefits.

The oil companies are generally viewed among the least amenable to change in the global economy. Yet as environmental, geopolitical, and local market conditions become increasingly unmanageable, and molecular technologies create new ways to harvest and package energy, the business environment of the energy industry may require much faster adaptation. Browne fits the role of an adaptive CEO. He directs the evolution of BP rather than its actions. He improves performance by enabling self-organization among people and business units, by increasing the connectivity throughout the enterprise, by explicitly managing diversity and recombination, and by paying careful attention to the feedback loops that create selective pressure in the organization, whether imposed by management or the market, by destabilizing his company and his industry. He appears to walk the walk as well as talking the talk of the Adaptive Enterprise.

Today, no one can prove that Browne's drive to make BP adaptive will make it the oil company with the greatest long-run profits. The data are consistent with the Adaptive Enterprise hypothesis: faster growth and more rapid response to regulation than its peers, but lower on measures of current profitability. The outcome won't be known for a while, but Browne may prove to be the pioneer of a new and coherent approach to leading a huge company. Along with the first-class performance that BP's shareholders are enjoying, the company is working to provide a "great place to work" for 110,000 people, and providing leadership to the world's discussion of growth and the environment. Above all, in directing the evolution of BP, Browne is focused on the capacity to respond:

How the world is changing, where advantage takes place not just today but in two years time, if you can align the right forces inside the company. How you develop people, because the people we need tomorrow are not the same as the people we have today. That is in itself quite a big change. That is, I suppose, the fundamental of evolution: trying to identify the capability and skill and experience content of the people who will lead the company tomorrow. How do you allow, on the one hand, a clear direction for evolution, and on the other hand, enough space for them to evolve in a way which you probably don't understand? Because they're going to be here way after you've gone.

You have to think about the company today, because you've made commitments, you've set expectations. But that's only part of the story, because you're actually thinking about the company over a period of years. And by definition, over a period of years, you will evolve. You must. Otherwise you will die.[18]

For the IPO in December 1999, my presentation included a slide that showed a miserable, shriveled, pithy orange, which is itself bred and improved from what it was in the Garden of Eden, let's say. Next to it, a slice of a juicy, beautiful orange from today. These show that our ancestors, without any knowledge of genomics, genetics, structure, function, proteins, anything reductionist, simply knew that plants when they breed create diversity.

—Russell Howard, CEO, Maxygen Inc.

9

BORN ADAPTIVE AT MAXYGEN

R USSELL Howard provides a unique window into the language and mind-set of the molecular economy. Few CEOs liken their organizations to sponges, amoebas, and stem cells, as Howard does.

Mountain View, California–based Maxygen's core competence is directed molecular evolution, a process of breeding molecules to develop products that can perform a variety of specialized functions, from warding off disease to increasing the cleaning power of laundry detergents. The company's processes and strategic vision are all about accelerating evolution, and its management and vocabulary keep reminding us that something new is coming. Maxygen, staffed with molecular-sciences Ph.D.s, doesn't have to learn about being adaptive—it was born that way.

Maxygen sees adaptation not only in biotechnology but everywhere in business. "We are an adaptive business," Howard tells us, "though this is not necessarily an innovation. The word *adaptation* describes the interaction between an organism and its environment. In the competitive business environment, this means access to money and investment—the financial environment, and the opportunity environment of who will buy what products. The guy who sells cantaloupe in the market at Marrakech is doing adaptive business, as his predecessors have been doing for 10,000 years. It's just the frequency of change and the speed of adaptation that are different."

In 1996, Maxygen was spun off from Affymax Research Institute, a subsidiary of what was then GlaxoWellcome. Led by Willem "Pim" Stemmer, now Maxygen's VP of research, a group of researchers at the parent company had begun playing with ways of improving on nature's ability to maximize genetic diversity. Intrigued by the new scientific platform that they could see emerging, they broke away from the mother organism with parental blessing. Today, the company has annual revenues of $31 million and a market cap of $261 million, and are doing business with pharmaceutical, agricultural, and chemical customers. In August 2000, at a time when many biotech companies were retracting into their shells, Maxygen completed the acquisition of ProFound Pharma, a Danish protein-pharmaceutical company, which provides Maxygen with scale, intellectual capital, complementary technologies, and commercial partners in the pharmaceuticals market.

Maxygen's reason for existence is to create and assess high-value candidate molecules which it then seeks to monetize, selling its products to partners for applications in human health, agriculture, and specialty chemicals. Of our four profiled organizations, Maxygen shows us the most insight into the development of the molecular economy. The company's entire production process is to create, connect, evolve.

A VERY LIVELY CELL LINE

In 1996, Maxygen was just the most recent mutation of a cell line being cultured in the portfolio of companies developed by biotech elder statesman Alejandro Zaffaroni. In his late seventies as the twenty-first century began, Zaffaroni has an illustrious history, beginning with his key role in building Syntex, creator of the birth-control pill, into a major pharmaceutical company in the 1950s. Since that time, he has maintained a biological model for growing wealth. When researchers come forward with ideas that do not fit within a parent company, rather than send them back to their knitting, he helps them set up new firms. And like Maxygen, each of Zaffaroni's eight separate enterprises is built on a new technological "platform" of scientific tools, rather than on a specific product. In effect, when a potentially valuable mutation occurs, Zaffaroni's approach is to ensure that it has an environment in which it can survive, rather than having to fight for its niche with established capabilities. In this he employs the biological lessons of diversity and reproduction through cell division. Board members and executives themselves are often passed along like high-performance genes to be inherited by the new thoroughbred company.

Maxygen's scientific platform is based on what dog breeders and farmers have been doing for millennia. Over a period of thousands of years, Mesoamericans, knowing only that "this plant produces more grain than the other one over there," managed to direct the evolution of corn simply by recombining elements existing in nature and selecting those that worked best. Selective breeding at the macrolevel of whole organisms was a key element in the agrarian revolution.

Maxygen founder Pim Stemmer was at Affymax, another Zaffaroni portfolio company, when he came up with a high-tech version of the same idea, technology he soon patented called MolecularBreeding. Stemmer and his team employed the natural process of genetic recombination (a.k.a. "sex"), concentrated in time, to maximize the genetic diversity of biological molecules that they thought might prove useful in commercial applications. As Russell Howard says, "Pim realized that nature creates high-quality diversity through recombination, and that mankind has actually used this algorithm for diversity creation with farmyard animals and crops. And wouldn't it be great and interesting if we could use that same principle in evolving genes for required commercial properties?"

The first step in Maxygen's MolecularBreeding is DNAShuffling, a rapid, low-cost process for building a diverse library of new DNA sequences or gene variants, simply by mixing and matching. "Nature has a way of providing rare solutions that could never in a million years have been predicted or designed from first principles," Howard tells us. What he's describing is the creation of new biological agents.

Next, for selective pressure, the scientists at Maxygen use MaxyScan, a proprietary screening system that selects for the desired mix of several commercial properties from among a library of variants. If the process sounds awfully random for something as precise as biotechnology, that's because it is. "We are essentially voyeurs," John Bedbrook, Maxygen's president for agriculture, adds. "We screen for things."

Researchers at Maxygen do have an outcome in mind, but they make no a priori assumptions about how it will be achieved. Moreover, they don't really care. "You don't need to understand something in its mechanistic basis before you improve it," Howard explains. "There's no Human Genome Project working on the breeding of Valentine's Day roses. But these flowers don't have thorns; they have wonderful long stems, a beautiful color, and a very light perfume. They are boldly engineered by people who do not have degrees in molecular biology. You can breed for success by defining criteria, taking the appropriate genetic material, and then applying this algorithm of recombination." Maxygen simply breeds a population of these kinds of molecules, using its DNAShuffling, screens these to select those that perform the best, breeds again, and so on. Rather than trying to engineer which molecules are most effective, it lets the results emerge.

The more traditional approach to drug development, called "rational design," minimizes randomness by seeking to predetermine the outcome. In rational design, researchers must first solve the structure of the protein and understand, in advance, how it will behave in different environments. Rational design is an expensive, labor-intensive process that can take half a decade to discover and develop a new biological agent. And with rational design, when you fail, you're back to square one. By contrast, the experience of rapid trial-and-error expands Maxygen's knowledge base, allowing researchers to find intermediate advances and new ideas for potential solutions.

Pim Stemmer goes on to explain it this way: "The problem with rational design is that you usually go after one physical parameter—such as temperature stability or pH level. It's very difficult to go after ten parameters simultaneously. But that's what nature does. When you breed an apple or breed dogs, you can get changes in many properties simultaneously. We select for a combination of properties that we don't understand rationally. You can make an apple more crisp, more flavorful, or more colorful. You can do it quite readily through breeding, but not very easily through a rational design process. Each property is a complex composite, usually involving a range of genetic factors."

The speed of innovation depends crucially on the diversity of the pool of genes, memes, or people on which the system can draw. "Usually, only two parents contribute to the recombinant," Stemmer says. "What's most important is that we can alter one of the rules of nature. We can create molecules bred from multiple parents."

In Maxygen's world, researchers access more diversity in every generation by multiplying the parents; this might complicate human lives, but bacteria don't file paternity suits. Roughly speaking, the company gets three generations of recombination in one.

MolecularBreeding gets Maxygen into the heart of the solution much quicker, shrinking the discovery process down from an average of six and a half years to less than two years. MolecularBreeding assumes not only that there are many different routes to a solution, but that most of these are non-intuitive. As with dog breeders, all that matters is the outcome.

Maxygen's breakthrough technology has essentially invented new ways for molecules to have sex. "And by sex," Howard goes on, "we mean recombination of pre-existing genetic diversity. It's really, you could say, a redefinition of sex."

Howard cites the example of one particular antibiotic to demonstrate the business significance of the company's approach. Maxygen worked with Eli Lilly to improve the productivity of *Streptomyces frandiae*, a bacteria industrialized twenty years ago and currently used to produce tysolin, a key compound used for manufacture of antibiotics, anti-cancer drugs, and anti-viral drugs. The antibiotic was developed commercially using a technique known as Classical Strain Improvement (CSI), which essentially involves inducing random mutations in a sequential fashion and then screening the results. And over the past twenty years, researchers have been improving the efficiency of tysolin production using CSI by about two or three percent.[1]

"We came along and, in collaboration with Lilly, had access to those organisms from twenty years ago—took them, just like they did twenty years ago, and bootstrapped some initial diversity by mutagenesis. Then we took the microbes that were slightly better than their parents at making this antibiotic, and braided them together in the equivalent of group sex, doing sexual recombination of multiple organisms simultaneously. It works beautifully for certain bacteria. And what we did in twenty months was better than what Lilly was able to do in twenty years.

"And the nice thing about it," Howard reminds us, "it is holistic. We have no idea as to what we've improved. We didn't care. This is holistic improvement of the microbe for the amount of production of something very discrete. Make more chemical. And I don't care whether the organism does it by altering its internal metabolic pathways, getting more carbon from the environment, better transport of the compound out of the cell— whatever the mechanism." John Browne says that giving up the illusion of control is very liberating; Maxygen takes it a step further and makes it profitable.

The "group sex" capability, coupled with the ability to scan the resulting compounds, represent developments that will become part of the technological infrastructure of the molecular economy. By using the techniques of nature rather than those of chemical engineers, scientists like those at Maxygen are reducing the costs of some highly desirable molecules by orders of magnitude. Howard explains: "In a chemical process that takes low-value chemical inputs, things available in barrels that are basically $5 a kilo or $10 a kilo, we can design a two- or three-step enzyme process to make something that is now worth $200, $500 a kilo. We use enzymes to make very specific, information-rich chemical conversions that go like a laser through the chemical space that's involved. Whereas a chemist would require ten or fifteen steps, in a biological process a single enzyme can replace ten chemical steps. So you can imagine that the complexity, the time, the cost of the infrastructure is all dramatically reduced, especially when enzymes, in general, work at low temperatures, low pressure, in aqueous solvent. Compare that with any organic process. There's a high temperature and pressure, which means cost of heating, and cooling, and power. And traditional organic processes work in organic solvents, which means danger and environmental risk. Enzymes are brilliant if you can get them to do their thing. And we are the masters at evolving enzymes to do what you want."

This capability is allowing one of Maxygen's business units, Codexis, to get into the business of providing hard-to-produce, expensive molecules to anyone who has a need for them.

Codexis' strategy has three stages. "First of all, cut the cost of goods of known processes," Howard begins. "Second, enable the manufacturer of molecules that people want today that are impossible to conceive of in commerce. They're simply academic curiosities. Then, third, use the technology to enable new molecules that will be our next generation of commercial molecules."

Because Maxygen's holistic approach doesn't require that anyone understand how the molecule functions, Codexis can invent new molecules designed to entirely novel specifications. Need a concrete additive that makes tires stick to your driveway while snow falls off? Breed one. What Maxygen is describing is the precursor of the signature production process of the molecular economy: compiling matter, from the bottom up, on demand.

It's as if Alan Kay were showing us the first dial-up modem or microprocessor in the early seventies, technologies that wouldn't cause a ripple in the business world for a decade, but would eventually power growth for half a century. It will be the application of these capabilities to industries beyond pharmaceuticals and agriculture that marks the transition from the second quarter of the molecular economy, in which technology is developed, to the third, in which it is applied throughout the economy.

Howard predicts that soon the company will be "using biologically derived molecules not for their receptor properties and their exquisite specificity of intermolecular interactions, but as substances that can be made with whatever dialed-in properties you want, inexpensively, in fermentation systems. Antifreeze proteins, synthetic spider web, 'cosmeceutical' proteins to remove dead skin from the face or unclog pores, biosensor proteins to detect environmental pollutants, proteins as components of nano-machines, etc.—you can make proteins that do all sorts of things. That's a wholly new area, but most of these applications, interestingly, will be for totally novel markets that people cannot conceive of today."

When it comes to monetizing molecules, Maxygen is the epitome. Create, connect, and evolve permeates the company's entire process, from MolecularBreeding to DNAShuffling to MaxyScan. But because Maxygen was born adaptive, evolution is built into not just its products but its strategy and management as well.

LETTING THE MARKET DECIDE

Maxygen's scientific platform—randomly creating a huge library of options, then screening through them with incredible speed—is also its business model. Neither one seeks to predict and control outcomes.

"It was immediately obvious that our technology platform was broadly applicable," president Simba Gill tells us. "That core asset represented a massive piece of value, and we recognized early on how important it was to protect and build on our intellectual property base." Protecting it did not mean guarding it closely and developing applications internally. Maxygen sought out partners promiscuously, making its corporate boundaries permeable, because the value lay in recombining its proprietary platform—promiscuous molecular recombination or group sex—with its partners' product-development goals.

"We all realized," Gill goes on, "that if the technology was as powerful as we believed, and as broadly applicable as we hoped, then to grow our business we would have to partner aggressively with people who were interested in using it in other areas. We weren't going to choose that focus ourselves. We were humble enough to acknowledge that we lacked not only the resources but the knowledge needed to extract maximal value from our platform."

The model that evolved was to partner with the experts in multiple areas, trying to retain some proprietary rights but always arranging to participate in some of the upside in the event that successful products were developed. "That's still the model we have today," Gill says. "In all our deals, we earn royalties from any product developed from use of our technology. In most cases, our partners are paying for almost all of our research and development costs. They're the ones who know how to develop products, and they actually do a lot of the early-stage work—for applications in agriculture, for example."

Science led to a platform, which led to a business model, which led to a certain organizational structure—or, perhaps, lack of organizational structure.

"Early on, we had no formal regular senior management meetings," Gill goes on. "I've worked in a lot of companies. And every other company I've worked in, large or small, would have a weekly meeting in top management. It would be an absolute requirement. And you'd have to get in a room and spend three hours talking about all of the key issues. We didn't do that at all for the first three years. Ours was much more Pim [Stemmer], Russell [Howard], myself, primarily, and a few other people, running around like madmen, literally, like headless chickens to the outside world. And then, Russell and myself just talking regularly, whenever we could, by phone, on planes, about what the right thing to do was."

Asked if Maxygen succeeded despite or because of this free-form style, Gill says, "I think if we had a typical disciplined structure, it would have been a huge negative.

"Under that corporate group, we created a core technology group. They need a harbor where they can develop core technologies that can be leveraged across the whole company, technologies we need to meet potential competitive threats from the outside. While we're all under a single corporate umbrella, the business units each have their own presidents working with their differentiated intellectual property to fulfill their own goals. Our technology platform lends itself to that automatically. It's less a question of the technology platform, than of the organization's willingness and ability to change direction very, very quickly. As a management team, we are willing to adapt very quickly, to pounce on an opportunity when we see it, to change the organization, to think about new developments, and to be always very open to any change in any direction." Maxygen calls this approach one of "planned opportunism."

Russell Howard elaborates on Maxygen's adaptive capability. "As a business, we're an organism with our threads of knowledge, of intellectual property, of expertise at our fingertips. The competitive business environment, the financial environment—the access to money and investment—and the opportunity environment—who will buy what products—are all continuously changing. Sometimes they are in sync with each other, and sometimes they're not. Sometimes conditions are good for our company, and sometimes they're bad. But our interaction with the environment is one of continual testing and probing, success and failure."

Maxygen's philosophy of adaptation went against the grain of traditional investors. Stemmer tells us, "Early on, the board members would always want the company to focus on areas that matched their expertise. Our board was dominated by pharmaceutical people and they wanted the focus to be on pharmaceuticals, which is still probably the world's most attractive industry in terms of net profit. Yet we had four major opportunities. Fortunately, we chose to let all four areas more or less compete and show what they could do. The result was surprising. Although our board, dominated by pharmaceutical people, never thought that agriculture could be a promising area for us, it was two $100 million deals in agriculture that allowed us to go public."

It was as if Maxygen's board was trying to do "rational design" in the face of the more adaptive, recombinant approach led by the science. "Rational design of business development is very similar to the problems that we encounter in rational design of proteins," Stemmer notes. "In my experience, it's best to go out to other companies, to listen, and to react rather than to go through arguments internally without looking at the outside." Maxygen established permeable boundaries and used them to access diverse market environments.

As Simba Gill describes it, "In a Darwinian, natural-selection sort of way, we let Pim and others in the company go out to the world asking, 'Tell us what you'd like to do with shuffling.' We let the environment drive the initial focus of the company and, as a result, consummated two very important agricultural partnerships with two of the world's largest players, Pioneer/DuPont and Syngenta. We were nimble and opportunistic enough to capitalize on their interest. Another deal, with Novozymes, the number-one industrial-enzyme company in the world, also understood the power of the technology immediately, and came to us."

"We found that agriculture companies like Pioneer/DuPont have both classical plant breeders and rational-design molecular biologists," Stemmer tells us. "We fit right in the middle of that. We're applying a plant breeder's perspective and recombination approach, using molecular-biology tools. The ag companies saw this as a bright future."

Nonetheless, Gill goes on, "There is a tension between a rational approach, which favors investing in pharmaceuticals because these always have a higher return, and a more adaptive approach, which favors exploring other areas and investing based on what comes back. We have done both.

"While the early deals actually were in agriculture and chemicals, we recognize, rationally, that we need to put money into those areas that have traditionally seen the highest returns: pharmaceuticals and vaccines. At the same time, we need to respond to the markets and feed those areas that actually are getting the deals."

By exploring the potential of the company's technology to add value in agriculture, in industrial enzymes and the chemicals business, and in protein pharmaceuticals and vaccines, Maxygen found that it could consistently produce molecules more versatile and useful than all of the parental genes. Researchers pushed the limits of the technology and discovered that it could be used with long genes, short genes, linear DNA, circular DNA, low-homology DNA, and high-homology DNA. In every field, the technology could improve genes and endow them with desired properties.

This has allowed Maxygen to capitalize on the breadth of its technology, maintaining a portfolio of applications in agriculture, protein pharmaceuticals, preventative and therapeutic vaccines, and specialty chemicals. The company's success results from the fact that during the early phases of its development, it deliberately remained very opportunistic and unfocused, able to evolve as its environment gave it feedback.

Maxygen did not set out at the beginning to target and capture a market. Instead, it let science take the lead. The lab created new capabilities, and once those capabilities proved themselves, management let the market decide where they should be applied.

Just as Maxygen focuses on connections with its external environment, it focuses on the nature of connections internally. Taking a cue from its technology platform, which relies on recombination as the molecular mechanism for creating genetic diversity, Maxygen applies the concepts of recombination and diversity to its people as well.

"In this good company," Stemmer tells us, "good people get recycled. There is a kind of executive breeding that happens in the Zaffaroni-family companies. Conceptual breeding goes on as well. Most of the Zaffaroni companies have a strong interdisciplinary approach, with engineers working alongside biologists and chemists, and this contributes to a culture of openness and innovation." Maxygen, too, has skilled biologists to nudge nature along, mathematical wizards to design the formats for screening, and equally skilled chemists to analyze the read-outs.

Maxygen grew up with 50 percent non-American employees. Gill himself was born in Africa of Indian parents and was raised in the United

Kingdom. Russell Howard is Australian, John Bedbrook a New Zealander, Pim Stemmer Dutch, and Alejandro Zaffaroni an Uruguayan.

"We're very thoughtful about the types of people we hire into the organization," says Gill. "We think about how they fit within current breeding stock. Some species breed with each other and don't breed with other species. You've got to make sure you bring something in that's the same species." With the acquisition of the Danish company, Maxygen's quotient of non-Americans jumped to 70 percent. "That's not deliberate," he says. "It's just that we attract different types of people, and we're very open to that." The company structure and organization, as well as the role of the founders and the management team, continue to evolve.

Part of this organizational flexibility comes from a management style that emphasizes accessibility. "As for hierarchy, there's no issue about talking to top management. We all have very open-door policies, and that boundaryless state is part of our company culture," says Gill. In our terms, Maxygen focuses on connectivity internally and externally to enable both people and business units to organize themselves around the opportunities presented by their environment.

CELL DIVISION DOESN'T HURT

Maxygen seems to have little trouble fostering self-organization and innovation through connectivity and diversity. How does it translate feedback from the market into selective pressure internally, especially for a company at which nearly 90 percent of the staff are working full time in pure research and where one-third of the 300 employees hold doctoral degrees?

"Somehow you have to duplicate the natural phenomena of selection and evolution; you need something that will mimic the natural environment. Top management in a company has to be the equivalent of selective forces in nature, which calls for a willingness to let people in the organization explore what they want to explore, to flourish and develop. If they don't deliver, then you've got to apply selective pressure," Simba Gill explains.

"I think as an organization, while we always want to retain the ability to become a complete organism, we also want to retain the stem cells, because they allow us to grow in any direction. We can become a liver, and still have the ability to become a lung or any of the other organs.

"I've had my long and painful stint in a big company, and one of the lessons I learned was that focus can actually destroy you. Companies like us are about creativity, and focus destroys creativity. If you centralize everything, you stifle entrepreneurialism. We can't have a single person driving all business negotiations, nor a group with complete control. We've still got a core corporate group, and we're always there acting as mentors and thought leaders."

Pim Stemmer brings the stem-cell analogy down to ground level. "In the beginning, you have sort of a broad vision. You're open to many different ideas. After a while, you start to focus on certain areas, and you are no longer open to alternative ideas. To build the value of the company, you have to focus on product development. At that point, openness to new ideas is even more reduced. There is a feeling that, after a certain time, new technology development does not really increase the value of the company further.

"This actually creates opportunities for spin-offs. You start out with a broad idea from which you could adapt in many ways, and the more mature the company gets, the less adaptable it becomes. In a sense, you may not want to fight that. If there is something really novel that is at a very different stage and needs to be nurtured, it may be better to spin it off, because the mother company has differentiated to an extent that it is no longer very efficient at nurturing babies.

"There's an irreversible differentiation that happens," Stemmer continues. "In order to develop drugs efficiently, you need to focus. This is quite incompatible with an innovative environment. Innovation cannot be compartmentalized." In other words, once you've learned to be a liver, you need to function as a liver and never recover the potential to differentiate in another direction.

Howard reinforces this point. "High-risk exploration takes a certain kind of mind-set. Most things fail, and you keep trying. When you shift from *explore* to *exploit*, when you finally decide to move in a particular direction, you are going to create a specific profit-making business, which is quite different than technology exploration. A profit-making business requires focus on particular products, expertise, and muscle in a specific area. To hit the opportunity quickly, you've got to have a competitive leadership group that are asking the right questions about applications, diligence, and execution. That's a very different set of managerial talents and corporate imperatives."

Naturally, everyone at Maxygen uses biological metaphors. When we ask CEO Russell Howard how he thinks about the company, he switches the metaphor to a different biological model. "We look at our business as an amoeba, with pseudopods reaching toward resources. If the pseudopods are reaching in the same direction, the organization moves. If, as at Maxygen, they reach in four different directions, you look at the organization and say, 'It's going to divide.'

"I think what we've done is to go from an amorphous amoeba that has multiple pseudopods testing different environments into a highly differentiated cell that will soon go through cell division. We are now a more complex cell, with a pseudopod out in the direction of agricultural products, another out toward chemical products, another toward protein pharmaceuticals, and another toward vaccines. Each of those pseudopods is differentiating in order to specialize in those fields.

"There comes a point when you can't all be within one cell. It's just physically impossible, as a natural competition arises between the groups, each serving different investors and industry customers. After a while, you get conflicting resource requirements, and conflicting priorities."

What does cell division mean in the corporate context? "The alternative is to spin companies out or sell them, or merge them with other entities," Howard says, "so that they're completely separate and no longer under the same corporate umbrella. In our case at the moment, we don't have any prejudice about what the solutions will be for each of our differentiated business units.

"Our concern is creating separate entities that each win in their businesses. To what extent do these entities need each other? Why separate if it's going to make them weaker? The strength of separation is to promote independence, selfish thinking, and local solutions. The weakness of separation is that other parts of the organization may come up with solutions that in a different context could be applicable to your business unit. In our current model, the corporate group at Maxygen is the core of intellectual property, corporate legal governance, business development, and strategic thinking for the whole business."

In late 2000, Maxygen began moving down one pathway to differentiation. In order to tune Maxygen to its environment, Howard embarked on what he refers to as "faster differentiation and devolution," using the term "devolution" very carefully. "What we think of as devolution is separation in a gradual process that's intellectual, corporate, legal, and managerial, positioning the new entity for its own path with an exit that may not be an IPO," he says.

"I don't regard the companies that we are creating as spin-outs in the sense of being ready tomorrow to go to an IPO. Often, when you say to investors, 'Oh, I'm going to spin out a company,' they automatically assume that you're creating an entity whose growth path is toward the public market," Howard continues. "We look at creating entities that will, by definition, enhance shareholder value. The exit for those companies could be an IPO, if appropriate to the public markets, and if there was the right form of investment that we wanted. They equally could be a highly valuable trade-sale where the business is sold to a leading company in that space, and for a nice five-times multiple on the investment of the shareholders. So I don't use the word 'spin-out' when I talk publicly, because people think just of that single path."

The devolution of the chemicals unit has already taken place. Codexis, whose three-stage strategy we described earlier, recently raised $25 million through the investment of Maxygen and several investment groups expert in the chemicals arena. As a newly developed organization with its own board of directors and separate business plan, Codexis has eighteen potential products and processes in its research pipeline, six product candidates in development, and three processes at commercial scale.

Off to a very promising start, Codexis uses Maxygen's Molecular-Breeding platform but is introducing new techniques of its own. Maxygen's current techniques focus on working with the individual gene, creating variations of it, and then selecting from the winners for which gene made the best protein for the industrial application. Codexis has a new technique for evolving the entire organism through whole genome shuffling, which was used to improve the *Streptomyces* organism discussed earlier.[2]

The Future Is All About Code

As we explored Maxygen's evolutionary path, we found that the company anticipates its own convergence of information and biology. "We not only do the physical recombination of genes *in vitro*," Howard tells us. "We also do it *in silico*. We've been working on this for four or five years—ahead of the curve, we believe.

"Maxygen has created an amazing database that we have not yet begun to exploit. How many companies have 10,000 variants of a protein that differ from each other only in two, or three, or one particular amino-acid position? Therefore, they are very closely related structural variances of each other for which a variety of functional or physicochemical properties have been measured. We have proteins where, for any variable, whether it's pH tolerance, or ionic-strength tolerance, or enzyme reactivity, or enzyme selectivity, or enzyme activity—whatever you want—we've got the variables measured. And we have 10,000 variables. And we've got proteins that are duds. We've got proteins that have moderate activity, the same as the parental gene or genes, and proteins that are superior in any criteria you look at," Howard continues.

"The next question is, if you do that N times on N different proteins, is there now a theme or a link which allows you to take the next protein, which you've never touched, and from that database come up with a new functionality not known? It's conceivable, absolutely conceivable. This is something really quite orthogonal to our current business model. But we're very aware of it. And we're looking for how to exploit this." So Maxygen's future, derived from molecular biology, will lie, at least in part, *in silico*. Code is code.

THE PAYOFF

Most companies we know would see the growth of a different business model based on other capabilities as a threat to their existence. The power of Maxygen's point of view lies, in part, in believing that it can adapt to whatever changes the environment brings, in John Browne's words, "the strength to seize the opportunities." Anyone as versed in biology as Russell

Howard would give some thought to organizational death as well. "Of course, life is characterized by death," he says, "but it is more characterized by reproduction, passing on the DNA, the thread that produces progeny and is the real essence of life." Samuel Butler, a nineteenth-century British satirist, quipped that a hen is just an egg's way of making another egg. Most businesses are the genesis of another business. They may spin off another company, and the parent may die, but the spin-offs survive and succeed. Through the successor companies, the patents, the processes, and the people that make up the corporate DNA will be passed on to proliferate and continue to evolve. "Though the original organization may die, I use the analogy not of death, but of life's continuous process of re-creation," Howard says.

Perhaps this thought itself is an element of Alejandro Zaffaroni's success. His companies tell an impressive story of high-risk success in developing leading technologies: introduction of the birth-control pill (Syntex, 1951) and founder of Alza, a leading company in drug delivery (1968), sold recently to Johnson & Johnson for $10.5 billion; then Inex (1980), a leader in cytokine research; Surromed (1989); Affymax (1989), a leader in combinatorial chemistry; Affymetrix (1993), dominating the field in microarray technology; and Symyx (1996), a leader in materials science using combinatorial chip technology.

"With Zaffaroni companies, there is always a continuous evolution in the way they're run," according to Gill. "They've all learned from each other's mistakes and successes, and they get better and better, able to operate at a much more accelerated pace, based upon the knowledge that has been transferred. What you've got in Zaffaroni companies is a massive amount of knowledge and experience that creates a great breeding stock for subsequent ventures."

Maxygen is a "second quarter" company that in our economic life-cycle theory embodies not only the science of the next ten years but the core concepts of this science in its management, strategy, and structure. This embodiment reached even deeper in its thinking, behavior, and language. Sponges, stem cells, and pseudopods find very real expression in the way Maxygen conceives and manages itself. At Maxygen, there is no debate about whether biology is metaphor or business model—it's just how the world is.

The payoff for Maxygen lies in its ability to explore continually evolving technology and applications, while also creating different units to exploit commercial opportunities not always closely related to the founding capabilities. It achieves this by, in part, giving up the desire to control the destinies of the differentiated units.

Over time, there should be another payoff for Maxygen. Although as of mid-2002 it had $220 million in the bank, the company must contend with scarcity of additional financing. As investors learn that a stake in Maxygen is equivalent to options in a long line of technological developments, rather than a simple bet on a single market and technology, Maxygen should enjoy greater access to funding, higher price-earnings ratios, and a lower cost of capital.

It's worth remembering that volatility isn't always a threat. It's a time when change creates new possibilities. The key thing is to have the strength . . . to seize those opportunities.

—Lord John Browne of Madingley[1]

10

BECOMING AN ADAPTIVE ENTERPRISE

Y OU'VE just read about four organizations living the adaptive life, but none of them awoke one morning and decided to become adaptive that day. So what starts a company down the path to the Adaptive Enterprise?

We said early on that business has always been adaptive to a degree, and it shouldn't be a surprise that, in most cases, the impetus is the environment. The U.S. Marine Corps understands that the unpredictability of the enemy and the nonlinearity of war make adaptibility imperative. Capital One perceived that interest rates and customer desires changed faster than anyone in the credit-card business responded, and the company created adaptive capabilities to fill that gap.

In some cases, adaptiveness is in the genes. Maxygen takes its cues from the molecular science it practices; evolution is its world.

Only BP is a story of an explicit management program aimed at increasing adaptiveness. John Browne's view is like Capital One's in that he sees value in adaptiveness that his competitors have yet to understand. But unlike Capital One, which was able to establish a new company with information-based strategy deep in its DNA, Browne must work to change the behavior and attitudes of a huge, well-established enterprise.

In nature, evolution requires that a new generation be born for progress to occur; the analogy in business is that a company cannot evolve, only an industry. BP is trying to demonstrate that this ain't necessarily so. Plants and animals have no known mechanism to change the behavior of their cells—their evolution depends solely on selection.

Businesses, however, can establish an objective and use that objective to define fitness, to apply selective pressure on the behavior of the individuals. If the individuals' decision-making behavior changes, the enterprise's capabilities will adapt.

TARGETING VOLATILITY

If your environment has not made you adaptive thus far, why should you take action? Why should you let yourself in for the same challenging, costly, uncertain kind of campaign that Browne is waging? The answer, we said at the outset, is that the connected economy is accelerating change and increasing volatility, creating the adaptive imperative. If destabilizing change has already hit you, you probably haven't begun to catch up with it. If it hasn't hit you, it will. As we mentioned in Chapter 5, the way a company addresses volatility affects its performance in terms of both growth and market value.

Most companies start down the path to the Adaptive Enterprise by taking aim at a specific source of volatility in its business and creating an isolated, adaptive response. In the fashion-retail industry, companies like Zara and Benetton have connected their manufacturing operations to point-of-sale data, pushing sense-and-respond to the limit, to act on the fickle dictates of their customers and avoid markdowns. Automobile and equipment manufacturers like John Deere and General Motors have overcome scheduling and work-flow challenges by creating operations that can Seed, Select, and Amplify (assembly plant scheduling) and Self-Organize (paint booths).

The following approach to becoming more adaptive works for just about any enterprise, profit-seeking or not-for-profit:

First, look for the sources of volatility in your business environment: raw-materials costs or availability, weather, market conditions, technological change, competitive activities. Then ask: How can I better anticipate this volatility? Is there a hidden factor driving it that I can isolate and identify? Is some new sensor available?

Red Lobster uses satellite data on the temperature in the Gulf of Mexico to learn how fast shrimp are breeding and thus hedge its bets in the futures market.

Second, assess the economic impact of that volatility. Are expensive assets deployed against contingencies? Or is significant business being lost because of an inability to respond? How many cars are on dealer lots because you can't sell from an empty shelf? How often is the exact car the customer wants in stock? If you could respond to customer demand more rapidly, you could free up inventory—something Toyota pioneered with its five-day order-to-delivery cycle in Japan. And how many fewer elevators does a building need when the system batches the stops efficiently? These are big numbers.

Third, what could be done to make these business areas more adaptive—do the seven management principles suggest any solutions? This is the hard part, because the memes aren't habits of mind in most organizations. In a moment, we'll outline a systematic approach to make them so.

Fourth, are there systems, rules, or other constraints that, if simply removed, would allow a more adaptive approach? Remember, first we shape our systems, and then they shape us. What constraints are built into our businesses that prevent effective response or adaptation? Often, these are systems that were installed in the name of control or efficiency, on the assumption of infrequent change or low volatility.

In sum, first identify important volatilities, then link them to significant costs or revenue opportunities, identify constraints, and consider adaptive solutions. This straightforward process can apply to any part of an enterprise. The hardest part is finding the solutions, because many of them are unfamiliar, and management doesn't know where to look. In time, the killer apps of adaptiveness will emerge and become as familiar as other management techniques. Here are seven ways that the Adaptive Enterprise is coming into being in applications that address the core concerns of every business.

Inventory Management

At Seagate Technology's high-tech manufacturing assembly plant in Asia, new behavioral rules for component handling, real-time monitoring, and triggering of inventory movements have helped to reduce days-of-supply inventory by 90 percent. Inventory turns have been accelerated more than fivefold, jumping from 50 to 270 turns sustained. While this kind of result is not yet common, dramatic reductions in inventory cost will become commonplace through new sense-and-respond technologies.

Radio frequency identification (RFID) is the next in a series of technology innovations designed to make a unit of inventory go farther. Bar codes, commercialized in 1966, were a great improvement toward sensing inventory levels in real time. With the advent of a new breed of electronic and radio units, however, many companies are rejecting bar-code systems' traditional trade-offs of poor print quality, relatively high manual labor, and the need for precise orientation.

RFID not only solves these problems but offers the promise of real-time inventory management, enabling a company to deal with market dynamics as they occur. This sense-and-respond capability relies on the combined use of bar codes, electronic product code (ePC), RFID units, and a warehouse management system that updates and tracks, in "real time" mode, inventory activities including receiving, put-away, inventory control (physical or cycle count), picking, and loading/shipping.

When Sainbury's invested in RFID technology for its chilled-food products, the U.K.–based supermarket chain reported improved speed and accuracy in distribution. In environments where Sainsbury's workers are using RFID, they can now unload, document, and process an entire truckload of food crates in just fifteen minutes—a fraction of the two and a half hours previously required.[2] The order system receives accurate inventory and code life data, enabling better forecasting, improved availability (fewer stockouts), and reduced waste (fewer instances of overstocking and consequent price reductions). The system is designed to operate automatically and to provide exception reports for anomalies such as miss-rotation, short-life products, and so on. RFID tags are attached to food crates, which are reprogrammed when the crates are reloaded;

since the pilot, Sainsbury's has developed plans to tag products at the individual-item level.

In the future, RFID technology will be used on such a scale that the price of tags and readers will drop significantly. Pilot programs have taken place in the retail industry for the past five years, particularly in Europe, which concentrates on case lots. Costs were typically $1.50 per tag and $30,000 per reader, plus infrastructure costs. Interest in RFID is increasing substantially in retail and consumer goods, leading tags to approach between 5 and 10 cents each and readers $70 each. Gillette just placed an order for half a billion tags. As other leading companies like Sainsbury's, Wal-Mart, Tesco, Home Depot, CVS, Target, and Procter & Gamble show commitment to the technology, providers are finding ways to lower the costs even further as acceptance increases.[3]

To take advantage of new capabilities to sense, make sure you build matching capabilities to respond. A firm's back-end systems and processes must allow it to respond to change and increased volumes of information. For example, manufacturers in replenishment-driven environments must be capable of same-day scheduling, which will allow their manufacturing facilities to replenish customers on demand.

Real-time inventory-management tools usually can provide additional data on products that transcend transit paths and supply levels. For example, in contrast with point-of-sale data, RFID adds the value of understanding customer behavior. How did the customer proceed through the store? What did she pick up and put back on the shelf? What did she select in its place? Which end displays are really the most effective? What behaviors did promotions encourage? Insight into consumer behavior is just as (or more) important a goal of tracking technologies as inventory management. And it can feed the agent-based models that will help explore innovations.

RFID also offers a solution for dealing with issues of tampering, safety, compliance, and theft. The pharmaceutical industry, for example, faces issues more about the visibility of inventory than understanding consumer behavior at the retail outlet. Using ePC and RFID technology, pharmaceutical manufacturers can track inventory through the supply chain and manage product-safety and -integrity issues. This means monitoring things like expiration date, temperature, and package security of controlled substances, and product-related data. Retailers may force the issue since they are being fined for having out-of-date drugs on their shelves.

Customer-Order Management

When order fulfillment was slow, when customization was expensive, when information flow was halting, the default response in most industries was "build to stock," investing in inventory until the right customer came along. Large inventory or stockouts occasionally rocked the supply chain, and customers would not get exactly what they wanted—but all in all, the trade-offs of build-to-stock were worth a reasonable delivery time to the customer.

Now many companies have developed the capabilities necessary to sense and respond quickly with customized processes, build-to-stock is no longer good enough. Real-time order management (RTOM) combines the customization component of "Customer Need to Order" with the speed and inventory component of "Order to Delivery." RTOM is a combination of technology, processes, and industry expertise that streamlines, links, and manages the process and information flow of these two mega-processes.

RTOM provides the ability to receive and fulfill an order as fast as is achievable to satisfy the customer. It also uses the information from the order to plot changing demand patterns—a learn-and-adapt capability. RTOM synchronizes inventory and capacities based on the information, helping companies commit and respond more accurately to customer requirements in the future.

RTOM is so new that most companies are still planning it rather than doing it. But at Dell Computer, perhaps the best-reported example, the results are in, and they are unequivocal. Rapid build-to-order manufacturing and order-fulfillment capabilities enable the company to outsource subcomponents, reduce inventory levels, and rapidly incorporate new technologies into product offerings.[4] Dell orders material as needed and schedules every line in every factory around the world every two hours. Typically, a factory runs with only five to six hours' worth of inventory on hand (including work in progress), thus increasing cycle time. Dell's inventory on-site was down from thirty-four days in 1995 to under five days in 2001, due to its customer-order management process and supply-chain efficiencies. And Dell has a total commitment to delivery times.

In part due to Dell's rapid order-management capabilities, the company writes off only between 0.05 and 1.0 percent of total material costs in excess obsolete inventory. And each customer has exactly the computer he wants.

American Airlines provides a similar example. In 1999, Chris was returning to Boston from Dallas. Arriving at the gate, he found the aircraft waiting but an unusual number of people milling around. It turned out that an entire plane of Montreal-bound passengers had been detained all day. At the same time, the Boston flight was lightly loaded, and there was a United flight to Boston just down the concourse.

The fulfillment issue in this case—matching passengers to available capacity—is often stymied by inflexible schedules, which cannot adjust to fluctuations in demand for seats bound for specific destinations. The entire system is vulnerable to volatility, stemming from uncontrollable delays caused by weather and mechanical problems. American Airlines' adaptive response has been to create a scheduling process that can re-assign aircraft to different flight numbers on the fly. Chris and the other Boston-bound passengers were told, "Sorry, this aircraft's going to go to Montreal, and we're switching you to United." Everyone reached their destinations as scheduled, and American Airlines made a larger number of customers happier.

Disney faces a similar problem in Florida, where, as you may have heard, the company runs a large theme park. Among the volatile elements in its business are how many customers will show up on a given day, and what those customers will want to do. What they want to do depends in part on the weather. So the requirements placed on the various aspects of the park—a particular ride, the food stands, the bathrooms, the shops—vary widely day-to-day. The capacity of each aspect is determined by the number of "cast members" working at each. Given that a major cost of running Disney World is payroll, the company doesn't want to overstaff; on the other hand, if the line is too long at the hot-dog stand, it could lose a juicy profit. So here is a source of significant volatility linked to a large cost. The key constraints are training—the cast member accustomed to climbing into the Goofy suit may not look good as Snow White—and union rules, which limit the tasks a given individual can perform and dictate that once an individual has been called in, he or she will be paid for a full day.

Disney is experimenting with a variety of adaptive techniques. Many of them start by taking the guest as an agent, and creating an agent-based point of view.[5] In a simulation, management can see guests moving around the park. Their choices of what to do next are affected by many things they do and don't know. Disney made a breakthrough in both load-leveling and customer satisfaction by posting waiting times at several places in the park, enabling guests to avoid walking long distances to an attraction with an unacceptable line. In this case, Disney does the sensing, and the guest responds.

If it wants to Learn and Adapt, though, Disney needs to observe the guests' behavior under different circumstances. The company is experimenting with different tracking approaches, but essentially imagine RFID tags for guests. That enables Disney to calibrate the agents in its models and try different approaches to modifying their behavior once they've arrived. The result should be that mismatches between the staff the company has scheduled and the desires of those who actually visit the park will decrease, costs will shrink, and guests will get more of what they want.

Pricing

Farmers selling at the market square reduce their prices at the end of the day. They have real-time information on their inventory, what they need in inventory tomorrow, and the condition of what remains in stock. They also have some empirically based views on the likelihood of further business today.

In the physical marketplace, all this information is local. In the national distribution systems of the industrial economy, on the other hand, such information is unavailable. As connections become feasible, and computers become able to handle national-scale information, the ability to set prices to the current market conditions has increased. Airlines are the best-established example. Their yield-management systems work so that the price they quote you is determined by the demand previously expressed (which determines which seat inventories are available) and their knowledge of likely future demand. But most businesses have not yet taken advantage of the opportunities this kind of yield management offers.

Today, sensors and connectivity can provide information about real-time market conditions and the "availability to promise." Software agents can incorporate knowledge about the likely future and rules for pricing. So it is increasingly feasible for every transaction to be priced in real time, reflecting the prevailing conditions. (And of course, for the pricing agents to learn from experience and continually adapt the pricing algorithms.) Time-based metrics become significant in pricing, product-mix, product-rationalization, and asset-optimization decisions. In high-fixed-cost industries, for example, Maxager Technology uses profit-per-minute information in addition to traditional profit-per-unit information to identify manufacturing constraints and bottlenecks. Time-based analysis increases profits and market share by shifting product mix toward higher cash-per-minute products and allowing the company more price flexibility.

This doesn't mean that every transaction will be a real-time bargaining session. Neither customers nor providers prefer this in all cases. But it does mean that price can be used to influence customer behavior, just as Disney is using knowledge of waiting times to help reroute guests to less overloaded attractions. Chris bought a theater ticket in London recently from one of the Shaftsebury Avenue vendors. Looking at his computer, the vendor was able to identify that the best available seat was only three rows in front of an available discounted seat at less than half the price. The behavior adapted, and the customer was happy.

Another example that's making a difference, and spreading rapidly, is road pricing. Pioneered in Singapore, whose central business district (CBD) attracts approximately 24,000 automobiles daily to an area of only 3.5 square miles, this system uses the same tags that allow automated toll payments to charge motorists to drive into the CBD.[6] Prices are posted for different times of day and days of the week. Depending on results, the authorities adjust the rates up to once a month. As at Disney, Singapore senses, and the motorists respond. CBD rationing is being implemented or considered in a dozen cities around the world.

In general, adaptive pricing offers another opportunity to put every resource to its best use.

Supply-Chain Management

You're stuck in the middle—a dynamic marketplace on one side, and supplier and distributor relationships on the other. Your end customers' needs and options are changing. Is your supply chain adaptive enough to keep pace?

The connectivity, speed, and processing power of technology today means that firms have unprecedented feedback on how well their current and anticipated customer demand matches supply. Leading companies are developing plug-and-play supply chains to respond to market dynamics quickly, and with low switching costs.

Modular supply-chain architecture features separation among multiple, interchangeable suppliers, with standard interfaces, such that system failures can be localized and supplier relationships changed as needed. Since it relies on Web-based technology, a modular supply chain can plug and play with a variety of suppliers. Relationships with suppliers and vendors can be rapidly changed, and capabilities redeployed to meet the changing environment and changing needs of the business.

With a modular supply chain, a company can achieve low interdependency and high recombination of the elements of its supply chain. AOL Time Warner, for example, developed a Web-based system by which employees could choose their requirements for shipping packages and envelopes, but not their specific providers. Many people who did not require FedEx's next-day service had assumed that trackability required FedEx. The system was able to assign them to other shippers with three-to-five-day service, and FedEx use dropped from 80 to 5 percent.[7]

Supply chain management follows a familiar pattern: Technology enables new types of relationships, but process and operational changes are also necessary for the new technology to be successful. In supply-chain management, the current challenge is how to balance the capacity for dynamic response with the proven benefits of partnerships and collaborations.

In the 1990s, GM, Ford, and Chrysler pushed their suppliers mercilessly for bottom dollar, dropping suppliers based on new information about the marketplace or competitors' bids. On the whole, quality was low, since suppliers lacked the incentives to invest. When Japanese car manufacturers partnered with their suppliers, American manufacturers were surprised to see the benefits of long-term collaborative relationships: supplier-led R&D and innovation, supplier-assumed risk (inventory holdings, just-in-time manufacturing, performance-based compensation), quality, partnership in evolution, and so on.

An adaptive supply chain is not a technology-enabled fallback to the former cost-based contracts of the Big Three. Cisco and others learned the hard way about the dangers of switching to unscrupulous suppliers.[8] Rather, successful firms align process with technology in their new relationships. Contracts can include gain-sharing and risk-sharing, reduced transaction costs, knowledge transfer, and other benefits that we used to see only in more long-term relationships—but we now see these in flexible but collaborative supply chains. More and better communication is an essential component of these new relationships. Dell, for example, provides suppliers with data, not just on which orders they have shipped but on how they are measuring up to Dell standards.

Yankee Research Group estimates that in the next five years, collaborative commerce can save companies $223 billion in reduced inventory and logistics costs.[9] As supplier relationships move from one-to-one and one-to-many to many-to-many, it will be ever more important for organizations to develop plug-and-play capabilities, both in terms of technology, and in terms of business relationships.

Another adaptive supply-chain initiative is event-driven management, a technology-enabled sense-and-respond mechanism. Event-driven management begins with customer demand and tracks and integrates all components of the supply chain to the point at which the delivery promise is met. The customer order triggers the process, from work orders to production orders, and from transportation requests to financial-settlement activities. By managing the entire order-fulfillment process, an organization can dynamically match supply to demand. Supply-chain event management enables businesses to monitor inventories, orders, demand, and constraints across the supply chain. By optimizing related business processes, organizations can resolve issues and problems (averting bloated inventories, for example) in real time.

At Unilever in the United Kingdom, factory managers use an adaptive approach that allows them to adjust their internal supply operations to changes in external demand. A single factory produces between twenty and one hundred different SKUs during a given week. These numbers alone might not represent a particular challenge, but significant complexity arises from the fact that each SKU is produced over a period of many hours, through a combination of batch and continuous (flow) processes. Each of these SKUs follows a semi-dedicated path through the factory, from mixer to silo to packing line. Silo volumes must neither overflow nor become empty. With fifty of these paths snaking their way simultaneously through the same networked factory, the potential conflicts are many, and there are all kinds of constraints that must be taken into account: color-sequence requirements, fixed maintenance schedules, delivery deadlines.

Traditional approaches to engineering this complex production network—optimization software and an expert (human) scheduler making revisions by hand—were unable to deliver a viable solution.

An agent-based simulation developed by BiosGroup helped Unilever see that by investing in a few links between transfer lines in the plant, operators could reroute certain functions to avoid out-of-service equipment. The simulation revealed that under actual conditions, the return on assets of this factory improved by increasing the investment. Though it becomes less efficient in a predictable world, it is more adaptive in the real one, where demand often varies from forecast.

An adaptive supply-chain approach is particularly useful today, when companies are competing in a volatile economic environment and are finding it increasingly difficult to forecast the future performance of their business or marketplace. An adaptive supply-chain operation dynamically matches supply and demand, better targets customers, and helps maximize revenue. It also enables a company to link order management with planning and forecasting and to develop separate operations for customer segmentation.

Product Development

Syngenta breeds tomatoes for superior taste and texture. Maxygen breeds molecules, and Capital One breeds bundled financial services. It's likely that your neighborhood deli breeds combinations of coffee (small, medium, large), muffin (blueberry, bran), and other breakfast foods (as does McDonald's on a larger scale). What does combinatorial product development (CPD) mean for your company?

The traditional product-development funnel is a weeding-out process, with more products proposed than can be supported. In contrast, CPD is a filling-in of the holes between products, capabilities, and markets—a rigorous testing of gaps. Based on "in-use" market data rather than "would-use" data, CPD relies on experimentation more than on personality, hypothetical speculations, or focus groups. It is also usually cheaper and faster than traditional product development. At the same time, CPD more closely meets niche needs because products appear to be bred for specific market segments.

CPD is based on the cross-fertilization of products, aspects, markets, and other assets or capabilities. While automation can help in well-structured situations, as at Maxygen and Capital One, other firms encourage recombination by moving employees around, by knowledge sharing, and by other management techniques. The key concept is that adaptive companies support experimentation.

As simulation techniques improve, CPD can even deal with questions of aesthetics and customer preference. BiosGroup created a user-guided evolutionary tool that allows designers at Honda to streamline what is normally a lengthy trial-and-error design process. Instead of the life-sized clay model that designers traditionally use, a Honda designer employing the Bios system begins with a chosen profile with aesthetic appeal. Then, working within technological constraints (such as wheelbase length, windshield angle, and size of engine compartment), the program is set free to evolve a group of designs. The designer then selects one appealing shape, modifies it, and evolves it further—or even uses two designs as "parents" for a new generation of shapes.

Because the user is always able to view both the current state of the design and all earlier mutations, any shape can be easily compared with its predecessors at every stage of the process. The program studies and learns the user's behavior and preferences. For example, if it learns that the designer often chooses a particular slant for a line, it will begin to generate more possibilities in that direction. The tool greatly accelerates the design process.[10]

Budgeting

The traditional model for budgeting was developed in the 1920s to help financial managers in large organizations such as General Motors, Siemens, or DuPont control costs and resource allocation. Now as then, traditional budgeting often serves as a control mechanism to subject business units to the financial discipline of a strong centralized staff. "Corporate" wants to avoid surprises, so units are held accountable for their commitments. Each manager sits on his or her resource allocation for a year, unable to fund new opportunities, expected to use full allocation despite outdated projects. Seventy-eight percent of companies do not change their budgets within the fiscal cycle.[11]

Traditional budgeting is time- and resource-intensive. A 1998 benchmarking study showed that the average company invests more than 25,000 person-days per billion dollars of revenue in the planning and performance-measurement processes; the average time taken for developing a financial plan is 4.5 months.[12]

For decades, the traditional budgeting model did its job well. But as organizations face increasingly volatile marketplaces, shrinking strategy and product life cycles, and more-agile competitors, traditional budgeting is becoming anathema—i.e., measures and processes created with good intentions, act as barriers to critical sense-and-response activities.

What are the alternatives to this rigid and expensive process? In a *rolling* budget, managers prepare rolling plans (usually quarterly) for cash forecasting but not necessarily cost control. This is a sharp departure from the traditional method, in which budgets were forecasts and commitments determined by a time-consuming process to build their understanding of, and commitment to, the figures against which managers were measured.

Rolling budgets—by allowing firms to allocate resources more flexibly—are more responsive to volatility drivers. Also, by facilitating empowerment throughout the organization, they provide a stronger link between the people best able to forecast and change action.

Some companies are even closer to the ideal for a sense-and-respond organization—*continuous* budgeting. Borealis, a Danish polyolefin-plastics company, faces a notoriously cyclical petrochemical market, with financial success largely dependent on oil prices. The introduction of a continuous-budgeting model in 1995 allowed the company to react quickly and flexibly to market changes, doubling its shareholder value and reducing costs by 30 percent through 2000.[13]

Information Technology Infrastructure

In the beginning, business correspondence was handwritten. Un-networked electronic equipment changed processes *within* companies through automation, but not *between* companies; files were printed out and delivered, with data re-entered upon receipt. Electronic networks grew, and e-mail and common file types such as the Microsoft Office suite reduced the data entry for each file transfer. Eager to reduce manual effort and the possibility of error or leakage, some large companies invested in Electronic Data Interchange and customized applications for their supply chain where firms "pay to play"—i.e., invest in integrating with the technology of their partners in order to do business with them.

Advanced as they may be, even technological investment thresholds are a form of inefficiency in a connected economy. When a firm's network of contacts and partners grows exponentially, and when it includes consumers, manual translation and individual integration are no longer feasible. And because there is still healthy competition between business and consumer systems, no single universal "Esperanto" system is going to emerge in the short term. Instead, translator applications will emerge to permit disparate systems to share data and services without requiring human beings to translate the conversation. These applications already exist in the elementary form of Web services.

Web services are business and consumer applications, delivered over a network, that users can select and combine through almost any device, from personal computers to mobile phones. Based on XML, a popular standard for data exchange, and other programming languages, Web services make B2B communication a plug-and-play affair by standardizing the way applications make themselves visible over a network. By using common protocol and standards, Web services allow "on-the-fly" (real-time) links among the online processes of different companies.

Southwest Airlines uses a Web services technology architecture for rapid development, deployment, and reconfiguration of new products and services. Despite disparate systems (and booking costs), website, travel agency, and call-center bookings all funnel through the same IT system. Consistent with its "simplicity and low cost" theme, Southwest avoided banner ads so that pages could be quickly loaded on different PC equipment, and designed the site to require only five clicks to book a ticket online, even one hour before departure. Unlike other airlines, the company did not seek to create new revenue streams on the site via new business partnerships, nor give e-mail capability or anything that could divert customer attention from buying tickets. "Every business decision made is an integrated one. Anything we do offline is mirrored online. There is a definite cohesiveness."[14]

What Can My Business Do?
A Comprehensive Approach

When a new technology appears, often its first job is to breathe new life into existing processes, making them better, faster, and cheaper. Businesses first used computers to do things like automate payroll checks, for example. Next, information technology is used to make existing products more valuable—think of the increased efficiency, safety, and comfort of automobiles due to their 100–150 or so microprocessors. Third, the technology becomes the basis of entirely new businesses like Yahoo! and eBay. Finally, as we approach the maturation of the information economy in its fourth quarter, information technology is enabling new organizational models, as coordination of remote activities enables everything from "follow the sun" design processes to call centers located in India that service customers ordering from Hawaii.

This progression occurs one application at a time, as each adoption of the technology sets the stage for the next. Numerical control of machine tools was introduced to save money and improve quality in manufacturing processes. Once the machine was computer-controlled, it enabled mass customization, generating additional value. As the technology became widespread, it created the opportunity for businesses like Autodesk, which made the dominant CAD/CAM software AutoCAD. This in turn created a software standard allowing companies to outsource their designs from third parties, who could submit AutoCAD files. A similar progression took us from word processors, to computer graphics, to Kinko's retail stores, to Kinko's running an in-house reprographics department; and from payroll, to cafeteria benefits, to using Fidelity as a third-party benefits administrator for defined-contribution self-service benefits packages.

Save money, create value, grow new businesses, and restructure your organization. This is the way that industrial and information technologies were absorbed by businesses, transforming them and the economy in the process.

Over the next decade, the process is going to be a little messier. Evolution will find its way into business in three ways at once. First, the products and processes of the information economy will continue to become more capable of adaptation as the third quarter of the information economy comes to a close. Second, as the fourth quarter gets under way, the memes of the Adaptive Enterprise will shape the form and process of organizations. And third, molecular technologies will develop into the next high-tech industry, and their products will begin to affect other industries' processes and products.

With all this going on, it's going to be hard to figure out where to look for the solutions to your volatility problems, and keeping up with molecular developments that will very likely change your business.

In Figure 10-1, we've broken the business apart into four areas: Process and Technology, Product, Organization, and Strategy. We think this is the order in which most businesses will start taking advantage of adaptive techniques, though of course each business will be different. Below, we look at how each of the seven Memes for Managing might affect each of these four business areas.

FIGURE 10-1 Action Points for Adaptive Management

	SELF-ORGANIZE	RECOMBINE	SENSE & RESPOND	LEARN & ADAPT	SEED, SELECT & AMPLIFY	DESTABILIZE	MONETIZE MOLECULES
PROCESS AND TECHNOLOGY	■ Let intelligent agents run your processes (e.g., bidding systems, markets, artificial intelligence) ■ Establish operational rules that maximize local-decision-making for greater adaptivity	■ Use recombinant designs and solutions ■ Seek symbiotic relationships (e.g., outsource knowledge, capabilities, processes)	■ Install feedback and smart response capabilities in every process (e.g., sensors, intelligent software agents)	■ Close the loop of continuous improvement by incorporating learned experience into your processes	■ Use agent-based simulation to explore multiple, diverse scenarios ■ Develop "screening" methods to eliminate non-performing processes	■ Favor connected and variable over adaptive and non-adaptive processes ■ Disrupt static processes and operate at the edge of chaos	■ Use molecular technologies to create products with new characteristics
PRODUCT	■ Create a community of contributors for product development	■ Use reusable modules and standards to rapidly refine and customize products	■ Install a feedback loop in every offer (e.g., real-time maintenance and upgrade information)	■ Establish institutional learning mechanisms ■ Exploit the learning value of failure	■ Actively test diverse options and roll out winners	■ Exploit the opportunities of short product lifecycles	■ Look for opportunities to reduce costs and add value by shrinking mass and using molecular technologies
ORGANIZATION	■ Manage the rules not the people ■ Establish rules for people that enable flexible processes and drive adaptive behavior	■ Seek diversity and encourage free, frequent interaction among people, partners, and communities	■ Create markets for talent (e.g., staffing markets)	■ Make knowledge management work	■ Use agent-based simulations to test rules and governance structures ■ Keep your "lineup" fresh by introducing new people often	■ Establish a policy of turnover to continually refresh the idea pool	
STRATEGY	■ Take advantage of self-organizing communities inside and outside your business ■ Use agent-based simulation to explore strategic options	■ Maintain a diverse portfolio and market your capabilities wherever they are valued ■ Maximize opportunities for recombining ideas and incorporate contributions of partners	■ Let the market guide your strategy ■ Build a business model around flexible technologies and processes ■ Install sensors to provide real-time input	■ Let strategy emerge from distributed decision-making ■ Use data-farming to explore new strategies	■ Experiment, don't plan	■ Maximize useful instability ■ View market adaptability as financial strength	

How to Begin

If we've succeeded so far, you've been provoked by the propositions, stimulated by the science, mesmerized by the memes, and captivated by the case studies—but now you've come to the "so what" moment. Are these ideas sufficiently mature to act on? Is the need urgent enough to warrant the investment?

As the diversity of the case studies should signal, the degree of urgency depends on the degree of mismatch between the rate of change of various elements inside your business and the environment in which you operate. Based on our discussions with executives among Cap Gemini Ernst & Young clients, we've developed three approaches for thinking about how an organization can identify worthwhile ways to become more adaptive.

○ *Volatility Diagnosis.* An initial approach is not unlike what businesses went through with reengineering. There, the triggering insight was that functional organization was wasting costly resources, and that analyzing an organization's processes could improve performance. The diagnostic approach was to identify "Non-Value Added" (NVA) time and activities, and reorganize processes to minimize it. What made this possible, of course, was information technology, providing the coordination between process steps that made the costly buffer inventories and other NVA activities unnecessary. Now, that same connectivity has changed the environment, making it even more volatile.

The triggering insight this time around is this: You've designed your business for stability, but the environment is constantly changing. The costs that need to be minimized are the costs of change, which are *maximized* by designing for an unchanging world. The equivalent of the NVA analysis is to identify the economically important sources of volatility, and find adaptive approaches to coping with it. We outline this thought process in more detail below.

○ *Stand on the Shoulders of Others.* Thus far, we've seen the most improvement in adaptiveness in seven business areas: inventory management, customer-order management, pricing, supply-chain management, product development, budgeting, and Web services. In these areas, enough companies have plowed the ground to make your task easier. We've provided a section on some of the best practices in each.

○ *Comprehensive Analysis.* As consultants, we couldn't leave you without a matrix. In our research for this book, we thought about four aspects of business—process, product, organization, and strategy—and looked for examples of the seven adaptive principles in each of the four. We screened our case studies this way, picking those that most amply filled out this framework. (The case matrices appear at www.itsalive-book.com.)

To thoroughly assess the opportunities to become more adaptive, you can do the same. First consider your processes, and how they can be more self-organizing, more recombinant, etc.; then move on to your products, organization, and strategy, and do the same thing, one meme at a time.

To guide you, we provided a filled-out, generic example, showing in shorthand the most important actions we know to pursue adaptiveness. Then we've taken publicly available information about General Electric and applied our screen: We learned that many of the programs that made Jack Welch famous fit the Adaptive Enterprise model closely.

Below, we look at how each of the memes for managing can affect each of these four business areas. Happily, we can do so by showing how each has been applied by one of the most successful enterprises of all time, General Electric.

PROCESS AND TECHNOLOGY

As enterprise-software packages like those from SAP, Oracle, and People-Soft took off in the nineties, critics feared that they would recreate the rigidities of the assembly line, this time through the constraints of inflexible software. But as of 2002, these vendors are embedding intelligent agents and other adaptive techniques into enterprise-software packages, to ensure that the software infrastructure is capable of evolving with the needs of the market.

Today, linkages extend beyond the firm all the way up and down the supply chain. As noted, soon RFID tags in the supply chain will support real-time tracking, rerouting, pricing, and the capability to know when and how these components can come together to meet a specific customer order. The result will be an adaptive, event-driven, demand-fulfillment process, integrated through adaptive information technology.

Process and Technology at GE

Sense and Respond. Many companies have difficulty forecasting when expensive equipment, such as magnetic resonance imaging (MRI) machines and jet engines, will need servicing and what servicing will involve. General Electric's MRI machines and jet engines have built-in sense-and-respond capabilities. GE monitors the productivity of its customers' equipment in real time over the Web. If there is a problem, GE employees will know right away. Soon, GE technicians will be able to implement software upgrades to GE medical equipment via the Web, without involving an on-site medical technician at all.

This connected capability has also greatly increased GE's ability to forecast when individual jet engines will need an overhaul. GE Engine Services can create a month-by-month projection that outlines the number of engines to be sent in for repair, the specific problems affecting each engine, and the "turn time," an estimation of how long servicing will take. Airlines use this schedule to forecast fleet maintenance a year or more into the future. Because they can see how many aircraft will be out of service during a given month, they can adjust their overhaul schedule to reduce the need for spares and smooth the demand for the overhaul center.[15]

Recombine. Also in its jet-engine division, General Electric has used a proprietary genetic-algorithm and expert system package called "Engineous" to help design the engine for the Boeing 777. While addressing stringent design specifications for the Boeing aircraft, GE engineers determined that simplifying the engine's compressor would go a long way toward meeting design goals. However, the compressor already had been refined to the point that human designers were struggling to find any incremental improvements. Engineous allowed a design to further evolve to improve its match with a large number of constraints.

After a number of critical design factors were input, one simple but profound rule was introduced: Design a compressor with only six stages, instead of the previous seven. "The benefit sought by reduced weight, a key operating variable. At this point, we were just looking for new ideas and were curious to see what Engineous would produce," says Peter Finnigan, a research manager on the project. As it turns out, the software produced very powerful results.

Engineous coded each design factor as a "digital chromosome," then mixed these chromosomes together to form trial designs. After a breeding and fitness-testing process similar to the Deere scheduling program, GE had a viable six-stage compressor design in less than a week.

Monetize Molecules. GE recently gave its Global Research headquarters in New York a $100 million renovation with a new wing devoted to nanotechnology. Currently, GE has nanotech and biotech initiatives to develop:[16]

○ New contrast agents for MRI machines. Such designer molecules would be injected into patients to help doctors better "see" early signs of Alzheimer's disease;

○ Nanomaterials for improved plastics for high-density recordable media;

○ Nanomaterials to cool ever smaller and hotter microprocessors;

○ Nanocomposites for power and aircraft systems to improve temperature resistance, strength, and toughness of structural materials; and

○ A roadmap for applying nanotubes to GE businesses wherever possible.

PRODUCT

The more information an offer can process or has embedded within it, the more valuable it is. This has always been true for computers and other information technologies, but it has now become the yardstick against which every offer's value—from your car to your refrigerator to the scale you weigh yourself on in the morning—is measured.

As the molecule plays the role of the bit in the next economy, it will become the unit of value on which most offers are based. The new measure will become how adaptive your product is. Does it self-organize, recognizing its context like a GSM phone finding its network? Is it as light as current molecular technology can make it, like a new cell-phone battery? Does it learn from experience, like a cell phone capturing an incoming number? Can customers apply selective pressure to its features, using feedback loops?

Product at GE

Sense and Respond. General Electric dishwashers are now equipped with the GE ExtraClean sensor, designed to continually monitor every cycle and adjust for soil content, water temperature, wash-cycle length, and the amount of water needed to clean dishes efficiently.

ORGANIZATION

The Industrial Age gave rise to organizational innovations such as mass production, three-shift work schedules, labor unions, and company towns. The Information Age has supplanted many of these with organizational innovations better suited to a knowledge- and data-based economy, though because we're only at the dawn of the information economy's fourth quarter, this cycle of innovation and the changes it induces are not yet complete. We can already point to a few information-era organizational innovations such as networked organizational structures, a free-agent workforce (with more mobility and shorter job tenure), and anytime, anyplace contributions to product development (open-source innovation and collaborative development).

In the Molecular Era, a new cycle of organizational innovations will begin, and the new approaches to management that emerge will more closely resemble the tactics of natural systems than of mechanical ones. Already we're seeing organizational boundaries becoming less distinct, attitudes toward experimentation and failure becoming less risk-averse, and corporate hierarchies giving ground to temporary, project-based, multidisciplinary teams.

Organization at GE

Sense and Respond. When Welch took over in 1981, a "not-invented-here" attitude prevailed at GE leading employees to think there was little they could learn from anything outside their business unit, let alone the company. In the early nineties, he realized that if GE was to succeed, it had to become faster, involve everyone, and communicate more effectively. He coined the term "boundaryless" to describe the new GE. By removing numerous layers of bureaucracy, GE sought to operate like a small company in which agents could more easily self-organize but retain the benefits that come with size. When Welch arrived, more than 25,000 people had the title of manager, another 500 were senior managers, and another 130 were vice presidents. There was a strict hierarchy in which memos were continually passed up and down through the chain of command. Welch abolished all of the managerial layers that existed between him and the business leaders, transferring the strategic-planning function away from senior managers and turning it over to the business leaders. This "delayered" ability to sense and respond helped to make GE both more agile and more flexible.

Recombine. In 1986, Welch created the Corporate Executive Council (CEC), composed of the top twenty-five to thirty executives in the company. The CEC meets every three months and is designed to do away with the "silo" architecture. The sole purpose of CEC meetings is to share best practices across the organization, facilitating recombination and thereby increasing the performance of the entire company. Welch refers to the sharing and recombination at GE as "integrated diversity." GE has taken new-product-introduction techniques from Chrysler and Canon; effective sourcing techniques from GM and Toyota; and quality initiatives from Ford and Motorola. Welch sees GE's ability to take good ideas, regardless of their origin, and use them as a key virtue.

Learn and Adapt. After Welch finished the major downsizing of the early eighties, he realized that he needed a way of instilling in the employees a feeling of involvement and importance at GE and, at the same time, improve operations. Recognizing that those closest to the work know it best and should be in charge of the day-to-day decisions, he devised Work-Out, a program to allow employees from all levels and all service lines to express their views and ideas. The sessions take the form of a town meeting, and, as ideas are expressed, they are taken into consideration and frequently put into action right on the spot. These meetings harness the talent of the lower-level employees, allowing for value to be created from the bottom up and at the same time greatly increase the recombination of ideas. Work-Out has been instrumental in reducing the layers of bureaucracy within GE, allowing it to sense and respond in real time.

Seed, Select, and Amplify. In the early eighties, inflation was viewed by most companies as the number-one threat to success. To help mitigate the impact of inflationary pressures on GE, Welch forced his business leaders to ask themselves whether or not they could be number one or number two in their market. Like Brooklyn Dodgers veterans, managers had to either find a way of maintaining their dominant position, nurturing their business to grow quickly into the number one or number two position, or close or sell the business.

In a second example, Welch reduced the GE workforce by more than 100,000 people in the first seven years of his tenure, and those who remained faced a very different reward structure. The company breaks employee performance down in the following manner: The top 10 percent are role models, the next 15 percent are strong performers, the middle 50 to 60 percent are the highly valued core, the next 15 percent are borderline, and the bottom 10 percent are the least effective. Welch both amplifies and selects—the top 10 percent are rewarded far more than anybody else, and the bottom 10 percent are provided with "exit strategies."

STRATEGY

"Strategy [is] not a lengthy action plan but the evolution of a central idea through continually changing circumstances."[17]

Adaptive strategy is about sensing and responding to the demands of a permanently volatile economy.

Besides current and foreseen advances in information technologies, developments in biological technologies will push adaptive rather than engineered approaches to strategy. These will further reduce response time and lower the cost of developing adaptive operations. Companies will pursue multiple, diverse strategic options.

Strategy at GE

Sense and Respond. Better sensing capabilities translate to faster response time, critical for your strategy to keep apace of the continuous changes in the marketplace. GE Capital's "digital dashboard" delivers performance metrics directly to decision-makers. This integrated tool allows them to seize business opportunities as they arise, to respond to a drop in interest rates or to a new player in the financial-services marketplace. Sensors can monitor performance (customer-representative response time), or they can help mitigate risk by providing early warning of important developments (loan defaults or late payments).[18]

Destabilize. In January 1999, Jack Welch destabilized GE when he announced the company's e-business strategy. Viewing strategic planning as "too safe," Welch created the idea of "DestroyYourBusiness.com" (DYB). For each business unit, a DYB unit was created with the mission of attacking the existing business unit by acting as an Internet-based startup. Once weaknesses were identified, the DYB team developed a plan to recombine the dot-com opportunity with the strengths of the existing business. One result was that GE Medical Systems was able to repel challenges from Neoforma, which was selling used equipment and damaging GE's new-equipment market. The DYB team realized that GE could probably perform this service better than the startup because of its logistics capability, and at the same time allow the company to reach new markets such as small clinics, and hospitals in the Third World.

In a 1998 speech to shareholders, Welch explained the worldview that makes GE an Adaptive Enterprise:

This company cannot be "managed" to perpetual double-digit growth. Management implies stewardship of an asset, orderly, structured, tightly controlled. . . . A manager controls things, keeps them in channels, builds and respects boundaries between functions and ranks, stays within internal and external company walls. The leader goes after those boundaries with a hammer, drawing the best ideas from anywhere: the factory floor, other businesses, other companies. The GE leader, in particular, sees this company for what it truly is: the largest petri dish of business innovation in the world. We have roughly 350 business segments. We see them as 350 laboratories whose ideas are there to be shared, learned, and spread as fast as we can. The leader sees that sharing and spreading near the top of his or her list of responsibilities.[19]

For Welch, "leading a big company is about assuring that it stays agile, unencumbered by bureaucracy, or lulled by complacency—keeping it a company that breathes information, loves change and is excited by the opportunity change presents."[20]

Taking Action

One of the appealing aspects of the Adaptive Enterprise from a leadership point of view is that you can start down the path without announcing an epochal change program. By working on one element of your business at a time, you can start to make the whole more adaptive. And as adaptive approaches succeed, they will multiply—that's why we want you to think of them as memes. And as they multiply, they will become a mind-set.

And, ironically, the systems of the enterprise will start to train the people. As films like *Modern Times* have showed us, the machine-age factory turned its workers into machines. They had no choice but to behave as the industrial engineers determined they needed to if they wanted to succeed in adding value. It will happen again—if the systems of the Adaptive Enterprise are functioning, they will require those who work with them to become adaptive, too.

THE NEXT TEN YEARS

The next decade will see businesses discovering and employing specific adaptive solutions. Real-time pricing and order management, for example, will become common "business objects." These will be the basis of the next wave of best practices, spread by software vendors able to install these capabilities within enterprises across a range of industries. They will spread as websites have, first for information, next for transactions, and increasingly now to support a community around a company's offers. Software agents—incorporating real-time pricing algorithms, say—will become branded, and compete. Some may work for a percentage of the gross margin.[21]

We mentioned earlier that we may be going back to a period like that of bacterial evolution, when small pieces of DNA floated around in a common environment, becoming incorporated into various bacteria. The same excellent approach to booking a rental car on-line that you find at Hertz.com seems to have appeal at Boston Coach. There will be enormous opportunity to improve productivity as these adaptive components become available to improve the way our economy uses resources to fulfill our desires.

So much will happen in the next ten years that we don't hope to be able to foresee it. But we should note that, as productivity continues to grow rapidly, the human lifespan increases, the nature of work evolves, and the skills rewarded by the economy shift, we can expect some major changes in the way people live, just as the industrial era moved people to cities, and the information era is blurring work and life.

Perhaps, as the Adaptive Enterprise spreads, it will train us to be as adaptive as we will need to be.

The year 2013 seems far away, a world hard to grasp, especially if during the next decade, as predicted, experiences change twice as fast as the past one. Extrapolating from our major trends—volatility, adaptive technology and management, and the molecular economy—to see how they might play out, we conclude that within ten years over half of our economy will be subject to radical change. But one thing an evolutionary and ecological perspective tells us for sure: if several major forces are at work, they will not progress in separate straight lines—they will interact chaotically, creating

PART IV
CONVERGENCE

unforeseen changes. We're sure, for example, that the focus on behavior at the bottom and emergence at the top will lead to an economic view built more around the individual and less around the corporation, but just how that will play out no one can say.

But even bigger things will be on our mind. In ten years' time, questions like "What is alive?", "Do we want to live forever?", and even "Do robots have rights?" will move from our peripheral vision to become the focus of social and political discussion. If our biology is changing, so will our ethics.

As this enormous computing power is combined with the manipu-
lative advances of the physical sciences and the new, deep under-
standings in genetics, enormous transformative power is being
unleashed. These combinations open up the opportunity to com-
pletely redesign the world, for better or worse: The replicating and
evolving processes that have been confined to the natural world
are about to become realms of human endeavor.

—Bill Joy, chief scientist, Sun Microsystems[1]

11

THE ADJACENT POSSIBLE

OUR objective in writing *It's Alive* is to tell the story of the forces of
change, already in motion, that will shape the economy during the
next decade. Some of these, like the Adaptive Enterprise, result from the
maturation of the information economy. Others, like the Molecular Economy, result from the appearance of the next technology foundation. Still
others result from the convergence of these two trends based on the rules
of evolution as their model for continual change.

In this final chapter, we want to imagine what will happen when these
trends mingle and merge. We can't claim precognitive powers; the three
big developments we just cited will interact in ways far too chaotic for any
precise predictions to hold up. However, we do think that by marshaling
the evidence we've assembled so far, and by carefully considering the technologies and trends as they have progressed over the past fifty or one hundred years, we can make an informed guess as to where and how some of
these technologies and trends will manifest themselves next.

In Chapter 2, we mentioned the concept of the "adjacent possible."
It's an attractive phrase to capture a provocative idea: that the next new
thing is built upon the possibilities created by all the previous new things.

The term neatly balances the inevitability of continued innovation with the understanding that not all of the things that *can* happen *will*. The future is a question of what each of these trends makes possible that *might* happen next. We don't say *will* because there are many adjacent possibilities that we haven't figured out that might happen instead. But based on the evidence, this is what we think. We're eager to hear what you think, and you can tell us at our website.[2]

THE MATURING OF THE MOLECULAR ECONOMY

The economic life-cycle model gives us useful questions to pose regarding the development of the molecular economy. In each previous life cycle, we've developed new ways of handling energy and physical distribution. And in each cycle, we've created crucial new products: both upstream as industrial goods and downstream as consumer products. We've summarized these developments with examples in Figure 11-1.

FIGURE 11-1　Selected Elements of Four Economies

	Economy			
	AGRICULTURAL	**INDUSTRIAL**	**INFORMATION**	**MOLECULAR**
ENERGY SOURCE	Muscle power	Coal, oil, electricity	Chemical (e.g. batteries, solar, piezoelectrical)	Molecular (e.g., ATP)
PHYSICAL DELIVERY	Animals, boats	Trains, automobiles	Planes	Distributed fabrication
INFORMATION DELIVERY	Human contact	Mail, telegraph, telephone, radio, television	Wired and wireless data networks	Neural interface?
INDUSTRIAL COMMODITY	Seeds, land, textiles	Steel, chemicals	Silicon, software	Nanomaterials Designs
KEY PRODUCT	Domesticated plants and animals	Automobile	Computer	Matter compiler? Personal hospital? Universal mentor? Experience machine? Social science simulator?

Future developments

What will be the "fuel" and the key raw materials for the molecular economy? What will the distribution and delivery systems look like? What will be the multibillion-dollar industry creating the commodity materials as this new century unfolds? What will be the transforming devices, the intermediate goods equivalent to transistors and chips, that make possible a vast array of new products and services in nearly every sector of the future economy?

Again, we can't give you detailed and specific answers you can take to the bank. However, we can frame the issues, and we can offer reasonable conjecture, that should give you a useful context for grasping the molecular future as it rushes toward you.

Alan Kay already provided a couple of clues to the energy source for the molecular economy when he described the flagella of cells rotating at enormous speeds. The cell is already the master of nanotech. We anticipate that the sources of energy for our molecular devices will be the same as the ones that power our cells, molecules that store energy that can be released through particular chemical reactions. Adenosine triphosphate (ATP) is "the motor driving [muscle] movement, the most widespread energy currency of the cell,"[3] but there are other such molecules in nature. Most of our energy today comes from a particular kind of reaction: the oxidation of carbon-based compounds such as wood, coal, and oil. But bacteria have discovered ways to live on carbon dioxide, on sulfur, and in a huge range of temperatures, by developing novel chemical pathways. Nanodevices will take advantage of these capabilities. The information economy uses far less energy per dollar of GDP—factories run on megawatts, PCs run on decawatts. Nanotechnologies will accelerate this trend both because they require little power and because they can produce it themselves.

Molecules in the cell are typically held together by much weaker bonds[4] than the covalent bonds of industrial chemistry. This means that the amounts of energy to be stored and used are much smaller than in man-made systems, even in microelectronics. As a result, the renewability of these energy sources should be assured—we could run this part of the economy on photosynthesis. And there's an attractive irony: We once ran agriculture on ATP, albeit the ATP of work horses and oxen. As we reduce our physical economy to nanoscale, we can do it again.

As for the commodity product at the core of the next infrastructure, it's awfully early to be making predictions. But at the moment, nanotubes and buckyballs, described in Chapter 3, have an early lead. Both have an amazing array of properties that make them attractive candidates for the key enablers of the molecular economy. They are strong, lightweight, conductive, recyclable, power-efficient, programmable, and non-toxic, and their size and configuration allows them to either enter or seal just about anything.

If we are correct in assuming self-organizing, recombinant software, ubiquitous connectivity, nanoscale fabrication, genome-based medicine, and mastery of the physical properties of matter at the molecular level, then we can logically extrapolate these trends into the future. Once we can take all of these for granted the way today we take PCs, the Web, the mobile phone, and Google for granted, what will emerge from this new reality as the next "adjacent possible"? We can see new developments starting in several different sectors, each of which has the potential to overturn the status quo in its particular realm.

1. The Matter Compiler

Agriculture once occupied 70 percent of the labor of the United States. Today, it accounts for less than 3 percent. The same process is occurring in the manufacturing sector, although the press still treats reduction in manufacturing employment as a sign of cyclical weakness rather than a sign of our economy evolving toward higher value-added jobs. Employment in manufacturing jobs as a percentage of total non-farm employment decreased from 39 percent in 1920, to 27 percent in 1970, to 13.5 percent in 2001.[5] Research at the Center for Business Innovation has shown that the mass of a dollar's worth of GDP in constant dollars has shrunk by 30 percent in the last decade from 2.9 ounces to 2.2.[6]

So, manufacturing is shrinking as a source of employment, and what we are making is shrinking in mass. In addition, our manufacturing technology is becoming more decentralized. The steel industry is moving away from integrated steel mills and toward smaller capacity mini-mills. We're also beginning to see special-purpose manufacturing decentralized far more broadly. Just as the printing press, formerly an industrial tool requiring highly skilled labor, has become a $75 component attached to every

PC, we've begun to "print" in 3-D. Rather than sending molds out to be manufactured in a lab, dentists in South Africa create crowns extruded from resin that is shaped from digital images. This suggests a next stage that will molecularize all our manufacturing processes.

In *The Diamond Age*, science-fiction author Neal Stephenson extrapolates these trends to an end state in which matter is free, and only the intangible aspects of design carry value. In Stephenson's world, every household has a machine called the matter compiler, connected to a network called the "Feed," which draws from vast "separation ponds." In these ponds, all material waste is taken to be recycled. Nanobots separate the molecules of the materials into their constituent elements ready to be pumped through the Feed as ions whenever needed. Stephenson describes the molecular disassembly line:

Dirty air and dirty water came in and pooled in tanks. Next to each tank was another tank containing slightly cleaner air or cleaner water. Repeat several dozen times. The tanks at the end were filled with perfectly clean nitrogen gas and perfectly clean water. . . . All the action took place in the walls separating the tanks, which were not really walls but nearly infinite grids of submicroscopic wheels, ever-rotating and many-spoked. Each spoke grabbed a nitrogen or water molecule on the dirty side and released it after spinning around to the clean side. Things that weren't nitrogen or water didn't get grabbed, hence didn't make it through. There were also wheels for grabbing handy trace elements like carbon, sulfur, phosphorus; these were passed along smaller, parallel cascades until they were also perfectly pure. The immaculate molecules wound up in reservoirs. Some of them got combined with others to make simple but handy molecular widgets. In the end, all of them were funneled into a bundle of molecular conveyor belts known as the Feed.[7]

The matter compiler is the apogee of mastery over matter at the molecular level. Since all raw materials are recyclable, there is no scarcity. Whenever a household requires something—from a hat to a hamburger—the necessary ions are pumped into the matter compiler, whose instructions cause the desired artifact to self-assemble. In the case of the hamburger, the design is fully depreciated—hence the cost to the consumer for life's basics are close to nil. In Stephenson's world, the indigent have access to anything whose design is fully depreciated—a T-shirt, a hot dog—from public matter compilers, provided free of charge as a by-product of the infrastructure that everyone is using. If the hat, on the other hand, is a new high-fashion item, then the owner will pay a handsome sum to the Armani of 2050 to obtain the instructions to be given to the compiler.

Fanciful as it sounds, aspects of the matter compiler have already arrived in parts of our economy. An increasing proportion of GDP doesn't require physical distribution—it travels over networks, wired and wireless. We spend more on the software we use on our PCs than on the PCs themselves. The preponderance of the cost of our automobiles is in the software used to make them or embedded within them, and much of the steel and other materials is recycled. In 2000, more than 14 million tons of steel were recycled from automobiles, enough to produce 48 million steel utility poles in the United States, which is one-third the total installed.[8] In addition, aerospace and automobile companies use desktop 3-D printers to build prototype plastic parts for functional testing. Design engineers can now see, physically touch, and test their new products without ever entering a workshop or lab. Some feel that this affordable device for rapid prototyping (one-fifth the price of an average RP system) will soon become as common in the offices of engineers as laser printers are today.[9] And Brandeis robot researcher Jordan Pollack has created software that designs robots by itself and has these machines build them.

In the molecular economy, molecular technology will have a profound impact on the fabrication of everything, not merely drugs and medical devices but components of any physical object. If you're in a manufacturing business today, isn't it time to start examining where the first opportunities for molecular technologies will arise in your operations?

2. The Personal Hospital

As we explored in Chapter 3, noninvasive sensing technology already allows individuals to keep track of many vital signs painlessly and inexpensively, without going to the hospital for a painful puncture. This medical innovation follows the well-established trend of all affluent households to be increasingly dependent on information, provided by the computers and embedded information devices in these households. Roll the tape ahead ten years, and the graying "yuppie" generation will be preoccupied with health.

This is the gadget-prone age cohort that helped change the stroller from a $35 disposable Kmart item to the $350 folding, adjustable, Aprica status symbol. How would you expect them to care for themselves? Suppose that Agilent and Kaiser Permanente get together to provide the "home health care appliance," a small device you keep in your bathroom that measures your body non-invasively. "Grasp the handle," they say, "deposit some of your precious bodily fluids in this thing 200 times per year, and we will give you a health-care plan 20 percent better, faster, and cheaper than anything available on the market today. " The device would be wirelessly connected to your PC, where a piece of software resides, also given to you by this consortium, which would accept your daily readings, compile them as part of a longitudinal record, and subject them to appropriate tests to see if any action is required. The software would also relay the data to the provider's database, where your genome would be stored to support epidemiological analysis for the good of all. While today this might arouse privacy concerns, by the time we become accustomed to reaping the benefits of knowing our unique genetic properties, this will seem the *sine qua non*.

This home health-care device would not merely facilitate diagnosis. It would begin changing the health-care industry from one dominated by care-giving hospitals treating the sick, to one in which value is created primarily through the analysis of enormous amounts of information about the healthy. The focus would shift from remedial to preventative. The software in the household PC would become an integrating capability for the individual or household to manage their own health. Quicken has already helped millions to keep in one place financial data from all of their banks, credit cards, investment funds—and increasingly, insurance and transaction data. By the fall of 2001, Quicken had captured 75 percent of the personal-finance market.[10] A "Quicken for Health" capability will allow individuals to retain all of their health records from APGAR to autopsy. Further, with an active Google-like capability, this system will continually search for new information relevant to your specific health-care concerns.

When the number of users grows, it will become apparent how important it is to link all clinical outcomes to an individual's genome. Just as people carry living wills today to indicate they will donate their organs for the common good, tomorrow they will carry "data donor" cards allowing the results of every test performed on them be contributed to a publicly available outcomes database, in which their genome is associated anonymously with all of the outcomes they've experienced. This repository of information could be the source of medical discovery for a whole new generation of molecular biologists whose products might be made available locally via the matter compiler.

Overall, when individuals are using molecular sensing and adaptive software to give themselves feedback when they are well, we will see a health-care industry transformed from one focused on physical intervention in times of trauma to one focused on continual feedback about wellness and well-being and learning about behavior. This will break the paradigm of insurance paying for the risks that individuals encounter in the physical world in favor of an already growing one: individuals and households paying for their own wellness via expenditures on vitamins, health clubs, inspirational books, and assorted therapies that they believe are healthful. As the feedback loops on all of this voluntary expenditure become more robust, health will start looking like any other industry, providing whatever it is that assists customers in meeting their desires to extend their life spans and live with greater satisfaction. If you're in health care, how far can you push the implications of this ultimate shift from remedy to prevention today?

3. The Universal Individual Lifelong Mentor

As the half-life of knowledge shrinks, while the human life span extends, we will no longer see education as a capital investment made early and maintained only occasionally for necessary upgrades. Continual learning, including but not limited to on-the-job learning, is slowly becoming an accepted part of the average person's life. Of course, if we extrapolate this trend based on our existing technologies, we should expect to have 75 percent of the labor force teaching in graduate schools. But if we extrapolate based on developments already in the works, we can see the possibilities of other models. Tim Berners-Lee, inventor of the World Wide Web, is currently working on something called the Semantic Web, which could do for meaning what Google has done for Web pages: make the universe searchable. This next-generation Web is intended to operate on words and logical relationships among them at the conceptual level. Using XML tags to denote meaning, software agents will create a smart network in which they will not only search and retrieve information upon request—they will carry out transactions on the user's behalf. By addressing the problem of understanding, and by combining the different jargons of various disciplines, these agents should encourage global, cross-disciplinary collaboration, and dramatically simplify navigating our unfathomably vast repository of knowledge. Berners-Lee is one of many working toward this goal.

Once again, Neal Stephenson has imagined something similar to this. In his 1992 novel *Snow Crash*, he envisioned a universal information-retrieval device as a hologram called the Librarian:

The Librarian daemon [an AI term for agent] looks like a pleasant, fiftyish, silver-haired, bearded man with bright blue eyes, wearing a V-neck sweater over a work shirt, with a coarsely woven, tweedy-looking tie. The tie is loosened, the sleeves pushed up. Even though he's just a piece of software, he has reason to be cheerful; he can move through the nearly infinite stacks of information in the Library with the agility of a spider dancing across a vast web of cross-references. The Librarian is the only piece of CIC software that costs even more than Earth; the only thing he can't do is think.[11]

Our mentor idea goes a step further, not merely responding to questions but anticipating developmental needs of its owner. We can imagine that if this product develops, people will become far more dependent on it than they are on their more passive devices such as cell phones and Black-Berries. An always-available, tireless, intelligent servant with your best interest foremost on its mind would be hard to resist.

If you're in information technology, or in education, isn't it time to be thinking about how this convergence of the two will change the models rather than how to automate what we've got?

4. The Experience Machine

Several startup companies have developed devices that "print" aromas by squirting tiny amounts of essential oils into the user's atmosphere over the Internet. You can buy a chair to sit in when you play videogames that executes the appropriate shakes, rattles, and rolls when your virtual car crashes, or when you're hit by the missile of an opponent. The digitally reproduced sound of your Dolby THX-equipped theater creates vibrations that are not heard but felt, and surgeons are wearing 3-D virtual-reality goggles to look at images of probes inside patients' bodies. We're well along the path to a world where all experiences can be digitized, and all digits can be experienced. Neuroscientists already speculate about creating affect directly. Rather than creating the experience to be detected by our natural senses and relayed to the brain, they imagine neurotransmitters acting on the brain directly so that the individual generates the experience from the inside out. This has become routine in medical research, where we can apply electric pulses to the brains of rats, cats, and rabbits to cause them to experience feelings of pleasure or aversion.

All of this points toward a kind of "experience machine," a combination of digital and chemical technologies that allows the mix of real and imaginary circumstances to be experienced by its user. As with other devices, this will begin as an expensive, elite capability, then become a mass-market product. The moving picture was, after all, a high-end technology before the television brought the same capability to the home, which, in turn, has become the home theater.

Some will object, saying that going to movies or the live theater or concert is a social experience that cannot be replicated by a solitary one, and we don't imagine that these shared-experience media will disappear. But it is already also possible to have shared experiences over the Net, as any player of EverQuest or Ultima Online will tell you. What is clear is that the entertainment industry will continue to change profoundly as we become more and more able to make experiences cross code from the digital to the biochemical realm.

When this happens, it will become difficult to distinguish entertainment from drugs. It is almost certain that we will be capable of creating experiences that are even more addictive to adults than today's video games are to children. It is beyond our purpose here to speculate on the issues of regulation, productivity, pornography and censorship, and ethics that surely come to bear. What we do know is that an experience machine will transform the entertainment industry, both because such powerful stimulation will increase consumers' willingness to pay and because, when an experienced object is reproducible digitally, it can be readily shared and edited by any household, just as I-movies are today. If you're in entertainment, isn't it time to start imagining your role in this "next big thing"?

5. Social-Science Simulators

For fifty years, social scientists have struggled with a stepchild stigma of being considered not quite legitimate in the eyes of "true" scientists who insist on rigorous protocols and high standards of proof. When we planned the first trip to the moon, different factions advocated two different approaches: a direct landing and takeoff, and the lunar orbiter with the descent-and-ascent model that was actually used in the Apollo program. The orbiter was chosen on the basis of carefully reviewed engineering criteria—chief among them energy consumption and reliability. Without the lunar module, the *Apollo 13* would not have returned.

Contrast that with the social-policy debates we have over issues such as the productivity implications of different tax structures or welfare programs. The social sciences offer no rigorous analytics or even criteria for assessing the efficacy of their policy recommendations.

The kind of agent-based simulation described earlier offers the beginnings of a capability to create more rigorous tools for social science, so that the term *social science* is no longer an oxymoron. The data-farming of the Marines is the beginning of a replicable experiment exploring questions about human behavior. Brookings Institution Fellow Robert Axtell's landmark simulation that recreates the initial growth and subsequent decline of corporations is another.

Today, when a tax policy is considered or an investment in economic development evaluated, econometric modules are used to assess the long-term impact. In the future, the Office of Management and Budget might be able to assess social consequences of changes in policy through agent-based models. Over time, these models could simulate an increasing range of social behavior.[13] Similarly in business, organizational changes would be simulated before they are put into place. Just as the home hospital will call forth an individual's physiological simulation, companies would have simulations of their corporate body based not just on averages, but on individual behavior. This might enable not only better organizational design, but successful career planning. Social science may have an efflorescence in the twenty-first century to match the progress of physical science and engineering in the nineteenth and twentieth.

The five developments we've imagined here may pale by comparison with what actually develops. Whether or not we're specifically correct in any one instance, the larger point is that it's easy to imagine a plausible scenario in which a new technology will overturn the status quo in the manufacturing industries, the health-care industry, education, entertainment, and government. Collectively, these represent more than half of the total economy.[13] With the advent of code crossing molecular technologies, the adjacent possible is no longer a world of incremental change. How will the economy work if these or similar developments take hold?

THE FURTHER EVOLUTION OF THE ADAPTIVE ENTERPRISE

We've said that during the next ten years we'll see the emergence of the Adaptive Enterprise, whose roots are in the principles of evolution. During the past two decades, businesspeople have been discussing biology as a metaphor for business, useful in developing a mind-set but difficult to apply. More profound changes have had to await the development of the rigorous techniques we've described.

Now that technologies like genetic algorithms and agent-based simulations have been developed, and the understanding of principles of adaptive management is emerging, enterprises will begin to embody these principles in their behavior, structure, and economics.

The economic theory we all grew up with is consistent with industrial points of view, built, like the management theory of the same vintage, in the mind-set based on physics. The molecular economy, by contrast, will draw heavily on the ideas of biology and adaptive systems, growing from the bottom up. Our economic theory, too, will evolve to reflect the mind-set of the coming day.

Physics is based on laws, while adaptive systems are based on rules. By laws, we mean top-down observations about the behavior of the universe that yield equations we can solve; by rules, we mean the bottom-up choices that govern the agents in their interactions, which we can simulate. The tools of classical physics[14]—especially differential equations—have led us to an economics of predictability and stable equilibrium, while evolutionary models acknowledge unpredictability and volatility, never reaching equilibrium.

Economics has begun to evolve in this direction. As noted earlier, the Santa Fe Institute has held two conferences on "The Economy as a Complex Adaptive System," the first one chaired by Ken Arrow, winner of the 1972 Nobel Prize in Economics.[15] The mind-set of this work is very much the same as we've explored in information, biology, and business in Part II, and the toolset is similar, as Josh Epstein's work illustrates.

Equally interesting is the development of "behavioral economics." Two behavioral economists,[16] whose work explores the psychological drivers of human decision making, won the 2002 economics Nobel Prize. The behavioral approach attacks the assumptions of classical economics from the bottom up. According to Richard Thaler, perhaps the discipline's leading advocate, "neo-classical economics has defined itself as explicitly 'anti-behavioral,' "[17] meaning that it makes idealized assumptions about how "homo economicus" behaves so that physics-like equations can be solved.

Thaler cites three of the sacred cows of the classical economist as contrary to fact—and common sense. The view of individual choices that economists have used is based on a "rational expectations" model, which assumes that individuals have access to all information and the capacity to process it, the will to implement the economically optimal decision, and the single-mindedness to act only in their own self-interest. The behavioral economists replace these ideas with "bounded rationality, bounded willpower, and bounded self-interest" and explore the implications of these assumptions. They explicitly look to other disciplines, particularly psychology, to learn how individuals with these presumed attributes behave. They find that they are far better able to explain phenomena like stock-price movements and market bubbles if they open the door to explanations that reflect findings such as that people give too much importance to the most recent evidence, or have a preference to avoid loss rather than to achieve gains.[18]

The behavioral economists are starting to look at how individuals truly behave. Perhaps we can couple what they are learning about individual behavior with the techniques of agent-based modeling, to simulate what will happen when heterogeneous groups of people come together to engage in economic activity, as we described in Rob Axtell's "Firms" model. What would an economic theory based on this bottom-up point of view look like?

In 1943, psychologist Abraham Maslow articulated a hierarchy-of-needs concept that has since found its way into the popular consciousness. At the bottom of this hierarchy, sketched as an inverted pyramid, are the fundamentals needed to sustain life, biological and physiological needs such as food, water, oxygen, and the means to achieve good health. A couple of levels higher on the pyramid, Maslow placed all the material things that contribute to our self-esteem, the things that we tend to spend much of our money on—houses, clothes, automobiles, yachts, and everything that LVMH produces. At the top of the pyramid, Maslow placed self-actualization, the feeling of fulfillment that people derive from realizing a vocation, satisfying an innate drive to perform certain activities, as a painter might feel driven to paint, or a musician to compose.

The development of bottom-up management models combined with broader measures may move our focus upward on Maslow's pyramid. Regarding health, it's clear we are on the verge of a breakthrough in our understanding of how to maintain and extend a healthy human life. Medical interventions are becoming less intrusive and painful, and the human life span will continue to expand. Futurist Ray Kurzweil estimates that today the life span of the newborn increases by six months every year, and that within fifty years, the average human life span will increase more than a year every year. Our mastery of molecular biology should make this extended life span a far healthier and more capable one, if we don't unleash too many inadvertent—or deliberate—plagues.

If molecular mastery makes the scarcity of raw materials an anachronistic concern, we should be in for a long-term boom. Connecting software automata should ensure that less and less labor is required to produce the stuff on which we currently spend our income. Molecular technologies will reduce the materials and energy requirements. This means that goods and services of high quality previously available only to the few would become part of a mass lifestyle. Of course, as recent research has shown, people regard their wealth more as a function of their standing vis-à-vis others than as any absolute standard of living,[19] so we might assume that such abundance will have little subjective effect on how people will feel. Until our new biological tools change human nature, people will want more than they have.

What might actually improve our subjective sense of well-being is the availability of almost limitless computing power to make more of human learning available to more individuals. The "sense, respond, learn, and adapt" cycle could help more people benefit from what wisdom we have. Finally, if the work of social scientists described in Chapter 4 progresses, we may have the beginnings of social science that can better help guide social and government processes.

This utopian vision—in which the accelerating progress of molecular technologies and understanding of adaptive systems leads us to a world in which we find ourselves more healthy, wealthy, and wise—is, of course, appealing but not certain or even likely. The capabilities described above may be created, but progress always has its downside. The Industrial Revolution spawned the hellish factories of Charles Dickens' London. The Information Revolution seems to be creating a more polarized, politicized, unequal, and vulnerable world. The key social downside of the industrial economy continues to be the condition of the environment, while that of the information era appears to be privacy. In the coming economy, the key issues will be ethical. These questions will range from the current debate on cloning to the rights we accord artificial entities once they appear to be conscious and feeling.

Nonetheless, we believe that in the adjacent possible, the economy that will develop in the future, we will have an enormous potential to create more rapid growth and greater surplus. As in the past, there will be a "Cambrian explosion" of experiments, followed by a pruning of the possibilities that result.

THE CONVERGENCE OF THE BORN AND THE MADE

The discovery of natural selection, the austere logic of reproducing systems, was not only Darwin's first step. He used this new logic to span three seemingly unbridgeable metaphysical chasms. He showed how selection united the nonliving and the living, the nonhuman and the human, and the physical and the mental into a single fabric of intelligible material causation.[20]

If information, biology, and business codes can be freely translated into one another, where will this take us? Any environment filled with things that connect with each other, from microbial soup to microchips, will evolve. Since code is code, the molecular, informational, and physical can now connect to each other in new ways, meaning that we can anticipate the co-evolution of the born and the made, of the real and the virtual, of the organic and the inorganic. Software will breed its own new generations, and new kinds of organisms will be manufactured in wet labs.

These recombinations will, if we choose, amount to directed evolutionary engineering. To find this useful rather than threatening, we will have to remove ourselves further from the center of things, much as Copernicus had to "stand on the sun" to comprehend the solar system.[21] Then, we might marvel at an extraordinary participation in our own evolutionary futures, to say nothing of the artifacts and devices that future factories will create and evolve. Of course, this evolutionary process won't stop with the economy.

Bacteria evolved into cells with nuclei. Those cells self-organized into multicellular plants and animals, which in turn became wonderful hosts for more bacteria. You have more bacterial DNA in your body than you

have of your own. In fact, bacteria dominates the earth's biomass. Standing on the sun, who would you say rules the earth?

As information, biology, and business converge into a single system of connected codes, many imagine a relationship between ourselves and our computers similar to that between bacteria and ourselves. Are we, the inhabitants of the connected economies, dwelling inside an increasingly autonomous silicon-based host? This theme is being explored in the popular arena by movies such as *The Matrix* and *A.I.: Artificial Intelligence*. In the academy, as well, scholarly books point to this convergence.[22]

Many balk at the notion of blurring carbon and non-carbon life. They ask: How can cold code be infused with warm wet life? How can the ineffable qualities of humans be passed on, into computers? In return, however, we must ask: How can we accept the concept of evolution yet believe that it stops with us?

Species do not spring into existence *de novo*. They emerge as founder populations that represent recombinations of codes, creating innovative organisms and differentiated species, ultimately co-evolving in even less-understood ecologies. And if they evolve from earlier forms, then might not humans evolve forms more intelligent than themselves? We believe the apes did it. Aren't we at least as capable as they were of such creative, connective evolution? Of course, we may be more capable of stopping it but what would be the ethics of that?

We are not trying to settle the definition of life, only to point out that it, like our other ethical concepts, are about to evolve. The convergence we've attempted to show in *It's Alive* says to us that it is evolution—the dynamics of self organization, recombination, selective pressure, coevolution, and emergence—that is in charge. True, we have a unique ability to consciously intervene in evolutionary processes. Equally true, we cannot with any confidence predict the outcome of our interventions.

To help you "imagine" just how profoundly different this world will be from the one we know, let us offer you one last quick image: that of Anne Foerst of MIT's Artificial Intelligence Laboratory.

Foerst is part of a team building a cute and cuddly robot named Kismet. Like the child it resembles, Kismet responds differently to different tones of voice, then wins you over with big eyes and subtle facial

expressions. In fact, Kismet's features are very intentionally designed to elicit nurturing behavior from adults. The more time and attention we give Kismet, the more it can learn from us.

The team's objective at MIT is to try to make robots in which intelligence is truly embodied. Movement, growth, balance, friction, digestion, social interaction—these all inform the way humans think. For robots to function as we do, they need the same or similar elements informing the way they think. Primarily, their intelligence needs to be distributed, as ours is, across different drives and capabilities. In other words, it's not enough to have a set number of answers programmed in for a set number of questions. Each drive must compete with others so that novel solutions for unanticipated problems can *evolve* through the selective pressure of success or failure. That's what gives a good robot "the juice," as they say at MIT.

And Foerst's role in all this?

She is not a computer scientist. She is a Lutheran minister. She is the theological adviser to MIT's God and Computers Project.

Welcome to the next wave of economic history.

Notes

INTRODUCTION

1. Kurzweil, Raymond, "The Laws of Accelerating Returns," published on KurzweilAI.net, March 7, 2001.
2. Margulis, Lynn and Dorion Sagan, *What Is Life*, Simon & Schuster (1995), p. 62.

1. ECONOMIC EVOLUTION: LEARNING FROM LIFE CYCLES

1. See www.smalltalk.org/alankay.html.
2. Gibson, William, *Neuromancer*, Ace Books, reissue edition (1995).
3. "2002 Route to the Top," *Chief Executive*, February 2002.
4. "'Build a Better Mousetrap': 2001 New Product Innovations of the Year," Market Intelligence Service, December 21, 2001.
5. "Economic Report of the President," January 2001.
6. The special items are costs—or less often, gains—excluded from a company's reported earnings. They include restructuring charges, asset impairments, merger and acquisition charges, and other significant, unanticipated, nonrecurring items.
7. Whaley, Robert E., "The Investor Fear Gauge," February 4, 2000, appearing at http://faculty.fuqua.duke.edu/~whaley/vix/. The CBOE Volatility Index was developed to measure investors' expectations about the volatility of the S&P 100. Index values are based upon option trading prices.
8. Computer Industry Almanac Inc.
9. "One World?" *The Economist*, October 18, 1997.
10. *Ibid.*
11. Saffo, Paul, "The Business World Turned Upside Down" in *The Biology of Business*, edited by John Henry Clippinger III, Jossey-Bass (1999) p. xvii.
12. Lohr, Steve, "IBM Opening a $2.5 Billion Specialized Chip Plant," *New York Times*, August 1, 2002, p. C1.
13. In 2001, CEMEX's profit margin of 15.6 percent dwarfed the industry average of 2.8 percent. Figures taken from "Adaptive Capabilities—Case Studies," a May 2002 presentation by Forrester Research senior analyst Tom Pohlmann.
14. Feder, Barnaby J., *New York Times*, February 7, 2003, p. c4.
15. Biotechnology Industry Organization, 2002, appearing online at http://www.bio.org
16. *Ibid.*
17. Biotech patents source: U.S. Patent and Trademark Office, *Technology Profile Report*, Patent Examining Technology Center, Groups 1630–1650, Biotechnology 1/1977–1/1998, April 1999.
18. We thank Rodrigo Martinez, Harvard Business School Life Sciences Project, for these examples.
19. "Digital Economy 2002," the U.S. Department of Commerce's fourth annual report on the IT revolution, p. v.

PART II: CODE IS CODE

1. Gershenfeld, Neil, "Draft: Executive Summary," Center for Bits and Atoms, MIT, July 16, 2002, appearing at http://cba/mit/edu

2. We are indebted to Evelyn Fox Keller for showing us how metaphorical even the rigorous, testable, code-based translation of genetic code to digital code really is.

2. GENERAL EVOLUTION: LEARNING FROM NATURE

1. Diamond, Jared, in the foreword to Ernst Mayr's *What Evolution Is,* Basic Books (2001), p. vii.

2. Kauffman, Stuart, *At Home in the Universe: The Search for Laws of Self-Organization and Complexity,* Oxford University Press (1995), p. 27.

3. Not to mention disease and epidemics, markets, social networks, ecologies, food webs, cooperation and competition, and roughly speaking, everything else.

4. Edited by Philip W. Anderson, Kenneth J. Arrow, and David Pines, Santa Fe Institute, Addison–Wesley, (1998).

5. Dawkins, Richard, "Son of Moore's Law," in *The Next Fifty Years: Science in the First Half of the Twenty-First Century,* edited by John Brockman, Vintage (2002).

6. Ambrose, Sue Goetinck, "Biologists Create Polio, Terrorists Could, Too: Genetic data available from public sources," *The Dallas Morning News,* July 12, 2002.

7. "The Smell of Trouble," *Technology Review,* January/February 2001.

8. Keller, Evelyn Fox, *Making Sense of Life: Explaining Biological Development with Models, Metaphors, and Machines,* Harvard University Press (2002), p. 199.

9. Sipper, Moshe, *Machine Nature: The Coming Age of Bio-Inspired Computing,* McGraw-Hill (2002).

10. Bacteria are more promiscuous. DNA floats around in their environment, and they may adopt sequences from many parents before dividing to form the next generation.

11. Mayr, Ernst, *This Is Biology: The Science of the Living World,* Belknap Press of Harvard University Press (1997), pp. 151–152.

12. This doctrine was hijacked a century ago by the Social Darwinists, who advocated selection based on their own views of moral fitness. But Darwinism was not "a doctrine of the strong celebrating the rightness of their power over the weak." (See "The Greatest Englishman Since Newton," a *New York Times* book review by John Tooby of Janet Browne's biography, *Charles Darwin: The Power of Place,* October 6, 2002.)

3. BIOLOGY AND THE WORLD OF MOLECULES

1. Feynman, Richard P., "There's Plenty of Room at the Bottom," a speech delivered at Caltech on December 29, 1959.

2. Alan has recently become a Senior Fellow at HP Labs.

3. See www.KurzweilAI.net.

4. This includes genomes data for bacteria, archaea, and eukaryotes. The number of genomes sequenced cited here includes data only for publicly available genomes through June 2002. It is estimated that hundreds of additional genomes are sequenced in private databases. Source for the number of genomes sequenced: David Ussery, Center for Biological Sequence Analysis, BioCentrum, Technical Uni-

versity of Denmark. Source for the cost per base pair: U.S. Department of Energy; "Testimony on Advances in Genetics Research and Technologies: Challenges for Public Policy" by Francis S. Collins, before the Senate Committee on Labor and Human Resources, July 25, 1996, and Raymond Kurzweil, "The Law of Accelerating Returns," published on KurzweilAI.net March 7, 2001.

5 "Scientists Prove How Geckos Stick," press release from Lewis & Clark College, Portland, Oregon, August 26, 2002.

6. Feder, Barnaby J., "The Rise of the Ting," *New York Times*, November 28, 2002.

7. Gross, Michael, *Travels to the Nanoworld: Miniature Machinery in Nature and Technology*, Perseus (1999), p. 25.

8. *Ibid.*, p. 33.

9. www.veeco.com.

10. Doug Schiff, 3rd Tech VP of marketing and business development, quoted in "3rd Tech Selling 'Picks and Shovels' for Nanostructures," by Sandra Helsel, Nanoelectronicsplanet.com, July 16, 2001.

11. Proteomics is a field of research that looks at proteins and their functions. Unraveling DNA and creating a map of the human genome is merely the first step toward developing successful medical treatments. Since most diseases are rooted in protein activity, to attack diseases, scientists must understand proteins and how they function.

12. Chadwick, Alan V., "Solid progress in ion conduction," *Nature*, Vol. 408, December 21–28, 2000, pp. 925–962.

13. "Societal Implications of Nanoscience and Nanotechnology," National Science Foundation, March, 2001, p. 7.

14. Barsoum, Michael W. and Tamer El-Raghy, "The MAX Phases: Unique New Carbide and Nitride Materials," *American Scientist*, July-August, 2001. pp. 334–343.

15. Gross, Neil and Otis Port, "The Next Wave for Technology," *Business Week*, August 31, 1998.

16. Woodbury, Dale, Emily J. Schwarz, Darwin J. Prockop, and Ira B. Black, "Adult rat and human bone marrow stromal cells differentiate into neurons," *Journal of Neuroscience Research*, Vol. 61, Issue 4, August 15, 2000.

17. "The Motley Fool Interview: Diversa CEO Jay Short," with Tom Jacobs, March 1, 2001.

18. CBI interview with Jay Short, November 28, 2000.

19. Interview with Tom Jacobs of Motley Fool.

20. Pollack, Andrew, "Scientists Are Starting to Add Letters to Life's Alphabet," *New York Times*, July 24, 2001.

21. Pollack, Andrew, "New Ventures Aim to Put Farms in Vanguard of Drug Production," *New York Times*, May 14, 2000.

22. Van Brunt, Jennifer, "Molecular Farming's Factories," *Signals Magazine*, February 19, 2002.

23. "Microchips in the Blood," *The Economist Technology Quarterly*, September 19, 2002.

24. *Ibid.*

25. Graeber, Charles, "Diagnosed in 60 Seconds," *Wired Magazine*, August 2002.

26. Kotler, Steve, "Vision Quest," *Wired Magazine*, September 2002.

27. Zoltán N. Oltavai and Albert Lázlo Barabási, "Life's Complexity Pyramid," *Science*, Vol. 298, October 25, 2002, p. 763.

4. Information and the World of Bits

1. Stoppard, Tom, *Arcadia,* Faber & Faber (1996).
2. For a treatment of how our understanding of the way genes work is evolving today, see *The Century of the Gene,* Evelyn Fox Keller, Harvard University Press (2000).
3. "Evolving Labor Market Strategies at HP," a presentation delivered by Chuck Sieloff and Kai Shi at the CBI's Embracing Complexity colloquim, August 2–4, 1998, described in the conference proceedings.
4. Epstein, Joshua M. and Robert Axtell, *Growing Artificial Societies: Social Science from the Bottom Up,* MIT Press (1996).
5. To see a run of Sugarscape, visit http://www.brook.edu/dybdocroot/sugarscape/default.htm.
6. http://www.ics.uci.edu/CORPS/dica.html
7. See it at www.red3D.com/cwr/boids
8. Kelly, Kevin, *Out of Control: The Rise of Neo-Biological Civilization,* Addison-Wesley (1994), p. 11.
9. Canter, Sheryl, "Programming Crowd Behavior: Point and Run," *PC Magazine Online,* April 1, 1996.
10. "THUMS: Toyota's Virtual Crash Test Dummy," at http://www.toyota.com/about/operations/design-rd/thum.html
11. Margulis, Lynn and Dorion Sagan, *Microcosmos,* Summit Books (1986), p. 85.
12. Margulis and Sagan, *What Is Life.* p.17.
13. Holland, J.H., *Adaptation in Natural and Artificial Systems,* University of Michigan Press (1975).
14. "Complex Job Scheduling: Evolving Solutions at Deere & Co.," a presentation delivered by Bill Fulkerson at the CBI's Embracing Complexity colloquium, July 17–19, 1996, described in conference proceedings.
15. Johnson, R. Colin, "Genetic algorithms design low emission engine," *EE Times,* June 30, 2000.
16. Lipson, Hod and Jordan B. Pollack, "Automatic design and manufacture of robotic lifeforms," *Nature,* Vol. 406, August 31, 2000, pp. 974–978.
17. Langton, Christopher G., "What Is Artificial Life?", Biota Publications, appearing online at http://www.biota.org/paperds/cglalife.html
18. Farmer, Doyne, "Toward Agent-Based Models for Investment," white paper published by the Association for Investment Management and Research (2001). pp. 61–70.
19. Initially created as a research partnership between Christopher Meyer and Stuart Kauffman, BiosGroup is now an independent consulting company based in Santa Fe, New Mexico. Cap Gemini Ernst & Young is a capital participant in BiosGroup; Meyer sits on its board.
20. Diamond, Jared M., "Life with the Artificial Anasazi," *Nature,* Vol. 419, October 10, 2002. pp. 567–569.
21. Stoppard, Tom, *Arcadia,* Faber & Faber (1996).

5. Adaptive Management

1. Toffler, Alvin, *The Adaptive Corporation*, McGraw-Hill (1984). p. 2.
2. Toffler, *The Adaptive Corporation*, p. 1.
3. Paraphrased from Alvin Toffler's *The Third Wave*, Bantam Books (1981).
4. Toffler, *The Adaptive Corporation*, p. 106.
5. Porter, Michael E., *Competitive Strategy: Techniques for Analyzing Industries and Competitors*, Free Press (1980).
6. Stalk, George and Thomas M. Hout, *Competing Against Time: How Time-Based Competition Is Reshaping Global Markets*, Free Press (1990).
7. "In the fast lane," *The Economist*, October 19, 2002, p. 58.
8. *Meme* is a word coined by geneticist Richard Dawkins to call attention to the idea that knowledge itself is alive: an evolving, adaptive system. The meme is like the gene—an idea that can replicate itself and become prevalent in an environmental niche. "Examples of memes are tunes, ideas, catch-phrases, clothes fashions, ways of making pots or of building arches. Just as genes propagate themselves in the gene pool by leaping from body to body via sperm or eggs, so memes propagate themselves in the meme pool by leaping from brain to brain. If a scientist hears, or reads about, a good idea, he passes it on to his colleagues and students. He mentions it in his articles and his lectures. If the idea catches on, it can be said to propagate itself, spreading from brain to brain." From Dawkins' *The Selfish Gene*, Oxford University Press (1990).
9. Ernst & Young, Embracing Complexity Conference Proceedings, 1999.
10. For more on the links of insect behavior to self-organizing systems in business operations, see "Swarm Intelligence: A Whole New Way to Think About Business" by Eric Bonabeau and Christopher Meyer, *Harvard Business Review*, May 2001.
11. "Linux Operating Environments Market to Reach $280 Million by 2006 Despite Decline Last Year," IDC Press Release, July 30, 2002; also Ewalt, David M., *Information Week*, "Just How Many Linux Users Are There?" June 13, 2001; and Ricciuti, Mike, "Open Source: Rebels at the Gate," *CNET News*, October 14, 2002.
12. Petzinger, Thomas, Jr., *The New Pioneers*, Simon and Schuster (1999). It states: "ANYTHING not expressly prohibited by the language of this agreement IS ALLOWED."
13. Gladwell, Malcolm, "The Tipping Point: Why Is the City Suddenly So Much Safer—could it be that crime really is an epidemic?" *The New Yorker*, June 3, 1996; and Tapellini, Donna, "Digital Crime Fighter," *CIO Insight*, June 1, 2001.
14. Herel, Suzanne, "Pilots May Pick Own Routes: Satellite technology could allow less communication with traffic controllers," *San Francisco Chronicle*, June 10, 2001.
15. Sculley, John and John A. Byrne, *Odyssey: Pepsi to Apple—A Journey of Adventure, Ideas and the Future*, HarperCollins (1987), p.32.
16. Gladwell, Malcolm, "Smaller: The Disposable Diaper and the Meaning of Progress," *The New Yorker*, November 26, 2001.
17. Warneke, Brett et al., "Smart Dust: Communicating with a Cubic-Millimeter Computer," *IEEE Computer*, Vol. 34, No. 1, January 2001. pp. 44–51.
18. Of course, corresponding increases in computing power and storage are needed to exploit this data. David Tennenhouse, Intel VP and director of research, estimates that the data traffic generated by sensors could create a 100 times increase above and

beyond the growth of the Internet today. Kanellos, Michael, "Intel Delves into Pervasive Computing," ZDnet.com, August 27, 2001.

19. Hu, Kang, Sean Skehan, and Rex Gephardt, "Implementing Smart Transit Priority System for Metro Rapid Bus in Los Angeles," City of Los Angeles, Department of Transportation, White Paper 01-3544, November 2000.

20. Haeckel, Stephan H., *Adaptive Enterprise: Creating and Leading Sense-and-Respond Organizations*, Harvard Business School Press (1999). Steve has generously acknowledged the contribution of the CBI's thinking to his title.

21. http://researchweb.watson.ibm.com/autonomic/overview/faqs.html#1

22. http://www.efi.org/products/power/contthrm.html

23. http://www.baseballhalloffame.org/hofers_and_honorees/hofer_bios/rickey_branch.htm

24. This account, based on conversations with Cannavino, appears in *Surfing the Edge of Chaos: The Laws of Nature and the New Laws of Business*, by Richard T. Pascale, Mark Millemann, and Linda Gioja, Crown Business (2000), pp. 23–24.

25. We used normalized standard deviation. Firms approximately one standard deviation from the mean were considered unstable. The number of firms in the stable group was 1,002. The number of firms in the unstable group was 552. The number of firms in the sample does not add up to 3,000 because we included only firms with ten years of data extending back to 2001.

26. "Delivering on the Promise of Pharmaceutical Innovation: The Need to Maintain Strong and Predictable Intellectual Property Rights," Pharmaceutical Research and Manufacturers of America, White Paper, April 22, 2002, p. 28.

27. Meyer, Christopher, "Survival Under Stress," *Sloan Management Review*, Fall 2002.

28. Leff, David N., "Can Electronic Pacemakers Go Genetic?", *BioWorld Today*, Vol. 13, No. 175, September 12, 2002.

29. Miake, Junichiro, Eduardo Marbán, and Bradley H. Nuss, "Biological pacemaker created by gene transfer," *Nature*, Vol. 419, September 12, 2002, pp. 132–133.

30. "Cargill Dow to Produce New Type of Plastic from Grain," GEAPS In-Grain Online, Vol. 20, No. 2, February 2000.

31. Based on updated research by the Center for Business Innovation, originally presented in Christopher Meyer, "What's the Matter?", *Business 2.0*, April 1999.

32. Based on updated research by Tim Simcoe, Center for Business Innovation, originally presented in "What's the Matter?" by Christopher Meyer.

33. Kelly, Kevin, *Out of Control: The Rise of Neo-Biological Civilization*, Addison-Wesley (1994), p. 2.

6. SEED, SELECT, AND AMPLIFY AT CAPITAL ONE

1. Letter to Shareholders, Capital One Annual Report, 1998.
2. At least until Q3, 2002. For 2003, Capital One estimates EPS growth of 15 percent.
3. Letter to Shareholders, AR 1998.

7. BREEDING EARLY AND OFTEN AT THE U.S. MARINE CORPS

1. Quoted in Heinl, Robert D., *Dictionary of Military and Naval Quotations*, Naval Institute Press (1966), p. 239.

2. Krulak, Charles C., "The Leadership Imperative," in *Corps Business* by David Freedman, HarperBusiness (2000), p. xii.

3. Marine Corps Doctrinal Publication 6, "Command and Control," Secretary of the Navy (1996), p. 46.

4. Kristof, Nicholas D., "How We Won the War," *New York Times*, September 6, 2002.

5. Borger, Julian, "War Game Was Fixed to Ensure American Victory, Claims General," *The Guardian*, August 21, 2002.

6. Cebrowski, Arthur, "Network Centric Warfare: Its origins and future," Naval Institute Proceedings, 1998.

7. "Command and Control," Secretary of the Navy.

8. Keller, Bill, "The Fighting Next Time," the *New York Times Magazine*, March 10, 2002.

9. Alberts, David S., John J. Garstka, and Frederick P. Stein, *Network Centric Warfare: Developing and Leveraging Information Superiority* (2nd Edition), DoD C4ISR Cooperative Research Program (1999), p. 2.

10. Luchetti, Aaron, "Marines Land on Merc Trading Floor to Swap Tips on Working Under Fire," *The Wall Street Journal*, December 16, 1996.

11. Marine Corps Doctrinal Publication 1, *Warfighting*, Secretary of the Navy (1996), pp. 13–14.

12. Horne, Gary E., and Alfred Brandstein, "Data Farming: A Meta-technique for Research in the 21st Century," in *Maneuver Warfare Science 1998*, edited by F.G. Hoffman and Gary E. Horne, pp. 93–100; and Horne, Gary E., "Beyond Point Estimates: Operational Synthesis and Data Farming," in *Maneuver Warfare Science 2001*, edited by Gary E. Horne and Mary Leonardi, pp. 1–7. Both texts published by the United States Marines Corps Development Command.

13. Arquilla, John and David Ronfeld, "Swarming and the Future of Conflict," RAND (2000), p. vii.

14. Leo, Alan, "The Soldier of Tomorrow," *Technology Review*, March 20, 2002.

8. CREATING THE CAPACITY TO RESPOND AT BP

1. Browne, Lord John, "Lord Goold Memorial Lecture: Marketing Strategy," speech delivered at Bradford University, November 23, 2001.

2. Lord Browne was kind enough to speak at length with us about BP on November 13, 2001. Any quotations without other attribution are drawn from the transcript of that discussion.

3. BP notes that ". . . operations span six continents, with nine plants and 24 sales offices. Production reached 42 MW in 2000 and 54 MW in 2001. In 2001 we expanded our solar business by investing in a state-of-the-art factory in Madrid, Spain, producing highly efficient photovoltaic systems. The anticipated annual production from the plant will be 60 MW by 2003, equivalent to approximately 20% of the world's current demand for solar energy." From http://www.bp.com/environsocial/environment/renewenergy/ourperform.asp

4. Average return on equity, 1995–2001.

5. "The Top 25 Managers of the Year," *Business Week*, January 14, 2002.

6. http://www.bp.com/companyoverview/objectives/s_o_objectives.asp

7. Remarks by Lee R. Raymond, speech delivered at the ExxonMobil 119th Annual Meet-

ing, May 30, 2001: http://www2.exxonmobil.com/Corporate/Newsroom/SpchsIntvws/ Corp_NR_SpchIntrvw_AnnualMeeting_010530.asp.

8. Buchan, David and Tobias Buck, "Refining BP's Management," *Financial Times*, July 31, 2002.

9. Dunn, Seth, "An Oil Company Proves Bush Wrong on Climate Change," March 26, 2002, a report from the Worldwatch Institute posted at http://www.tompaine. com/feature.cfm/ID/5334

10. Browne, Lord John, from "Technology and Business—a Progress Report," a May 11, 2001 speech at Imperial College of Science, Technology and Medicine.

11. Echikson, William, "When Oil Gets Connected," *Business Week*, December 3, 2001.

12. Browne, from "Technology and Business."

13. Hall, Nina, "Passing the Acid Test," *Frontiers: The BP Magazine of Technology and Innovation*, December 2001.

14 "An Oil Company Proves Bush Wrong on Climate Change."

15. Jurgens, Rick, "BP Chief Touts Fight Against Global Warming," *Contra Costa Times*, March 12, 2002.

16. Lee R. Raymond at ExxonMobil annual meeting, May 30, 2001.

17. Jurgens, Rick, "BP Chief Touts Fight Against Global Warming."

18. From CBI interview with John Browne on November 13, 2001.

9. BORN ADAPTIVE AT MAXYGEN

1. Zhang, Ying-Xin et al., "Genome Shuffling Leads to Rapid Phenotypic Improvement in Bacteria," *Nature*, Vol. 415, pp. 644–646.

2. *Ibid.*

10. BECOMING AN ADAPTIVE ENTERPRISE

1. "Lord Goold Memorial Lecture: Marketing Strategy."

2. Andrews, David, "Trial by Ice," *Supply Chain Systems*, Vol. 21, No. 3, March 2001: http://www.idsystems.com/reader/2001/2001_03/tria0301/tria0301.htm

3. Abell, Peter, Roddy Martin, and Kara Romanow, "ePC and RFID Are for Real," *AMR Research Alert*, August 26, 2002.

4. Roth, Daniel, "Dell's Big New Act," *Fortune*, December 6, 1999; IDC, "The Lessons of Dell's Online Success," IDC, June 1998; "Web Commerce as If Customers Mattered" *Fast Company*, November 1, 1998; www.dell.com; E&Y Center for Business Knowledge.

5. All of the ideas described here have been discussed by Disney management, but many have not been implemented as of the beginning of 2003.

6. Kaur, Sharmilpal, ". . . but many did not leave cars behind," *Straits Times*, April 20, 2001.

7. From presentation made by Sarah Copp at the 2002 Global Supply Chain Sales Summit, March 2002, Washington D.C.

8. Cisco reported a $2.2 billion write-down from bad data, essentially from Cisco's suppliers setting up fake e-mail addresses so that Cisco could not contact them to stop production. See "Inside Cisco's $2 Billion Blunder," by Paul Kaihla, *Business 2.0*, March 2002.

9. "The Collaborative Commerce Value Statement: A $223 Billion Cost Savings Opportunity Over Six Years," *The Yankee Report*, June 15, 2001.

10. Clippinger, John H., III, editor, *The Biology of Business: Decoding the Laws of Enterprise*, pp. 204–205.

11. Juergen Daum, "Beyond Budgeting: How to become an adaptive sense-and-respond organization," *The New New Economy Analyst Report* (www.juergendaum.com), May 22, 2001.

12. *Ibid.*

13. *Ibid.*

14. Chabrow, Eric, "Slow but Steady," *Information Week*, March 12, 2001.

15. Pool, Robert, "If It Ain't Broke, Fix It," *Technology Review*, September 2001.

16. Forman, David, "The World's Largest Companies Bet on Nanotech R&D," *Small Times*, July/August 2002, pp. 22–29.

17. Slater, Robert, *The GE Way Fieldbook: Jack Welch's Plan for Corporate Revolution*, McGraw-Hill (1999), p. 194.

18. Whiting, Rick, "GE Capital's Dashboard Drives Metrics to Desktops," *Information Week*, April 22, 2002.

19. Welch, Jack, "Speech to Shareholders," April 22, 1998, in Slater, Robert, *The GE Way Fieldbook: Jack Welch's Plan for Corporate Revolution*, p. 204.

20. Welch, Jack, "Letter to Shareholders," February 12, 1999, in Slater, Robert, *The GE Way Fieldbook: Jack Welch's Plan for Corporate Revolution*, p. 220.

21. Will software agents need agents? Creative Artists Agency, take note.

11. THE ADJACENT POSSIBLE

1. Joy, Bill, "Why the Future Doesn't Need Us," *Wired Magazine*, April 2000.

2. www.ItsAliveBook.com

3. Gross, Michael, *Travels to the Nanoworld: Miniature Machinery in Nature and Technology*, Perseus Publishing (1999), p. 27.

4. Hydrogen bonds, electrostatic attraction between parts of molecules, and the so-called van der Walls' forces.

5. Bureau of Labor Statistics, U.S. Department of Labor.

6. Pounds per real GDP dollar, from 1989 to 1999.

7. Stephenson, Neal, *The Diamond Age*, Bantam Books (1996), p. 8.

8. According to the Steel Recycling Institute.

9. Jacobson, Joseph, "The Desktop Tab," *Communications of the ACM*, Vol. 44, March 2001, pp. 41–43.

10. Wood, Christina, "The Cult of Quicken," *On Magazine*, November 2001.

11. Stephenson, Neal, *Snow Crash*, Bantam Books (1992), p. 107.

12. Agents are sometimes called bots, reflecting that software robots are working for us to automate work as mechanical robots were expected to in the industrial era. (Not surprisingly, just as our machine tools don't look like Klaatu, our bots don't talk to us like Isaac Asimov's robots—yet.) In Asimov's novel *I, Robot*, the author envisioned a world in which the work was done by machines controlled by software agents with three key rules: (1) A robot may not injure a human being or, through inaction, allow a human being to come to harm; (2) A robot must obey the orders given it by human beings, except where such orders would conflict with the First

Law; and (3) A robot must protect its own existence as long as such protection does not conflict with the First or Second Laws. The most provocative situations arose when these "values" came into conflict, confusing the software.

13. CBI analysis. Data from the U.S. Department of Commerce, Bureau of Economic Analysis.

14. Quantum physics, with its intrinsic uncertainty, threw a monkey wrench into the classical model and moved the mind-set from certainty to probability.

15. Conference proceedings: Philip W. Anderson, et al., *The Economy as an Evolving Complex System; The Economy as an Evolving Complex System II*, edited by W. Brian Arthur, Steven N. Durlauf, and David A. Lane, Proceedings Volume XXVII, Perseus Books (1997).

16. Daniel Kahneman, professor of psychology and public affairs at Princeton University, and Vernon L. Smith, professor of economics and law at George Mason University.

17. Mulainathan, Sendhil and Richard H. Thaler, "Behavioral Economics," NBER Working Paper No. 7948, October 2000.

18. Odean, Terrance, "Are Investors Reluctant to Realize Their Losses?" *Journal of Finance*, Vol. 53, No. 5, October 1998, pp. 1775–1798; Shefrin, Hersh, and Meir Statman, "The Disposition to Sell Winners Too Early and Ride Losers Too Long: Theory and Evidence," *Journal of Finance*, Vol. 40, No. 3, July 1985, pp. 777–790.

19. According to a branch of economics known as "Prospect Theory."

20. Tooby, John, "The Greatest Englishman Since Newton," a *New York Times* review of Janet Browne's *Charles Darwin: The Power of Place*, October 6, 2002.

21. Thanks to Dick Morley for this helpful thought.

22. See, for example, *Flesh and Machines: How Robots Will Change Us*, Pantheon Books (2002), by Rodney Brooks, director of the MIT AI Lab, and *Investigations*, Oxford University Press (2000), by Stuart Kauffman of the Santa Fe Institute.

Acknowledgments

If you've been paying attention at all, you know that we believe in open boundaries, diversity of thought, and continual selective pressure as the way to make something evolve toward higher fitness. If that something is a book, you expose your thinking early and often to a wide variety of people. We've been lucky enough to benefit from the insights and advice of Noubar Afeyan, Brian Arthur, Eric Bonabeau, Antonio Damasio, Juan Enriquez, Joshua Epstein, Joel Freidman, Seth Godin, Stephan Haeckel, Evelyn Fox Keller, Kevin Kelly, Ray Kurzweil, Jaron Lanier, Rodrigo Martinez, Tom Petzinger, Alan Weber, and Mick Yates. There could be no better reason to write a book than the opportunity it afforded for conversation with these remarkable thinkers.

Equally stimulating were our interviews with executives from our case study organizations who stole time from crushing calendars to help us understand their situations. Our meetings numbered in the dozens, but we'd particularly like to thank Lord John Browne and Adam Kroloff of BP; Russell Howard and Pim Stemmer of Maxygen; Rich Fairbank, George Overholser, and Tatiana Stead of Capital One; and Lt. Gen. Paul Van Riper, Al Brandstein, and Gary Horne, all associated with the U.S. Marine Corps, for their generous time and commentary.

We want to acknowledge the essential support of Cap Gemini Ernst & Young worldwide, without whom there would be no Center for Business Innovation. In particular, we would like to thank our colleague John Parkinson, whose meticulous critique gave us much useful commentary. Because this book required extensive new research into future trends, the entire staff of the Center for Business Innovation made contributions to our knowledge base, and many offered helpful comments on various drafts. Jennifer Cline provided support throughout, and readied the text.

Rafe Sagalyn, our agent, once again wisely guided us through the publishing process, and John Mahaney was active and terrific as our editor at Crown, supported by Shana Wingert and Tara Delaney Gilbride.

The research team of Will Clifford, Prabal Chakrabarti, Cindy Cho, and Yusi Wang identified so many wonderful new examples we couldn't resist printing too many. And William Patrick, though he edited Stan's earlier *Future Perfect,* didn't know what he was getting into when he undertook to help us with the writing of *It's Alive.* His enthusiasm for the subject helped propel the project; his graceful prose, we think, propels the reader. (If ever you found this not to be the case, it was our writing, not Bill's.)

But our greatest gratitude must be reserved for the leader of the team that managed the research and writing process, Johanna Woll. Confronted with a boundless demand for more data, and with authors alternately intractable and inert, Johanna resolutely pushed this work to completion with good thinking, good sense, and good grace. Without Johanna, *It's Alive* would have died.

Finally, our collaborations thrive, we think, because of our respect for our complementary strengths and the perspectives they add. Please forgive us for using this space to express our mutual enjoyment of fifteen years of working together.

CHRISTOPHER MEYER
STAN DAVIS
Cambridge, Massachusetts

Glossary

Adaptation A characteristic of an agent that improves its ability to survive and reproduce in its environment. Also used to describe the process of genetic change within a population, as influenced by natural selection.

Adenosine Triphosphate (ATP) A compound that serves as fuel for cells. Used in synthesizing molecules, contracting muscles, transporting substances, and performing other tasks.

Adjacent Possible A term coined by Stuart Kauffman to refer to the space of possibilities that are not actual, but one step away from the actual.

Agent A physical, computational, or living system which has goals, sensors, and effectors, and decides autonomously which actions to take and when based on its internal state and that of the environment.

Agent-Based Model A simulated environment composed of many participants, which are formulated as interacting autonomous software or artificially intelligent agents. Each agent is endowed with traits, makes decisions, and acts based on a set of rules.

Amino Acid The molecular building block from which proteins are synthesized. There are twenty main amino acids in the proteins of living things, and the properties of a protein are determined by its particular amino acid sequence.

Antibody Any of a large number of proteins that are produced normally after stimulation by an antigen and act specifically against the antigen in an immune response.

Artificial Intelligence (AI) The branch of computer science concerned with making device perform functions that are normally associated with human intelligence, such as reasoning and optimization through experience.

Artificial Life (ALife) The discipline that studies "natural" life by attempting to recreate biological phenomena from scratch within computers and other artificial media.

Artificial Neural Network Collections of mathematical models inspired by the way the densely interconnected, parallel structure of the mammalian brain processes information. Artificial neural networks emulate some of the observed properties of biological nervous systems and draw on the analogies of adaptive biological learning.

Atom The smallest unit of a chemical element, about a third of a nanometer in diameter. Atoms make up molecules and solid objects.

Atomic Force Microscope (AFM) A tool used to image surfaces at the atomic level and move nanoscale particles into patterns. Much like a phonograph, a tiny probe typically between two and 30 nanometers wide is brought into direct contact with the sample surface. The probe is attached to the end of a cantilever that bends as the tip moves across the sample's surface. The deflection is measured allowing the AFM to detect variations in the vertical surface topography of the sample.

Bacteria Single-celled, prokaryotic organisms that can survive in a wide variety of environments.

Biosensor An analytical device incorporating a biological or biologically derived sensing element to produce either discrete or continuous digital electronic signals.

Biotechnology The deliberate manipulation of living organisms at the cellular or molecular level for commercial applications.

Buckyball A spherical fullerene ranging in size from 20 to 500 carbon atoms.

Catalyst A substance able to accelerate a chemical reaction but not affected by the overall reaction.

Cell The basic structural and functional unit of most living organisms.

Chaos Theory A branch of mathematics that explores the statistical regularity hidden in seemingly random systems that are extremely sensitive to changes in initial conditions.

Chromosome A structure in the cell nucleus that carries DNA.

Coevolution Evolution in two or more agents in which evolutionary changes in one agent influence the evolution of the other agent.

Combinatorial Chemistry The simultaneous synthesis of large numbers of new chemical compounds that are systematic variants of a chemical structure.

Complexity Theory An interdisciplinary field studying systems composed of many and varied parts that interact in complex and non-linear ways.

Deoxyribonucleic acid (DNA) A molecule encoding genetic information.

Directed Evolution The process in which the mechanisms of "natural" selection are employed at the molecular and single cell level to cause and then identify evolutionary adaptations to novel environmental challenges.

Ecosystem A community of agents interacting with each other and their environment.

Emergence Behaviors of a system arising from the interactions of agents but that cannot be predicted from the properties of the agents.

Enzyme A protein capable of catalyzing a chemical reaction.

Eukaryotic cell A cell with a distinct nucleus. Almost all multicellular organisms are eukaryotes. Compare with prokaryote cells.

Evolution Change in the heritable traits of organisms through the replacement of genotypes in a population.

eXtensible Markup Language (XML) A widely accepted format of sharing information over the Internet in a way that computers can use, regardless of their operating system.

Fitness A relative measure of an organism's ability to successfully reproduce.

Fullerene A class of cage-like carbon compounds composed of fused, pentagonal and/or hexagonal carbon rings.

Fuzzy Logic A technique used to handle approximate information, as opposed to binary, in a systematic fashion.

Gene The basic unit of inheritance composed of a sequence of nucleotides coding for a protein (or, in some cases, part of a protein).

Gene Shuffling Performed by fragmenting a family of related gene sequences into a pool of random DNA fragments that are then reassembled to create a collection or "library" of recombinant DNA molecules.

Genetic Algorithm A class of algorithms used to find solutions to difficult-to-solve problems, inspired by and named after biological processes of inheritance, mutation, natural selection, and the genetic crossover that occurs when parents mate to produce offspring.

Genetic Programming A computational method based on using evolutionary concepts-recombination, mutation, and selection-to allow computer programs to be evolved according to some user-defined goal.

Genome The complete genetic profile of an organism.

High-Throughput Screening (HTS) A process in which large batches of compounds are rapidly tested in parallel for binding activity or biological activity against target molecules.

Inorganic Compounds that do not contain carbon as the principal element.

Meme The word coined by Richard Dawkins for a unit of culture, such as an idea, skill, story, or custom, passed from one person to another by imitation or teaching. Memes reproduce, mutate, are selected, and evolve in a similar way to genes.

Metabolism The chemical processes that occur in a living organism in order to maintain life.

Micorarray A chip used for matching known and unknown DNA samples based on base-pairing rules and automating the process of identifying the unknowns.

Microbe A general term sometimes used to refer to microscopic (not visible to the unaided eye) organisms.

Micro-electromechanical systems (MEMS) The fabrication or micro-machining of materials to make stationary and moving structures, devices, and systems of a nominal size scale from a few centimeters to a few micrometers.

Molecule The smallest particle of a substance that retains all the properties of the substance and is composed of one or more atoms bonded together.

Mutation A change in genetic material that results from an error in replication of DNA. Mutations can be beneficial, harmful, or neutral.

Nanometer One billionth of a meter.

Nanotechnology The manipulation, precision placement, measurement, visualization, and modeling of matter at the sub-100 nanometer length scale to create functional materials, devices, and systems.

Nanotube A cylindrical shaped fullerene usually made of carbon atoms.

Natural selection The differential survival and reproduction of organisms that differ from one another in one or more usually heritable characteristics. Through this process, the forms of organisms in a population that are best adapted to their local environment increase in frequency relative to less well-adapted forms over a number of generations.

Nucleotide A unit building block of DNA and RNA. A nucleotide consists of a sugar and phosphate backbone with a base attached.

Nucleus A region of eukaryotic cells, enclosed within a membrane, containing the DNA.

Organic A term used to refer to carbon-based compounds. Often used to describe compounds both derived from and not derived from living organisms, but historically the first carbon and hydrogen compounds described were indeed derived from living organisms.

Organism A living thing.

Parthenogenesis Development from an egg cell that has not been fertilized.

Prokaryotic cell A cell without a distinct nucleus. Bacteria and some other simple organisms are prokaryotic. Compare with eukaryotic cells.

Proteins Chain molecules made up of a sequence of amino acids responsible for carrying out many important cellular functions.

Proteomics The study of protein expression and protein-protein interactions.

Quantum Mechanics A model of the behavior of matter at scale of atoms and electrons.

Recombination An event, occurring by the crossing-over of chromosomes, in which DNA is exchanged between a pair of chromosomes.

Selective Pressures Environmental forces that result in the survival of only certain organisms with characteristics that provide resistance.

Self-Assembly A bottom-up technique wherein elements of a system arrange to form highly ordered structures without external manipulation.

Self-Organization A bottom-up process wherein agents, behaving in accordance with simple rules, interact in response to local information and generate emergent properties.

Species A group of actually or potentially interbreeding populations.

Stem cell An unspecialized cell that gives rise to differentiated cells.

X-Ray Crystallography A technique in which the pattern produced by the diffraction of x-rays through the closely spaced lattice of atoms in a crystal are recorded and then analyzed to reveal the nature of a molecule.

Index

About the Authors

CHRISTOPHER MEYER is director of the Center for Business Innovation in Cambridge, Massachusetts. He is also a founder of Bios Group, Inc., a Santa Fe–based venture that develops applications of complexity theory for business. With more than twenty years experience in general management and economics consulting, he is an authority on the evolution of the information economy and its impact on business. He was listed among *Consulting Magazine*'s "25 Most Influential Consultants" in 2001, and served on *Time*'s Board of Technologists in 2002. With Stan Davis he was co-author of *Future Wealth,* published in 2000, and *Blur,* published in 1998.

STAN DAVIS is an independent author and speaker based in Boston, as well as a senior research fellow at the Center for Business Innovation. He is well known as a visionary business thinker who advises leading companies and fast-growing enterprises around the world. In addition to co-authoring *Future Wealth* and *Blur,* he has written nine other influential books, including *2020 Vision, The Monster Under the Bed,* and the bestselling *Future Perfect,* published first in 1987, reissued in 1997, and recipient of Tom Peter's "Book of the Decade" Award. His books have sold over one million copies and appear in 15 languages. *Successful Meetings Magazine* listed him as their number-one speaker in the December 1999 cover story "21 Top Speakers for the 21st Century."